The Translations of Nebrija

A VOLUME IN THE SERIES

Studies in Print Culture and the History of the Book

EDITED BY

Greg Barnhisel
Robert A. Gross
Joan Shelley Rubin
Michael Winship

The Translations of Nebrija

LANGUAGE, CULTURE, AND CIRCULATION IN THE EARLY MODERN WORLD

Byron Ellsworth Hamann

University of Massachusetts Press

Amherst and Boston

ISBN 978-1-62534-170-9 (paperback); 163-1 (hardcover)

Designed by Sally Nichols
Set in Palatino
Printed and bound by Sheridan Books, Inc.

Library of Congress Cataloging-in-Publication Data

Hamann, Byron Ellsworth, 1972–
The translations of Nebrija : language, culture, and circulation in the early modern world /
Byron Ellsworth Hamann.
pages cm. — (Studies in print culture and the history of the book)
Includes bibliographical references and index.
ISBN 978-1-62534-170-9 (pbk. : alk. paper) — ISBN 978-1-62534-163-1 (hardcover : alk. paper)
1. Encyclopedias and dictionaries—Early works to 1600—History and criticism. 2. Nebrija,
Antonio de, 1444?–1522—Criticism and interpretation. 3. Translating and interpreting—
History. 4. Language and languages—Etymology—History. 5. Lexicography—History.
6. Sociolinguistics—History. I. Title.
AE3.H36 2015
031.02—dc23
2015030471

British Library Cataloguing-in-Publication Data
A catalogue record for this book is available from the British Library.

Του Ματθαίου, της Δάφνης και της Λουκίας

Contents

Maps and Figures

MAPS

FIGURES

ix

Acknowledgments

Many thanks to Linda Arnold, Liza Bakewell, Doris Bartholomew, Mary Bellino, Jeff Blomster, Mary Clayton, Rick Copp, Karen Dakin, Joe Dietl, Juan Manuel Domínguez Chacón, Dawn Dyer of the Bristol Reference Library, Caitlin Earley, Constantin Fasolt, Salvador Ferrando Palomares of the Archivo del Real Colegio Seminario de Corpus Christi, David Freidel, Amanda Gluibizzi, Julia Guernsey, Brian Halley, Jay R. Hamann, Nancy D. Hamann, Tamar Herzog, Matthew Hunter, Scott R. Hutson, Manuel Hermann Lejarazu, Michael O. Hironymous of the Benson Latin American Library, Aaron Hyman, John Kamys, Christian Kleinbub, Andrew Laird, Yolanda Lastra, Dana Leibsohn, Steve MacIsaac, Father Lorenzo Maté of the Biblioteca del Monasterio de Santo Domingo de Silos, John Monaghan, Barbara Mundy, Philip Nagy of the Vanderbilt University Library Department of Special Collections, James Oles, John O'Neill of the Hispanic Society of America, Pagona Papadopoulou, Ian Parks, Jacek Partyka of the Jagiellonian Library, Etna T. Pascacio, John Pohl, John Powell of the Newberry Library, the Program for Cultural Cooperation between Spain's Ministry of Culture and United States Universities, Gregory Rami of the Library of the American Museum of Natural History, María Salvador Cabrerizo, Cayetano Sánchez Fuertes, O.F.M., of the Archivo Franciscano Ibero-Oriental, Doris Schweizer of the Freiburg University Library, Larry Scott of the Stanford University Library Department of Special Collections, Adam T. Sellen, Kyle R. Triplett and Jessica Pigza of the New York Public Library Rare Book Division, Nancy P. Troike, Alexander Wilkinson, Virginia Yanez-Gonzalez of the Taylor Institution Library, and Ben Zook.

A Note on Typography

Because this is a book about words (words in many languages, used in different ways), I adopt stylistic conventions from lexicography:

Lexical items appear in italics.
Dictionary entry forms appear in bold.
Quoted dictionary definitions appear in double quotation marks.
Glossed interpretations appear in single quotation marks.

For example, Nahua people in sixteenth-century Central Mexico drank chocolate as a beverage. They called it *cacahuatl,* and when the Europeans arrived, the Nahuatl word *cacahuatl* became *cacao* in Castilian. A number of entries for chocolate-based beverages can be found in Alonso de Molina's 1555 Castilian–Nahuatl dictionary, beginning with the Castilian entry form **Beuida de cacao y maiz** ('beverage of chocolate and maize'), which is translated to Nahuatl as "cacaua atl" (literally, 'chocolate water'). Two entries later, we find **Beuida de cacao con axi** ('beverage of chocolate with chile'), which is translated to Nahuatl as "chillo cacauatl" and "chilcacauatl," both of which literally mean 'red chocolate water.'

Combining the second and third conventions above, when a quoted dictionary translation includes its entry form, the entry form is in bold, followed by the translation in normal type, and both parts are enclosed with double quotation marks: "**Beuida de cacao y maiz.** cacaua atl"; "**Beuida de cacao con axi.** chillo cacauatl, chilcacauatl."

More generally, missing letters from abbreviated words have been added in brackets ("cõ" becomes co[n], 'with'; "aqlla" becomes aq[ue]lla, 'that'). The spelling of author names has been standardized (I use Nebrjia throughout, and not the variants of Lebrixa or Nebrissensis; names printed as "Iuan" and "Ovdin" become Juan and Oudin). The spelling of early modern book titles, however, has not been modernized.

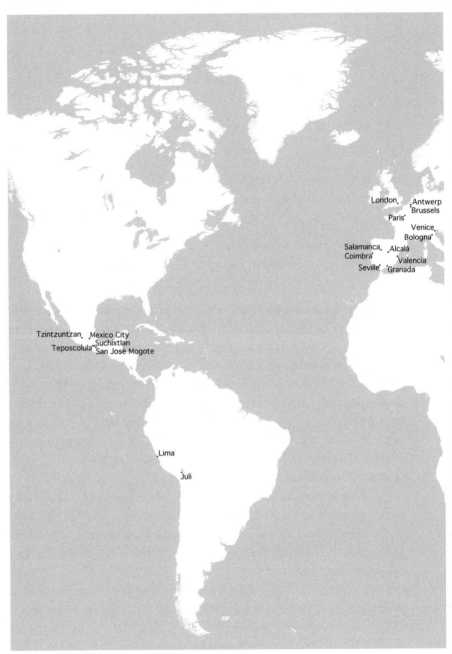

MAP 1. Global locations discussed in this book, in the Americas, Europe, and Asia

MAP 2. Iberian locations discussed in this book

The Translations of Nebrija

TRANSLATE [TRADVZIR], from the Latin verb *traduco, -is,* meaning to carry something from one place to another, or to direct it. *[According to] grammarians:* traduco, *to lead someone to a place, or from place to place, to transport; from* trans *and* duco. In the Latin language it has other analogous meanings, but in Spanish it signifies the turning of a statement from one language to another, as in translating a book from Italian or French into Castilian.

TRANSLATE [TRASLADAR], to move something important from one place to another, such as translating the body or relics of a saint.

TRANSLATE [TRASLADAR], sometimes means to interpret a text from one language to another, and it can also mean to copy: and this is called translated. Some are simple copies and others are notarized.

SEBASTIÁN DE COVARRUBIAS OROZCO,
Tesoro de la lengua castellana, o española (1611)

Introduction

T his is a story of words connecting the world. It tells how a best-selling
Renaissance book linked pagan Rome, Muslim Spain, Aztec Tenoch-
titlan, Elizabethan England, the Spanish Philippines—and beyond.[1] It is a
story of moveable type and inkwells, of illuminated manuscripts and
archaeological ruins. Above all, it is a story of translations.

In the early modern European world, translation had two primary meanings. Both had to do with movement, with transfer. One involved spatial
translation: the movement of things from one place to another. This kind
of translation was often linked to the travels of saintly relics. In the Middle
Ages, these sacred translations could happen in a number of ways: through
gifts, purchases, thefts. But in the sixteenth century a new, emergency translation developed, as holy fragments were rescued from Protestant attacks
and carried to safe havens in Rome, Iberia, and the Americas.[2]

The other early modern meaning of translation was linguistic: the movement
from one language to another. This would eventually become the concept's primary meaning. When we think of translation today, we usually have the translation of languages in mind. But in fifteenth-, sixteenth-, and seventeenth-century Europe, the association of translation with physical movement was just as
important. Thus the quotations that open this introduction—taken from our
earliest monolingual Spanish dictionary—define both **Traduzir** and **Trasladar**
first in terms of spatial transfer, and then in terms of linguistic transfer.[3]

This book explores the interconnected implications of these two senses
of translation—as well as the idea of translation as copying, which appears
in the second definition of **Trasladar**. It follows the travels and transformations of a groundbreaking Castilian–Latin text, the *Vocabulario* or
Dictionarium of the humanist professor Antonio de Nebrija (fig. 0.1). First
published in 1495, by the early 1600s Nebrija's work had been reprinted
thirty-four times in nine European cities.[4]

But the far-flung editions of Nebrija's dictionary were not all alike. Their

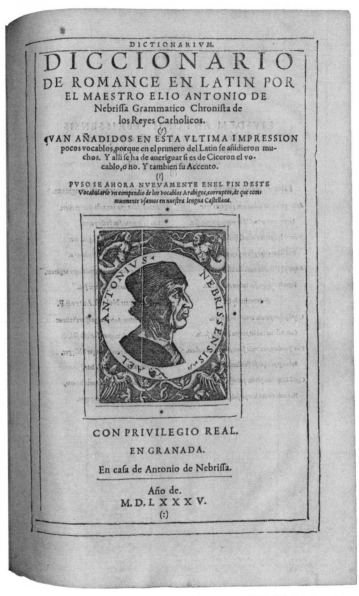

DICTIONARIVM.

DICCIONARIO
DE ROMANCE EN LATIN POR
EL MAESTRO ELIO ANTONIO DE
Nebriſſa Grammatico Chroniſta de
los Reyes Catholicos.
(?)
¶VAN AÑADIDOS EN ESTA VLTIMA IMPRESSION
pocos vocablos, porque en el primero del Latin ſe añidieron muchos. Y alli ſe ha de aueriguar ſi es de Ciceron el vocablo, o ho. Y tambien ſu Accento.
(?)
PVSO SE AHORA NVEVAMENTE ENEL FIN DESTE
Vocabulario vn compendio de los vocablos Arabigos, corruptos, de que com̃
munmente vſamos en nueſtra lengua Caſtellana.

CON PRIVILEGIO REAL.

EN GRANADA.

En caſa de Antonio de Nebriſſa.

Año de.
M. D. L X X X V.
(:)

FIGURE O.1. Title page of the 1585 Granada printing of Nebrija's *Dictionarium*, with a woodcut portrait of Antonio de Nebrija in the style of an antique coin. Image courtesy of Vanderbilt University Special Collections and University Archives.

lists of entries were in constant flux, revised first by Nebrija himself and later by his heirs and pirate printers. As a result, the Castilian–Latin entries in the Salamanca printing of 1495 are not the same as the entries in the Salamanca printing of 1513, and the contents of these two versions are, in turn, different from versions printed in Granada (say, in 1536) or Antwerp (say, in 1545) or Seville (say, in 1610).[5] The constantly changing nature of "Nebrija's Castilian–Latin dictionary" has been underappreciated, but it is of fundamental importance. Paying attention to the book's ever-developing contents can transform our understanding not simply of Nebrija's humanist legacy, but of early modern history on a global, cross-cultural scale.[6]

Nebrija's book opens up planetary vistas because of the conceptual richness of *translation*. As a bilingual dictionary, this Castilian–Latin text was a tool for moving between languages. But Nebrija's translating tool was also a physical object, paper and ink, and copies of it were *spatially* translated throughout the world—within Europe, across the Americas, and to Asia. As they traveled, these translating tools were transformed. Their Castilian word lists were used to create new dictionaries, dictionaries for translating languages other than Latin. In other words, as copies of Nebrija's constantly changing Castilian–Latin dictionary were physically translated across the globe, they were linguistically translated as well.

Nebrija's Castilian–Latin text gave birth to multilingual offspring. Usually these descendants were bilingual (Castilian–Arabic, Castilian–Tuscan, Castilian–Mayan, Castilian–French), but sometimes they involved three languages (Castilian–Latin–Nahuatl, Castilian–English–Latin). In turn, second-generation translations of Nebrija inspired dictionaries for yet other tongues—Nebrija's grandchildren, if you will. In the Americas, Castilian–Nahuatl became Castilian–P'urhépecha. In Asia, Castilian–English became Castilian–Tagalog. The later we move through the sixteenth century, the more complicated these genealogies become. In many cases, relationships between dictionaries are straightforward: one parent produces one child. But in some cases dictionaries are descended from two or even three progenitors.[7] Take Francisco de Alvarado's Castilian–Mixtec dictionary, published in Mexico City in 1593 (fig. 0.2). Alvarado (a Mexican-born Dominican friar) gathered his Castilian categories from three sources. Two were indigenous-language dictionaries also published for missionary purposes in Mexico City, one for translating Castilian to Nahuatl (Alonso de Molina, 1571) and one for translating Castilian to Zapotec (Juan de Córdova, 1578). Alvarado's third source was from Europe: the Castilian–Latin

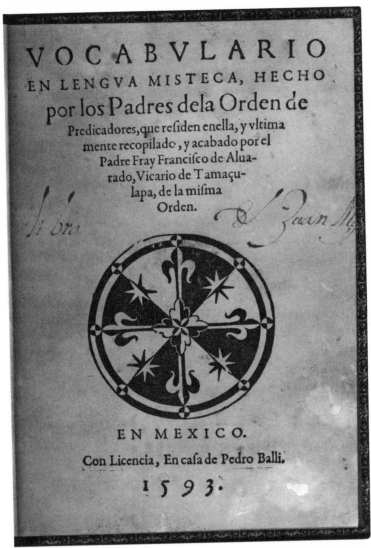

FIGURE 0.2. Title page of Francisco de Alvarado's *Vocabvlario en lengva misteca,* 1593. Image courtesy of the Nettie Lee Benson Latin American Collection, University of Texas Libraries, The University of Texas at Austin.

Dictionarium of Nebrija himself. More specifically (as we will see in the next two chapters), Alvarado used a copy of Nebrija from the Antwerp lineage, spawned in 1545 and amplified in 1553.

Whenever Nebrija's constantly changing word lists were used to create new dictionaries, the process involved both stasis and transformation. Terms inherited from Castilian–Latin dictionaries could be used in a frozen or fossilized way. For example, missionaries in New Spain sometimes tried to collect Native American equivalents for Castilian words that Nebrija used to translate ancient Latin concepts. In response, Native American collaborators created indigenous-language neologisms for antique Mediterranean terms. Thus we encounter a Nahuatl phrase for 'Roman senator' (**Senador romano**) and Zapotec approximations of pagan Roman divination (by animal entrails, by flocks of birds). We even find a P'urhépecha neologism for 'mosque' (**Mezquita**).[8]

But category fossilization, although a constant problem, is not the whole story. The ever-shifting word lists in Nebrija's constantly reprinted dictionary were themselves adjusted and transformed by new cultural contexts.[9] In some cases, words loaned to Castilian from other languages were added to Nebrija's core list, such as Caribbean terms for 'maize' (**Maiz**) and 'chiles' (**Axi**) in the New World. Sometimes Nebrija's categories inspired new variations, as when his **Espuma qualquiera** ('foam in general') was modified in Central Mexico to create an entry for **Espuma de cacao** ('chocolate foam,' the Nahuatl *cacauapoçonallotl*). And occasionally Castilian terms were actually invented to accommodate unfamiliar new concepts. Such is the case with *abaxador,* a Castilian neologism coined in 1555 by the Franciscan friar Alonso de Molina in order to translate the Nahuatl *tlatemouiani*.[10] When using Nebrijan translations, then, we should always keep two frameworks in mind: the inherited word lists of printed sources, and the local linguistic environment being gathered into a new dictionary.

The following chapters pursue Nebrija's translations across the early modern world. Chapter 1, "Nebrija and the Ancients," follows the European travels—and transformations—of Nebrija's Castilian–Latin text.[11] We will explore how entries in this dictionary changed over time, and how these changes in content allow us, now, to reconstruct a *genealogy of vocabularies*—a tangled family tree in which earlier editions of the *Dictionarium,* copied and revised, spawned descendent generations both legitimate (legally licensed) and bastard (pirated printings) (fig. 0.3). This genealogical history is continued in chapter 2, "Arabic, Nahuatl, Tuscan, Tagalog . . . ," which charts the reworking of Nebrija's Castilian–Latin dictionary into other languages, beginning in Iberia (Castilian–Arabic, 1505) and ending in the Philippines (Castilian–Tagalog, 1613).

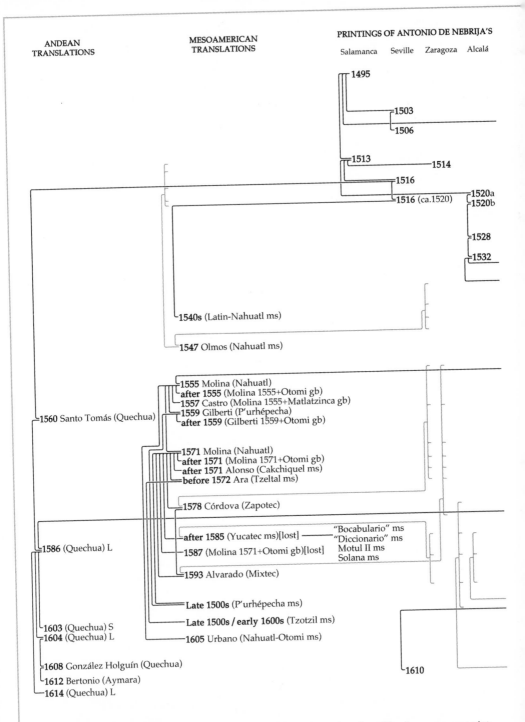

ANDEAN
TRANSLATIONS

MESOAMERICAN
TRANSLATIONS

PRINTINGS OF ANTONIO DE NEBRIJA'S

Salamanca   Seville   Zaragoza   Alcalá

1495

1503

1506

1513

1514

1516

1516 (ca.1520)

1520a
1520b

1528

1532

1540s (Latin-Nahuatl ms)

1547 Olmos (Nahuatl ms)

1555 Molina (Nahuatl)
after 1555 (Molina 1555+Otomi gb)
1557 Castro (Molina 1555+Matlatzinca gb)
1559 Gilberti (P'urhépecha)
after 1559 (Gilberti 1559+Otomi gb)

1560 Santo Tomás (Quechua)

1571 Molina (Nahuatl)
after 1571 (Molina 1571+Otomi gb)
after 1571 Alonso (Cakchiquel ms)
before 1572 Ara (Tzeltal ms)

1578 Córdova (Zapotec)

after 1585 (Yucatec ms)[lost] ——— "Bocabulario" ms
"Diccionario" ms
1586 (Quechua) L   1587 (Molina 1571+Otomi gb)[lost]   Motul II ms
Solana ms

1593 Alvarado (Mixtec)

Late 1500s (P'urhépecha ms)

Late 1500s / early 1600s (Tzotzil ms)

1603 (Quechua) S
1604 (Quechua) L   1605 Urbano (Nahuatl-Otomi ms)

1608 González Holguín (Quechua)

1610

1612 Bertonio (Aymara)
1614 (Quechua) L

FIGURE 0.3. The Translations of Nebrija, 1495–1614. Abbreviations: gb = glossed book; ms = manuscript; q = quarto size; f = folio size; L = Lima printing; S = Seville printing; V = Venice printing. Gray connecting lines indicate that identifying a specific parent edition was not possible.

CASTILIAN – LATIN *DICTIONARIUM* 1495–1610

Valencia   Granada   Antwerp   Estella   Antequera

EUROPEAN
TRANSLATIONS

ASIAN
TRANSLATIONS

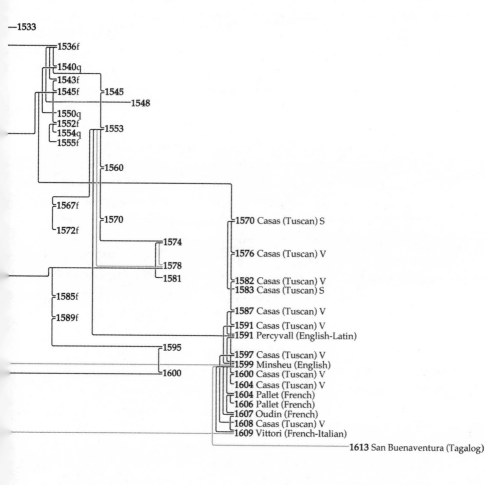

1505 Alcalá (Arabic)

—1533

1536f

1540q

1543f

1545f   1545

1548

1550q

1552f   1553

1554q

1555f

1560

1567f   1570

1572f

1574

1578

1581

1585f

1589f

1595

1600

1570 Casas (Tuscan) S

1576 Casas (Tuscan) V

1582 Casas (Tuscan) V
1583 Casas (Tuscan) S

1587 Casas (Tuscan) V

1591 Casas (Tuscan) V
1591 Percyvall (English-Latin)

1597 Casas (Tuscan) V
1599 Minsheu (English)
1600 Casas (Tuscan) V
1604 Casas (Tuscan) V
1604 Pallet (French)
1606 Pallet (French)
1607 Oudin (French)
1608 Casas (Tuscan) V
1609 Vittori (French-Italian)

1613 San Buenaventura (Tagalog)

But translation—even seemingly simple word-to-word translation—always involves transformation. In some cases, the transformations are violent. As the old saying goes, translation becomes betrayal.[12] And so having reconstructed a global genealogy of vocabularies in chapters 1 and 2, in the second half of this book I pay close attention to examples from the Americas, and to visual and material evidence, in order to explore the processes and implications of translation, transformation, and betrayal. Chapter 3, "From the Shores of Tripoli to the Halls of Montezuma," centers on the descendants of Nebrija in Oaxaca and Central Mexico. Three case studies—one Zapotec, one Mixtec, and one Nahuatl—illustrate the complicated issues that arise when words from missionary dictionaries are used today to interpret Mesoamerican archaeology, art, and hieroglyphic writing. Linguistic evidence is brought into dialogue with objects and images to reexamine what we think we know about prehispanic Native American culture. Visual and material evidence is also central to chapter 4, "Margins of Vocabularies." But here—inspired by historians of reading who insist that books are not simply bearers of information but physical objects as well—our focus is on the very process through which translations of Nebrija were created. The margins of a half dozen Castilian-to-indigenous-language dictionaries are hand-annotated with additional Castilian-to-indigenous-language entries. These riotously inked borders are visually and conceptually complex. They preserve, and dramatize, the social and bodily spaces produced through linguistic research: complex connections that linked speakers of different languages to lexical frameworks set down in black ink by previously printed texts.

This is a book about caution and context. But above all, it is about new possibilities. Mapping the translations of Nebrija isn't simply an antiquarian undertaking about how books beget other books. Our understandings of early modern dictionaries and their cultural worlds are radically transformed, our historical visions made more powerful, if we think about the translations of Nebrija in a global sense. Nebrija's Castilian–Latin vocabulary inspired a great deal of innovative and invaluable linguistic research, in the sixteenth century and beyond. Thinking about the planetary reach of Nebrijan translations allows us to work with these rich sources in new ways.[13]

This introduction began with quotations from the earliest monolingual dictionary of "Castilian, or Spanish." Languages of course change over time, and Sebastián de Covarrubias's 1611 *Tesoro* provides an important record of the meanings of Castilian words—such as *traduzir* and *trasladar*—four centuries ago. But the *Tesoro* contains only around 5,500 entries—a quarter of the nearly 20,000 entries found in the 1495 printing of Nebrija's dictionary.[14] The genealogical network of Nebrijan translations offers us vastly expanded resources for understanding the subtleties of early modern Castilian. Since the core lists of Castilian terms basically overlap in all the translations of Nebrija, we can often discover the early modern meaning of an archaic term by activating this network of relatives. Thus the archaically spelled **Abahar**, a Castilian entry that appears on the first page of Alonso de Molina's 1555 Castilian–Nahuatl *Vocabulario* (a work in turn based on the 1545 Granada printing of Nebrija) is translated for us into early modern English (and Latin as well) in Richard Percyvall's 1591 *Bibliotheca Hispanica:* "**Abahar**, to smoke or to fume, *Euaporo.*"

Because Nebrijan translations form a global network, the interlinguistic research made possible by this family of dictionaries need not be centered on Castilian. Transatlantic vistas are opened for scholars of Italian, who can move from Cristóbal de las Casas's *Vocabvlario de las dos lengvas toscana y castellana* (first edition 1570) to Alonso de Molina's Castilian–Nahuatl *Vocabulario* (1555), because both dictionaries borrowed their Castilian categories from a 1545 Granada printing of Nebrija. Eurasian vistas open for scholars of French, who can move from Jean Pallet's *Diccionario mvy copioso de la lengua española y françesa* (first edition 1604) to Pedro de San Buenaventura's *Vocabvlario de lengva tagala* (1613), because the Castilian entries in both were generated from John Minsheu's *A Dictionarie in Spanish and English* (1599)—a work with many parents, including two different printings of Nebrija's Castilian–Latin *Dictionarium*. The translations of Nebrija have long been used by anthropologists to study indigenous languages and cultures in the New World. Only recently have we begun to realize how much these translations can contribute to the history of Castilian as well—to say nothing of other European languages, or Tagalog.[15]

Finally, because Nebrija's dictionary was used as a linguistic model throughout the early modern world—in the Americas and Asia as well as in Europe—the translations of Nebrija have important implications for how we imagine the geographies of that world. They challenge its division into a "colonial" Philippines and Latin America allochronically separated from a

Europe that was "early modern."[16] The pages you are about to read, then, are as much concerned with events within the phantasmal frontiers of Europe as they are with the world beyond.[17] And so with this global vision in mind, let us set off along the paper trails forged five centuries ago by Nebrija's Castilian–Latin text.

1
ᴏNebrija and the ᴄAncients

Antonio de Nebrija was born in the Andalusian town of Lebrija in 1441 (map 2). He was baptized Antonio Martínez de Cala. At age fourteen he began studies at the University of Salamanca. Five years later, around 1463, he moved to Italy and enrolled in the University of Bologna.[1] There he studied Latin grammar and classical philology, and became inspired by the new approaches to ancient languages being developed by Italian scholars. Antonio brought these ideas back with him to Iberia in 1470, and he began teaching them at the University of Salamanca in 1475.[2]

In 1481 he published an influential book for learning Latin: *Introductiones latinae*. The first edition of one thousand copies quickly sold out; it would be reprinted dozens of times.[3] Manuscript copies circulated as well, such as the illuminated version featured on this book's front cover (Nebrija is at center, teaching a class). With the *Introductiones,* Antonio Martínez de Cala began to sign his works Elio Antonio de Nebrija (or, in Latin, Aelius Antonius Nebrissensis). The three-part structure was borrowed from classical Roman names; *Aelius* itself was an ancient family *gens* chiseled on stone monuments in the area around Lebrija—a town called Nebrissa Veneria in Roman times (hence, Nebrissensis).[4]

In 1487, Nebrija left his post at Salamanca and became private tutor to Juan de Zúñiga, Grand Master of the Knights of Alcántara and later Archbishop of Seville. (Zúñiga also appears on the cover illumination, seated at left; his son kneels before him). Nebrija enjoyed this patronage until Zúñiga's death in 1504, and was extremely productive during these seventeen years. He continued to publish new scholarship on ancient Latin, including a Castilian translation of the *Introductiones* for total beginners (the original version had been written entirely in Latin).[5]

Perhaps because of this translation, Nebrija became interested in the Castilian language as an object of study in its own right.[6] And so in 1492, in Salamanca, he published two revolutionary works. One was a book of Castilian grammar, the first grammar of a vernacular language ever printed in Europe. It was modeled, appropriately enough, on the Latin grammar Nebrija first published a decade before.[7] Nebrija's other 1492 work would change the future of linguistic research throughout the world: a Latin-to-Castilian *Lexicon* (word list or vocabulary). It was not the first Latin–Castilian dictionary to be published in Spain—Alfonso Fernández de Palencia had authored a two-volume *Universal vocabulario* in 1490—but it would be the most influential.[8] In part, this was because three years later Nebrija reversed his 1492 *Lexicon,* turning it into a Castilian-to-Latin *Vocabulario.*[9]

The 1492 *Lexicon* and the 1495 *Vocabulario* provide us with starting points for the subsequent translations of Nebrija. A number of well-known Latin glossaries had already been compiled in the Middle Ages, but Nebrija avoided them when creating his own dictionaries.[10] Instead, he gathered his terms directly from Latin texts by ancient authors. In many ways, this primary-source approach is not surprising, given Nebrija's typically humanist scorn of medieval Latin. The introduction to his 1495 Castilian–Latin *Vocabulario* complains about the "barbarity" of the Latin used in Spain— even the Latin taught at the University of Salamanca itself.[11] Traces of Nebrija's extensive scholarship can be seen in his Latin–Castilian entries, which occasionally mention ancient authors by name: Apuleius, Aristotle, Augustine, Festus, Galen, John the Evangelist, Marcianus of Heraclea, Nonius, Plautus, Pliny, Priscian, Seneca, Solinus, Theophrastus, Varro, Virgil, Vitruvius.[12] These author citations first appear in 1512, when Nebrija published a revised version of his Latin–Castilian dictionary, twenty years after the first edition. For example, the first page of Latin–Castilian entries under "M. ante. e." (that is, words beginning *Me-*) includes references to Quintilian, Pliny, Festus, Marcianus of Heraclea, John the Evangelist, and Augustine:

Me. vox est capraru[m] siue ouium Quintiliano autore
Meconites gemma est Plinio papaueri similis
Meddix. icis. inquit Festus magistratus est nomen
Medibilie. inquit Festus pro eo quod medicabile
Media gemma est Plinio a medea inuenta

Medialis gemma Martiano eadem est que media
Medians. in euangelio Joannis por cosa mediante
Mediator mortis ab Augustino dictur diabolus[13]

Most of Nebrija's sources, it is important to point out, were pagan authors; only a few were Christian (Augustine and John the Evangelist being predictable exceptions). Many of the same pagan authors were also cited by Nebrija in his *Libro de las antiguedades de españa* ('Book of the antiquities of Spain'), a short pamphlet on Roman Iberia printed sometime in the 1490s.[14] As far as we can tell, the only neo-Latin source used regularly by Nebrija was Theodorus Gaza's Greek-to-Latin translation of Aristotle's *Historia animalium,* published in Venice in 1476. (Gaza supplied Nebrija with a number of Latin terms for plants and animals.)[15] In general, however, Nebrija avoided post-antique sources and their supposedly corrupt language. His dictionary privileged Latin as it was written over a thousand years earlier, preserved in the words of ancient texts.

When Nebrija started to prepare the Castilian–Latin *Vocabulario,* he seems to have begun with the Latin–Castilian entries in his 1492 *Lexicon.* Unfortunately, Nebrija's working methods for creating the 1495 dictionary (and, for that matter, the *Lexicon* itself) are uncertain. María Lourdes García Macho suggests that he must have used some sort of card file to transform the Latin–Castilian work into its Castilian–Latin sibling. This is just a hypothesis—no handwritten entry-notes by Nebrija have survived—but we do know that annotated "slips" were used to compose books elsewhere in early modern Europe.[16] Whatever his method, it is clear that Nebrija reworked the entries of the Castilian–Latin *Vocabulario* to make it easier for Castilian-speaking users to consult. If Latin terms from the 1492 *Lexicon* did not have direct correlates in Castilian, they were often cut. For example, the 1492 *Lexicon* included six different entries for Latin terms related to the worship of idols (fig. 1.1):

Idolum.i. por el idolo o estatua. gr.
Idolopoeia.[a]e. por ficion de idolo.
Idolatra.[a]e. por el servidor de idolos
Idolatria.[a]e. por el servicio de idolos
Idolium.ij. por el sacrificio de idolos
Idolotitum.i. por aquello mesmo

Jchnuſa.e.la iſla que agora es cerdeña
Jco.icis.ici.por berir.acti.i.ra.
Jconium.ij.ciudad de capadocia.
Jconia.e.por eſta meſma ciudad
Jcos.nei icon.interpretatur imago
Jcon.is.por cierta figura en la oratoria
Jconicus.a.um. coſa debuſada delo natural.
Jconium.ij. por una ciudad de lycaonia
Jchtbis.is. interpretatur piſcis.
Jchtbiocolla.e. por el caçon peſcado
Jchtbiocola.e. por la colaper.
Jchtbiopbagi.pueblos que biven de peces
Jchtbiotropbium.ij.por eſtanque de peces
Jcterus.i.por la oropendola ave conocida
Jcterus.i. por la itericia dolencia deſte color
Jctericia.e. por eſta meſma dolencia
Jctericus morbus.por aquello meſmo
Jctericus.a.um.por coſa doliente della
Jctis.idis. interpretatur muſtela ſilueſtris
Jctus.a.um.participium ab ico.is.
Jctus.us. por el golpe o berida
   Jda.e.por un boſque de creta iſla
   Jda.e.por otro boſque deſtrota
Jdeus.a.um. por coſa deſtos boſques
Jdas.e. eroc fue enamorado de marpiſa
Jdalium.ij. monte z lugar de cipro iſla
Jdalius.a.um.por coſa d eſte lugar
Jdalia.e. por la dioſa venus deſte lugar
Jdalis.idis. por la meſma dioſa venus
Jdcirco.coniunctio.por porende
Jdea.e.interpretatur forma z ſpecies.
Jdcm.in maſculino.por el meſmo.
Jdcm. in neutro genero.por lo meſmo
Jdentidem.aduerbium. por una z otra vez
Jdios.interpretatur proprius.
Jdioma.atis.por propriedad de lenguaje
Jdiograpbon.eſcriptura de propria mano
Jdiota.e.el que no ſabe ſino lo ſuio
Jdoction.interpretatur nature accomodatum
Joos.interpretatur ſpecies uel forma.
Jdolum.i.por el idolo o eſtatua.gr.
Jdolopoeia.e.por ficion de idolo
Jdolatra.e. por el ſervidor de idolos
Jdolatria.e. por el ſervicio de idolos
Jdolium.ij.por el ſacrificio de idolos.
Jdolontum.i.por aquello meſmo.
Jdomeneus.i.por un rei de creta
Jdoneus.a.um. por coſa idonea

Jdoneior. comparatiuum ab idoneus
Jdos. interpretatur ſpecies
Jdume.es. region es de paleſtina judea
Jdumea.e. por aquella meſma region
Jdumeus.a.um. por coſa deſta region
Jdus.uum.por las idus del mes
   Jebus. la que ſe llamo deſpues ieruſalẽ.b.
   Jebuſeus.principe fue de aquella tierra
Jeci.ieciſti. preteritum eſt a iacio.is.
Jeconias.e. principe fue delos judios.b.
Jecorinus.i. por un cierto peſcado
Jecinus. oris. por aquello meſmo
Jecur.oris.por el bigado.
Jebenna.e.buego del inſierno.b.
Jebu. rei fue delos judios. b.
Jeiuna.e.por la tripa aiuna
Jeiunium.ij.por el aiuno.
Jeiunitas.atis.por aquello meſmo
Jeiuno.as.iciunaui. por aiunar. n.v.
Jeiunus.a.um.por coſa aiuna
Jeiunus.a.um.por coſa deſſabrida
Jens.euntis. participium ab eo is.
Jento.as.ientaui.por almorzar.
Jentaculum.i.por el almuerzo.
Jepte.juez fue delos judios.b.
Jeſſe.padre fue del rei david z bijo de obetb.b
Jes.ietis.ciudad de acaia tierra de omero
Jeſus.triſyllabum. por nueſtro ſalvador
Jeſuites.e.por el jeſuato fraile de jeſu.
Jetro.ſuegro fue de moiſen profeta.b.
Jgitur.coniunctio. por aſſique
Jginus.i. iſtoriador fue latino
Jgnarus.a.um.por coſa no ſabidora
Jgnauus.a.um.por coſa perezoſa mucbo
Jgnauia.e.por aquella grande pereza
Jgnauitas.atis. por aquello meſmo.pr.
Jgnauiter.aduerbium.por perezoſa mente
Jgnis.ignis. por el buego
Jgniculus.i. por el buego pequeño
Jgniarium.ij.por encendedero de leña
Jgneo.uel igneſco. por encender ſe. n.v.
Jgneſcor.eris.por aquello meſmo.pr.
Jgneus.a.um. por coſa de fuego
Jgnis ſacer.por el fuego de.S.marçal
Jgnicomans.tis.por lo q tiene raios de fuego
Jgnifer.a.um.por coſa que trae fuego
Jgnigena.e.por coſa engendrada de fuego
Jgniſpicium.ij.por la divinacion en fuego

FIGURE 1.1. Folio 75v of Nebrija's 1492 *Lexicon*, with idol-related entries. © Biblioteca Nacional de España, Madrid, *I1778.

In contrast, the 1495 *Vocabulario* contains only four Castilian entries on idol-worship (for 'idol', 'idolatry', 'to worship idols', 'idolater')—meaning that some Latin conceptual subtleties from 1492 (such as the category of *idolopoeia*, 'idol-literature') were left out (fig. 1.2):

Idolo en griego. idolum.i. phantasma.atis
Idolatria. idolorum cultus
Idolatrar. idóla colere.
Idolatra servidor de idolos. idolatra.[a]e.

At the same time, Nebrija also added Castilian terms to the *Vocabulario* that had not appeared anywhere in the *Lexicon*—perhaps because their Latin translations were of dubious antique pedigree.[17] This was certainly the case with 'papal indulgence', **Indulgencia del papa**, and 'mosque', **Mezquita**, both included in 1495 but with no equivalents in 1492:

Indulgencia del papa. indultum.i.
Mezquita. [a]edicula macumeth[a]e

The 1495 *Vocabulario*, then, was not simply a transposition of the 1492 *Lexicon*. Although physically speaking the two books share the same size and layout (both are large folio volumes, their pages divided into two 48-line columns), the 1492 Latin–Castilian *Lexicon* had more pages (153 folios or 306 pages) and thus more entries (29,343) than the 1495 Castilian–Latin *Vocabulario* (101 folios or 202 pages, with 19,393 entries). But although the 1495 *Vocabulario* included fewer separate entries than the 1492 *Lexicon*—even as it added concepts such as *papal indulgence* and *mosque*—both volumes were grounded in the same corpus of ancient Latin texts, and covered the same core repertoire of concepts.[18]

North and South: 1503, 1506, 1512–1513, 1514, 1516, "1516" [circa 1520]

Nebrija's dictionary projects developed gradually, over time. In 1503 the Latin–Castilian *Lexicon* and Castilian–Latin *Vocabulario* were published together, in a single volume, by the famous Seville-based Cromberger printing house. This one-volume work was apparently popular; another printing was issued by the Crombergers in 1506. These may be the first pirated editions of Nebrija's dictionaries—something the Crombergers are known to have indulged in on a number of occasions.[19] The contents of the

Juzgado. iudicatio.onis.iudicatus.us.
ꝙeincipientibus ab.i.uocali.
conjuncion.et.q5.atq5
i   Ia adverbio de tiempo. iam
Iañes sobre nombre.ioannes.is.
Iazer.iacco.es.iacui.cubo.as.cubui
Iazija.cubitus.us.cubatio.onis.
bernia o irlanda isla ocidental.inuerna
Ibernia esta mesma isla. ibernia.e.
da.itusitus.profectio.onis
Idolo.statua.e.simulachrum.i.spectru.i.
Idolo en griego.idolum.i.phantasma.atis
Idolatria. idolorum cultus
Idolatrar. idola colere.
Idolatra servidor de idolos. idolatra.e.
Idropesia.ueternus.i.aqua intercus
Idropesia en griego. hydrops hydropis
Idropico.ueternosus.a.um.hydropicus.a.u
Idropesia de aire. tympanitis.is.
Idropesia de umor.ascytis.is.
Idropesia de carne.hyposarca.e.
edra arbol conocido. hedera.e.
Iedra en griego esta mesma. cyssos.i.
Iedra blanca.hedera alba
Iedra negra. hedera nigra
Iedra tercera.belir.icis. similar.acis
Iedra baxa. chamecyssus.i.
Iegua.equa.e.iegua pequeña. equula.e.
Ieguada de ieguas. equaria.e.
Ieguarizo que las guarda.equarius.ij.
Ieguarizo que echa garañon.peroriga.e.
Ielo o elada.gelu.glacies.pruina
Iema de uevo.uitellus.i.luteum oui
Iema de vid.gemma.e.oculus
Iema de vino.uinum meracum
Iermo o desierto.desertum.i.solitudo.inis
Iermo en griego.eremus.i.
Ierma cosa.desertus.a.um.desolatus.a.um.
Ierro.error.oris.erratum.i.erratio.onis
Ierno marido de tu bija.gener.eri.
Ierno marido de tu nieta.progener.eri.
Ierva de ballestero.ueratrum.i.
Ierva de ballestero en griego. helleborus.i.
Ierva de santa maria.athanasia.e.
Ierva de san juan. hypericon.i.
Ierva rabonera.borit.saponaria.e.
Ierva puntera.sedum.i.
Ierva puntera en griego.aizous.i.

Ierva de golondrina.chelidonia.e.
Ierva buena.mentha.e.
Ierva mora.solatrum.i.halicacabus.i.
Ierva mora esta mesma.strichnum.i.
Ierva cualquiera.herba.e.
Ierva en griego.botane.es.
Iesca de buego.fomes.itis.esca.e.
Iesca de bongo.fungus aridus
Iesso especie de piedra.gypsum.i.
Iezgo ierva conocida.ebulus.i.
glesia.templum.i.edes sacra
Igual cosa.equus.a.um. equalis.e.
Igual cosa.par paris.parilis.e.
Igual mente.eque. equaliter
Igual de edad.equeuus.a.um
Igual peso.equilibrium. equimentum.i.
Iguala enel pleito.transactio.decisio
Igualarse enesta manera. decido.transigo
Igualar.equo.as.exequo.as.equipero.as.
Igualar con otro.coequo.as.aut.adequo
Igualar lo aspero.sterno.is.straui
Igualdad.equalis.e.atis.equamentum.i.
Igualdad.equabilitas.parilitas.atis
Igualdad de dia z noche. equinoctium.ij.
Igualdad de dia z noche.equidium.ij.
jada de pescado.abdomen.inis
Ijada de pescado. sumen suminis
Ijares.hypochondria.orum
liaca dolencia de tripas.ileon
Iliaco doliente dela ijada. iliacus.a.um
Ilicita cosa. illicitus.a.um
Ilicita cosa por religion.nefandus.nefarius
Ilicito enesta manera. nefas
magen de alguna cosa.imago.inis
Imagen enesta manera.simulachrum.i.
Imagen enesta manera. effigies.ei.
Imagen pequeña.imaguncula.e.
Imagen sacada delo natural. icon.onis
Imaginar.imaginor.aris
Imagen representar.imagino.as.
Imaginacion. imaginatio. onis
Imaginaria cosa. imaginarius.a.um
Image sacar o otra cosa.effigo.is.effiguro.as
Immortal cosa. immortalis.e.eternus.a.um
Immortalidad.immortalitas.eternitas
Immortal mente.immortaliter.eterne
Imola ciudad de italia.forum cornelij
Impaciente no sufrido.impatiens.tis
.b.iiij.

FIGURE 1.2. Folio 219r of Nebrija's 1495 *Vocabulario,* with idol-related entries. © Biblioteca Nacional de España, Madrid, *I1778.

one-volume editions from 1503 and 1506 are the same as those of the combined Salamanca publications from 1492 and 1495, but they differ in orthography. The use of *y* is preferred over *i* in the Castilian entries, and *u* over *v*—so that the entry for **Cabezcaido** ('crestfallen') in 1495 becomes **Cabezcaydo** in 1503 and 1506, and the entry for **Cantar el cuervo** ('to sing, the crow') in 1495 becomes **Cantar el cueruo** in 1503 and 1506. These spelling shifts may reflect Andalusian traditions of spelling and speaking; Seville was over 460 kilometers south of Salamanca, close to the Atlantic coast (map 1).[20]

That the two Sevillan printings were issued in such rapid succession—a mere three years apart—suggests they sold well. Whether authorized or not, their success may have prompted Nebrija to begin a revised edition. He had returned as a professor to Salamanca in 1505, following the death of his patron Juan de Zúñiga the previous year.[21] We don't know when the revision process started, but after his manuscript was ready Nebrija brought it to a printer he had worked with before: Arnao Guillén de Brocar. Guillén de Brocar then coordinated production with two different printers in two different cities, Burgos and Salamanca (map 2).

This method of "concurrent printing"—in which different parts of a single volume were printed in separate houses—was a standard early modern production strategy.[22] Its use in this instance may relate to the personal travels of Nebrija and Guillén de Brocar. Nebrija was actually living in Burgos for part of 1512, overseeing the publication of at least one other work. His hands-on authorial oversight was—like concurrent printing—a fairly common practice in the chaotic world of early modern publication. An author's presence could help assure that a project actually left the press.[23] Nebrija returned to Salamanca in 1513, which probably explains why part of his new dictionary was printed there as well.[24] Guillén de Brocar, in contrast, was not living in either Burgos or Salamanca. In 1511 he had relocated his business from Logroño (in northern Iberia) to Alcalá (300 kilometers to the south and close to Madrid), so may have felt that during this period of transition it was better to outsource printing to other workshops. Burgos and Salamanca were good choices as production sites, equidistant from Alcalá. Burgos was 250 kilometers to the north, and Salamanca was 250 kilometers to the west (map 2).[25]

And so in late November 1512—twenty years after the original Latin–Castilian *Lexicon* of 1492—a revised and somewhat expanded Latin–Castilian

Dictionarium was printed in Burgos by the publishing house of Fadrique de Basilea.[26] It contained 33,138 entries, slightly more than the 29,343 entries of the previous Latin–Castilian editions. Also included in the volume was a new section, "Oppidorum nomina" ('Names of towns'), a Latin-language gazetteer of 10,407 Latin and Greek place names. A few months later, in 1513, the Castilian–Latin section of Nebrija's revised *Dictionarium* was printed in Salamanca by Lorenzo de Liondedei.

This Salamanca printing marks the first substantial transformation in Nebrija's core Castilian–Latin word list—the first of many, and these will allow us to track genealogical relations across time and space. The Castilian–Latin section published in 1513 was notably shorter than previous editions. It contained only 15,943 entries, as compared to the 19,393 entries of the 1495 *Vocabulario*. The reasons for this reduction are twofold. First, as García Macho has chronicled in detail, Nebrija removed hundreds of entries which he felt involved problematic Latin terms—those that were too technical or were obviously medieval concoctions. That is, the revisions served to further Nebrija's battle against the "barbaric" Latin being used in Iberia.[27]

At the same time, Nebrija also removed almost all of the personal and place names that had been integrated into the word lists of the 1495, 1503, and 1506 printings. Excised entries include (among many others) **Aaron sacerdote ermano de moisen**, **Aben en aravigo**, **Xalon rio de calatayud** and **Xatiua cibdad de aragon** ('Aaron priest brother of Moses,' 'Aben in Arabic,' 'Xalon river in Calatayud,' 'Xativa city in Aragon'). One reason for this culling may be that Nebrija felt his new gazetteer section made redundant the inclusion of place names elsewhere in the volume.

Yet despite these various deletions, the overall result was growth. The joint Latin–Castilian / Castilian–Latin printings of 1503 and 1506 contained a total of 48,736 entries; the three parts of the 1512–1513 volume—Castilian–Latin, Latin–Castilian, and gazetteer—totaled 59,488 entries. This expansion was trumpeted on the 1512 title page: "Dictionary of Antonio de Nebrija, now finally enlarged and revised, in which are added more than 10,000 words. . . ."

Two more printings of this revised Latin–Castilian / Castilian–Latin dictionary quickly followed. Both were based on the 1512–1513 version, and both were apparently approved by Nebrija and Guillén de Brocar: a Zaragoza printing in 1514, and a Seville printing in 1516.[28] In turn, the 1516 Seville volume served as the model for a pirated copy, which also purports to have been printed in 1516 but more likely dates to around 1520.[29] In the space of two decades, then—from 1503 to around 1520—six printings of Nebrija's bidirectional dictionary appeared in Iberia. And so at this point we must begin to trace the ever more complicated genealogies of Nebrijan sources and offspring.

We have already seen how the 1503 Seville printing, although obviously modeled on the 1495 Salamanca printing, introduced its own variations in spelling, variations which were repeated in the Seville printing of 1506. These same spelling variations make it clear that Nebrija based the 1513 Castilian–Latin revision on his own 1495 *Vocabulario,* and not on one of the (possibly pirated) Seville printings from 1503 or 1506 (see fig. 0.3).[30]

In addition to the decreased number of entries in the Castilian–Latin section, another key change in 1513 involved the order of words in the entries for the letter Z. In contrast to the first three printings, several Z words were printed out of alphabetic order in 1513. The entry for **Zebra animal conocido** ('Zebra, well-known animal') was followed by **Zumbar** and **Zumbido** ('to buzz,' 'buzzing'), which in turn were followed by **Zebratana, Zorra o raposa, Zorra pequeña**, and finally **Zorzal aue conocida** ('blowgun,' 'vixen or female fox,' 'small vixen,' 'thrush, well-known bird'). This incorrect ordering was repeated in the 1514 Zaragoza printing, as well as in the two Seville printings dated 1516. These Zaragoza and Seville printings also feature the reduced and revised entry lists of the 1513 Salamanca printing, and even reproduce the original (dated) preface to the 1513 Castilian–Latin section. All of this makes clear that the Zaragoza and Seville versions of 1514 and 1516 were not based on the Seville printings of 1503 and 1506, or indeed on the original Salamanca volumes from 1492 and 1495.

If we turn to the details of spelling, important variations emerge after 1513. Overall, the 1514 printing follows the spellings of the 1513 printing quite closely. Yet a few telling variations are introduced: frequent use of the cedilla, as in **Conoçido, Conoçida,** and **Peçe** ('well-known' [masculine], 'well-known' [feminine], 'fish'), in addition to subtle respellings.[31] Since these alterations do not reappear in the volumes dated 1516, it is clear that the (first) 1516 printing was based directly on the 1513 printing, and not on the 1514 descendant.

In turn, the two volumes dated 1516 introduced their own spelling variations, variations which connect them to each other and separate them from their 1513 source. These patterned variations may have to do with where the 1513, 1514, and 1516 volumes were printed. The 1513 and 1514 versions were printed in Salamanca and Zaragoza, in northern Iberia. The 1516 versions, in contrast, were printed in southern Seville. As we have seen, such orthographic transformations also separate the 1503 and 1506 Seville printings from their 1495 Salamancan model. Major contrasts include the use of *i* and *u* and *v* in 1513 and 1514 versus *y* and *b* and *u* in 1516, so that entries for **Ierua** and **Ciudad** ('grass' and 'city') in 1513 and 1514 are changed to **Yerba** and **Cibdad** in 1516.[32] Another spelling variation (one we will use for tracking the connections linking later printings of the *Dictionarium*) has to do with the word *vihuela*, 'lute.' In the original 1495 volume (and in the reprintings of 1503, 1506, 1512, 1513, and 1514), *vihuela* was spelled without an *h*—as **Viuela**—and so was alphabetized between the words **Vituallas** and **Vizcocho** ('victuals' and 'hardtack'). In the 1516 volumes, however, an *h* was added—**Vihuela**—but the word was left between **Vituallas** and **Vizcocho**, out of alphabetical order.

In turn, the two "1516" Seville versions can themselves be distinguished by subtle details. The spacing of words on their title pages is different.[33] The pages of one edition (probably the 1516 original) are foliated in roman numerals, whereas the other lacks pagination (compare figs. 1.3 and 1.4).[34] Finally, the two versions have slightly different spelling variations for certain Castilian words: the foliated edition has **Carniceria este mesmo, Camara lo q[ue] assi se faze, Xarafe de medicina,** and **Xarafe para gomitar** ('butcher-shop, the same,' 'stool, passed thus,' 'medicinal syrup,' 'syrup for vomiting'), but the unfoliated edition has **Carniceria esta mesma, Camara lo que assi se haze, Xaraue de medicina,** and **Xaraue para gomitar.** These variations are important, for (as we will see in chapter 2) they help resolve uncertainty about the model for the earliest surviving indigenous-language dictionary from New Spain.

Alcalá and Valencia: 1520, 1520, 1528, 1532, 1533

Nebrija lived and taught in the university town of Salamanca for about twenty years total, from 1475 to 1487 and then on and off again from 1505. But in the fall of 1513—the same year the Castilian–Latin section of his revised dictionary was printed—he left Salamanca for good to begin a new job at the University of Alcalá.[35]

It was a dynamic moment in the history of this relatively new institution.

Camaras ſin dolencia.aluɩ citatio.
Camara lo q̃ aſſi ſe faze.aluɩ excrementum.
Camaró peſcado.gammar⁹.i.g.cāmaros.
Cambiar.cōmuto.ae.permuto.as.
Cambio.cōmutatio.permutatio.onis.
Cābiador.meſari⁹.ij.argētari⁹.ij.trapezita.g.
Cambiador aſſi.nſimularius.ij.
Cambio de lugar.vectur⁹.e.
Camello de vna corcoba.camellus.batrian⁹
Camello de dos corcobas.camellus arabic⁹.
Camellero que los cura.camelarius.ij.
Camelleria officio de aqueſte.camelaſſa.g.
Caminar andar camino.facio iter.
Caminar querer.habeo iter.
Caminador o caminante.viator.oris.
Camino real.via pſularis.vł regia.vł publica
Camino para ſeruidumbre.actus.us.
Camino tal para yr a pie.iter itineris.
Camino como vereda.ſemita.g.cirames.us.
Camino eſtrecho τ hondo.callie.is.
Camino por do algo lleuan.veha.e.
Camino de ſctiago eñl cielo.via lactea gala=
Camiſa de varon.ſubuculalinthea.   (xías.
Camodar.preſtigior.aris.vnde preſtig̃ator.
Campana.cimbalum.i.tintmabulum.i.
Campanario.turris cimbalaria.
Campanero q̃ las tañe τ faze.cimbalarius.ij.
Campo raſo coma vega.campus.i.
Capeſino coſa detal campo.agreſtis.e.ruſtic⁹
Campero el que lo guarda.camparius.ij.
Can perro o perra.canis.is.
Canal de madera cauada.canalis.is.
Canal pequeña aſſi.cananicula.g. canalicul⁹.
Canal de teſado.imbrex.icis.
Canal maeſtra.imbrex deliciaris.
Canal dela res que ſe come.imbrex.icis.
Canal de molino.incile.is.
Canalado fecho a canales.canaliculatus.
Cana coſa con canas.canus.a.um.
Canas los meſmos cabellos.cani.orum.
Canaſta grande.caniſtrum.i.qualus.i.
Canaſta deſta manera.calatus.i.qualum.i.
Canaſta como cucuano.cophinus.i.
Canaſtillo pequeño.q̃ſillũ.i.calatiſcus.i.
Cacer cōſtelaciō.cancer.cācri.g.carcinos.
Cácion.cātus.us.cantio.onis.cātilena.
Cácionero.odarum vel carminum liber.
Candado cerradura.ſera.e.
Candela.candela.g.lucerna.g.no.
Cādelero en q̃ las ponen.cādelabrũ.i.no.
Candelero el que las faze.cādelarius.no.
Cādiota vaſija de cādia.cadus cretenſis.
Candil de azeyte.lucerna.g.candela.g.

Candil de vna mecha.lucerna monimyxos.
Cādil ð muchas mechas.lucerna. polimixos.
Candileſos de judios.lucerna ēneamyxos.
Canela eſpecia conocida.cinnamũ.i.
Cangilon vaſo de barro.congius.ij.
Cāgrejo peſcado.cancer.cancri.g.carcinos.
Canoa naue de vn madero.monoxylum.i.
Canon en griego.canon canonis.i.regula
Canoniſta q̃ eſtudia canones.canoniſtes.g.
Canoniſta en latin.pontificij.iuris ſtudioſus.
Canonigo de ygleſia.canonicus.i.
Canonizar.in numerum diuorum refero.
Canonizado.in numero dinorum relatus.
Canonizacion.apotheoſis.g.
Canſar a otra coſa.laſſo.as.fatigo.as.
Canſado.laſſus.a.um.defeſſus.a.um.
Canſancio.laſſitudo.deſatigatio.onis.
Canſarſe.laſſeſco.is.defatiſco.eris.
Cantaro vrna fictilis.cantharus.g.
Cantar el tordo o zorzal.trutilo.as.aul.
Cantar el eſtornino.piſcito.as.aul.
Cantar la perdiz.cacabo.as.aui.
Cātar la tortola o paloma.gemo.is.
Cātar la paloma torquaza.plauſito.as.
Cantar la grulla.gruo.is.grui.
Cantar el ciſne.drenſo.as.aul.
Cantar o piar el halcon o açor.pipio.is.
Cantar el gorrion.pipillo.as.aul.
Cantar el bubo.bubulo.as.aui.
Cantar el milano.lipio.is.lipiui.
Cantar el buytre.pulpo.as.aui.
Cantar el cueruo.crocito.as.aul.
Cantar la cigueña.glotoro.as.aul.
Cantar el aguila.clango.is.
Cantar la lechuza.cucubo.as.aui.
Cantar el autillo.vlulo.as.aui.
Cantar el alondra.mitilo.as.aul.
Cantar el abejuruco.zingulo.as.aul.
Cantar la golondrina.trinſo.as.aui.
Cantar la graja.frigulo.as.aui.
Cantar la gallina.gracillo.as.aul.
Cantar el gallo.cucurrio.is.iui.
Cantar el pauon.pupillo.as.aui.
Cātar el anſar o graznar.gracito.as.
Cantar o graznar el anade.tetrino.as.
Cantar todas las aues.garrio.is.
Cantar o chillar el morcielago.ſtrido.is.
Cantar la cigarra.fritinio.is.iui.
Cantar el grillo.grillo.as.aui.
Cantar el abeja o zumbar.bombilo.as.
Cantar la rana.coaxo.as.aui.
Cantar el hōbre cano.is.canto.as.aui.
Cantar amenudo.cantito.as.ani.

FIGURE 1.3. Folio xvii recto of the 1516 Seville printing of Nebrija's *Dictionarium,* with entry for **Camara lo q[ue] assi se faze** (near top of the left column). © Biblioteca Nacional de España, Madrid, *R2700.

Camaras sin dolencia.alui citatio.
Camara lo que assi se haze.alui excrementum
Camaro pescado.gammar.i.g.camaros.
Cambiar.comuto.ae.permuto.ae.
Cambio.comutatio.permutatio.onis.
Cabiador.mesari.ij.argetari.ij.trapezita.g.
Cambiador assi.nsummlarius.ij.
Cambio de lugar.vectura.g.
Camelo de vna coxoba.camellus bactrianus
Camello de dos coxobas.camellus arabicus
Camellero que los cura.camelarius.ij.
Camelleria officio de aqueste.camelasta.g.
Caminar andar camino.facio iter.
Caminar querer.habeo iter.
Caminador o caminante.viator.oris.
Camino real.via psularis.vl regis.vl publica
Camino para seruidumbre.actus.us.
Camino tal para yr a pie.iter.itineris.
Camino como vereda.semita.g.traines.tis.
Camino estrecho z hondo.callis.is.
Camino por do algo lleuan.vecha.g.
Camino de sctiago est cielo.via lactea galaxi=
Camisa de varon.subucula linthea.   (as.
Camodar.prstigior.aris.rude prstigiator.
Campana.cimbalu.tintinnabulum.i.
Campanario.turris cimbalaria.
Campanero q̃ las tañer fazc.cimbalarius.ij.
Campo raso como vega.campus.i.
Capesino cosa de tal capo.agrestis.e.rusticus
Campero el que lo guarda.camparius.ij.
Can perro o perra.canis.is.
Canal de madera cauada.canalis.is.
Canal pequeño assi.canalicula.g.canaliculus
Canal de tejado.imbrex.icis.
Canal maestra.imbrex deliciaris.
Canal dela res que se come.imbrex.icis.
Canal de molino.incile.is.
Canalado fecho a canales.canaliculatus.
Cana cosa con canas.canus.a.um.
Canas los mesinos cabellos.cani.orum.
Canasta grande.cmistrum.i.qualus.i.
Canasta desta manera.calatus.i.qualum.i.
Canasta como cuenano.cophinus.i.
Canastillo pequeño.quasilis.i.calatiscus.i.
Cacer costelacio.cancer.cacri.g.carcinos.
Cacion.catus.us.cantio.onis.catilena.
Cacionero.odarum vel carminum liber.
Candado cerradura.sera.g.
Candela.candela g.lucerna.g.no.
Cadelero en q̃ las poné.candelabrum.i.no.
Candelero el que las haze.cadelarius.no.
Cadiota vasija de cadia.cadus cretensis.
Candil de azeyte.lucerna.g.candela.g.

Candil de vna mecha.lucerna monimyxos
Cadil de muchas mechas.lucerna.polimyxos
Candilejos de judios.lucerna cheamyxos.
Anela especia conocida.cinnamu.i.
Angilon vaso de barro.congius.ij.
Agrejo pescado.cancer.cancri.g.carcinos.
Anoa naue de vn madero.monoxylum.i.
Canon en griego.canon.canonis.i.regula.
Canonista q̃ estudia canones.canonistes.g.
Canonista en latin.pontinci iuris studiosus
Anonigo de yglesia.canonicus.i.
Canonizar.in numerum diuorum refero.
Canonizado.in numero diuorum relatus.
Canonizacion.apotheosis.g.
Ansar a otra cosa.lasso.as.fatigo.as.
Cansado.lassus.a.um.defessus.a.um.
Cansancio.lassitudo.defatigatio.onis.
Cansarse.lassesco.is.defenscor.eris.
Antaro.vrna fictilis.cantharus.g.
Cantar el tordo ozorzal.trutilo.as.aui.
Cantar el estornino.piscito.as.aui.
Cantar la perdiz.cacabo.as.aui.
Catar la tortola o paloma.gemo.is.
Catar la paloma torqua za.plausito.as.
Cantar la grulla.gruo.is.grui.
Cantar el cisne.drenso.as.aui.
Cantar o piar el halcon o açor.pipio.is.
Cantar el gorrion.pipillo.as.aui.
Cantar el buho.bubulo as.aui.
Cantar el milano.lipio.is.lipiui.
Cantar el buytre.pulpo.as.aui.
Cantar el cueruo.crocito.as.aui.
Cantar la ciguena.glotoro.as.aui.
Cantar el aguila.clango.is.
Cantar la lechuza.cucubo.as.aui.
Cantar el autillo.ylulo.as.aui.
Cantar el alondra.mitilo.as.aui.
Cantar la a bejuruco.zingulo.as.aui.
Catar la golondrina.trinso.as.aui.
Cantar la graja.frigulo.as.aui.
Cantar la gallina.gracillo.as.aui.
Cantar el gallo.cucurrio.as.aui.
Cantar el pauon.pupillo as.aui.
Cantar el ansar o graznar gracito.as.
Cantar o graznar el anade.tetrino.as.
Cantar todas las aues.garrio.is.
Cantar o chillar el morciciago.strido.is.
Cantar la cigarra.fritinio.is.aui.
Cantar el grillo.gryllo.as.aui.
Cantar el abeja o zumbar.bombilo.as.
Cantar la rana.coaxo.as.aui.
Cantar el hobre.cano.is.canto.as.aui.
Cantar a menudo.cantito.as.aui.

66

FIGURE 1.4. Unfoliated recto of the "1516" Seville printing of Nebrija's *Dictionarium,* with entry for **Camara lo que assi se haze** (near top of the left column). © Biblioteca Nacional de España, Madrid, *R2219.

The Complutensian Polyglot Bible project (based at the university for over a decade, and on which Nebrija had been an adviser) was nearing completion. The Greek/Latin New Testament was printed in 1514, and the four-volume Hebrew/Greek/Latin/Aramaic Old Testament in 1517. We saw earlier that Nebrija's collaborator, the printer Arnao Guillén de Brocar, had resettled in Alcalá in 1511. It was a good business move. Guillén de Brocar became printer for the Complutensian Bible (even designing special fonts for the volumes), and continued to bring Nebrija's work to press. Nebrija actually lived in a house near Guillén de Brocar's workshop, which allowed him to oversee their many projects.[36] Before Nebrija died in 1522, he and Guillén de Brocar had published nearly a dozen books in Alcalá, including two 1520 versions of the *Dictionarium*.[37] After Guillén de Brocar himself died in 1523, his son-in-law and partner, Miguel de Eguía, continued the tradition of printing Nebrija's works.[38] Between 1524 and 1533, Eguía published eighteen Nebrijan titles in Alcalá, including 1528 and 1532 printings of the *Dictionarium*.

Overall, the four Alcalá dictionaries (1520, 1520, 1528, 1532) are quite similar—as one might expect, given the close relationship of Guillén de Brocar and Eguía. The layout of their pages is nearly identical, sharing the same initial and final entries. The contents, however, subtly shifted over time. Spelling variations make it clear that Guillén de Brocar used the 1513 Salamanca printing as a model for his first 1520 version, and not the more recent 1514 and 1516 printings from Zaragoza and Seville. The second 1520 version, in turn, mimics the page layouts of its earlier Alcalá sibling (and not the layouts of the 1513 printing). Exactly why Guillén de Brocar issued *two* printings in 1520 is unknown, but, significantly, one of them (presumably the first) retained the out-of-order Z section which had emerged in 1513. This glitch was corrected in the presumably second printing (also dated 1520): **Zebra animal conocido** was (at last) followed by **Zebratana**, and then **Zorra o raposa**, **Zorra pequeña**, **Zorzal aue conocida**, **Zumbar**, and **Zumbido**.[39] In turn, when Miguel de Eguía printed his Alcalá version of 1528, he used the Z-corrected 1520 version as a model.[40]

The 1532 printing was itself based on the 1528 printing, sharing with it spelling variations not found in the copies from 1520.[41] One of these is the spelling of the word *lute*. As we saw above, the earliest versions of Nebrija's dictionary spelled the term somewhat archaically as **Viuela**, and thus alphabetized it between **Vituallas** and **Vizcocho**. The 1516 Seville printings used a more contemporary spelling, **Vihuela** (the spelling still used today). The

1520 Alcalá versions spelled the term **Viyuela**; but in 1528, and again in 1532, the more contemporary **Vihuela** was chosen.

At the same time, the 1532 printing also incorporated a number of spelling revisions that set it apart from the printings of 1520 and 1528 (and, indeed, from their 1513 source), such as **Cassador de escritura** ('canceller of writing,' 1532) versus **Cassador de escriptura** (1513, 1520, 1528) and **Visitar yr a ver** ('visit, go to see,' 1532) versus **Visitar ir auer** (1513, 1520, 1528). These 1532 revisions are important, for they enable us to see that *this* was the specific printing later copied by other publishers. For example, in 1533 an edition of the *Dictionarium* was published in Valencia by Francisco Díaz Romano—whether pirated or not is uncertain (map 2).[42] By the 1530s, Díaz Romano had a dozen different printings of "the" *Dictionarium* to choose from, but many details in his version make clear that he used the 1532 Alcalá volume as a model. The Valencian printing has a properly alphabetized *Z* section, and it shares spelling variations with the 1532 version that are different from the printings of 1520 and 1528. For example, the 1533 printing uses the **Visitar yr a ver** spelling of 1532, and not the **Visitar ir auer** spelling of 1513, 1520, and 1528.[43]

Exactly why Miguel de Eguía stopped printing Nebrija's works after 1533 is unclear. He continued to publish books by other authors until 1546 (his last work was printed in the town of Estella), and was still alive in 1548.[44] One tempting explanation is that in 1534 Nebrija's sons Sancho and Sebastián themselves began to publish their father's texts. They had attempted to gain monopoly rights over Antonio's writings since his death in 1522, and it may be that in the early 1530s they finally succeeded.[45] And so is to their story, and to the Andalusian city of Granada, that we now turn.

The Sons of Antonio and the Granada Expansion: 1536 to 1555

Thus far, we have seen how the first revision and reorganization of the Castilian–Latin section of Nebrija's 1495 *Vocabulario* took place in 1513. Dozens of entries (including personal names) were removed, and geographical terms were gathered in a separate gazetteer. Subsequent printings, from 1514 to 1533, involved minor adjustments (spelling variations, correcting the order of the *Z* entries), but the core list of Castilian entries remained the same. All of that changed in 1536.

When their father died in 1522, Sebastián and Sancho de Nebrija promptly sought a royal decree granting them monopoly privileges for the printing of his works. This would effectively block any further publications by Arnao Guillén de Brocar (legal publications, that is; piracy was always an option). They were initially successful in their suit, but were immediately defeated by a counterclaim: in July 1523, the crown extended Guillén de Brocar's permission to print the writings of Nebrija. But he did not enjoy this privilege for long: he died before the end of the year.[46] Nevertheless—as we have seen—Guillén de Brocar's son-in-law continued to print Nebrija's works for the next decade.

Although ultimately unsuccessful, the 1522 petition by Sebastián and Sancho suggests that they were already thinking of becoming publishers themselves. But not in Alcalá. They quickly severed all ties to that city—in July 1523, preparing to leave, Sebastián even claimed as his own a set of manuscripts that his father had deposited with the university. (As we will see, one of these documents, described as a "Vocabulario de medicina encuadernado en pergamino," or vocabulary of medicine bound in parchment, may have played an important role in the 1545 Antwerp expansion of the *Dictionarium*.)[47] By 1524 Sebastián and Sancho were gone. Their whereabouts over the next decade are uncertain, but late in 1534 they began a career as publishers in Granada. They started by reprinting several of their father's works: *Vafre dicta philosophorum* ('Artful sayings of the philosophers,' versified biographies based on a third-century text by Diogenes Laertius), *Libri minores* ('Minor books,' a compilation of Latin works for teaching, including Aesop's Fables), *Hymnorvm recognitio* ('Collected hymns,' their Latin carefully edited by Nebrija), and *Homiliae per diversos avtores in Evangelia* ('Homilies by several authors on the Gospels,' a selection of sermons by Church Fathers).[48] Two years later, in 1536, they published their own version of the *Dictionarium*.[49]

It was significantly different from previous versions: a total of 300 new terms were added to the Castilian–Latin word list, including **Jazmin, Queso fresco**, and **Vituperio** ('jasmine,' 'fresh cheese,' 'criticism'; see appendix A, section 1). Strategically, the new entries were marked with asterisks, making the lexical additions immediately visible to potential buyers (fig. 1.5). Attention to spelling variations makes it clear that Sancho and Sebastián used the 1532 Alcalá printing as their model (as opposed to earlier Alcalá printings, or the 1533 Valencia version).[50] In the end, then, the two brothers

Villania enla criança,rusticitas.atis.
Vmbre qualquiera vara,vimen.inis.
Vimbrera arbol,vitex.icis.agnus castus.
Vinagre vino corrompido,acetum.i.
Vinagrera vaso para el,acetarium.ij
Vinar baruecho.Isfringo,is.
Vinar viña,repastino.as,aui.
Vinatero que trata vino,vinarius.ij.
Vinatero este mesmo,vinitor,oris.
Vinda vanda altranes,balteus inuersus.
Vinniebla yerua conocida,canis lingua.g.cynoglossa
Vino generalmente,vinum.i temetum,i.
Vino puro sin agua,merum.i.
Vino rebotado o desuanecido,vappa.æ.
Vino cozido,defrutum.i.
Vino bastardo,vinum passum.
Vino de mosto torcido,vinum tortiuum.
Vino agua pie,lora,æ,vinum secundarium,
Vino espesso de mucha hez,rubellum.i.
Vino de trigo,zithum.i.
Vino de mançanas,sicera.æ.
Vino aguado,vinum dilutum vel mixtum.
Vino con especias,myrrhina,æ.
Vino con miel,mulsum,i,œnomeli.
Vino blanco,amincum vinum.
Vino tinto,vinum rubeum.
Vino dorado,vinum giluum.
Viña lugar de vides,vinea.æ.
Viñadero que la guarda,vinitor,oris.
Viñedo lugar de viñas,vinetum.i.
Violeta flor conocida,viola.æ.
...de violetas,violaceus.an..g.hyothinus,a.u.
...oer de violetas,violarium,ij.
...cosse madera,subscus.udis.
...de saca,sagita.
Virei rei por otro,prorex.g..
Virgo de donzella,flos etatis,rugiou.
Virgen o donzella,virgo.inis,virguncula,æ.
Virginidad,virginitas,atis.
Vihuela instrumento musico,lyra,æ,barbitus.i.
Virtud generalmente,virtus.utis.
Virtud por la fortaleza o esfuerço,virtus,utis;
Virtuoso,studiosus,a,um,et non virtuosus,
Visage,distorsio,onis,uel vultus,us.
Visagra de mesa,mense vertebra.
Visitar yr a ver,viso,is,inuiso,is.
...ar a menudo,visito,as,aui.
...le cosa que se puede ver,visibilis,e.
...en sueños,visum,i,oroma,atis.
...que parece de noche,phantasma,lemures...
...oso,strabo,onis,ludnius.ij.
...osa,straba,æ,ludnia,æ.
...ta,visus,us,visio,onis.
...ta de ojos,oculorum acies.

Vstuario de vestiduras,vestiarium.ij.
Vstallas para hueste,commeatus,us.
Vihuela,lyra,æ,barbitus.i.
Vituperio,opprobrium.ij.
Vizcocho, pan dos vezes cozido,copta.æ.
Vizconde,vicecomes.itis.
Vocal letra que suena por si,vocalis,is.
Vocatiuo caso,vocatiuus,i,vocandi casus.
Voluntad razonable,voluntas,atis.
Voluntad antojo,appetitus.us.
Voluntad de dios,numen.inis.
Voluntarioso,voluntarius,a,um.
Voluntariosamente,volenter.aduerb.
Votar hazer voto,voueo,es,voui.
Votar assi,vota suscipio vel concipio;
Voto desta manera,votum.i.
Votar dar el voto,suffragor.aris.
Voto desta manera,suffragium,ij,punctum,i,
   Vulgar cosa comun,vulgaris,e,
Vilgarmente,vulgariter.aduerb.
Vuestra cosa,vester,a,um.

De incipientibus ab. X. littera.

Xabon,sapo,onis,smegma,atis.
Xabonero,saponarius,ij,saponari,i..æ.
Xibonera yerua,herba fullonum,boruh.
Xiquima de bestia,camus,i.
Xara mata conocida,lada,æ,cistos.
Xaramago yerua conocida,armoracia,æ,siluestris raphanus.
Xarafe de medicina,potio,onis,
Xarafe para gomitar,tropis.is.
Xenabe o mostaça,sinapis.is.
Xergo o sayal,sagum.i.
Xeme medida,semipes,edis.
Xergon,culcitra stramenticia.
   Xibia pescado conocido,sepia.æ.
Xibia pequeña,sepiola.æ.
Xibion para plateros,sepium.ij.
Ximia o mona,simius,ij,simia.æ.
Xugosa cosa,succidus,a,um.

De incipientibus a. Z. littera.

Zangano de colmena,phucus.i.
Zaque para agua,ascopa,æ.
Zarço o garço de ojos,glaucus.i.
Zarca o garça de ojos,glaucopis.idis.
Zargatona yerua,herba policaria.Psylliu,ij.
Zargatona simiente,psyllium.ij.
   Zebra animal conocido,ege mula syria,
Zebratana,Zarbatana,æ.no.
   Zorra o raposa,vulpes.is.
Zorra pequeña,vulpecula,æ.
Zorzal aue conocida,turdus.i.
Zumbar,susurro,as,bombilo,at,
Zumbido,susurrus,i,bombus.i.

¶FINIS.

Kkk iij

FIGURE 1.5. Final page of the 1536 Granada printing of the *Dictionarium*, with new entries marked by asterisks. The first new entry on this page is **Vinniebla yerua conocida**, the eleventh entry in the left column. © Biblioteca Nacional de España, Madrid, *R27141.

profited from their failed 1522 attempt to gain monopoly rights over their father's works. They were able to use a rival's well-ordered and spelling-modernized edition as the basis for their own.

But in addition to the new entries added in 1536, another important change involves the word for *lute*. We saw earlier that Nebrija used the archaic spelling of **Viuela** in the earliest editions of his work. In contrast, the Seville printings dated 1516 and the Alcalá printings of 1528 and 1532 updated this spelling to **Vihuela**. The word itself, however, was left after **Vituallas**, out of alphabetical order. In the 1536 printing, this spelling and relative placement were maintained, following the 1532 model. (**Vituperio** was added in 1536, so it was placed after **Vituallas** - **Vihuela** and before **Vizcocho**.) But Sancho and Sebastián also added a second *vihuela* entry— **Vihuela instrumento musico**—which they placed further up the page (see column 1 of fig. 1.5). Yet even this new entry was misalphabetized: it was placed between **Virginidad** and **Virtud generalmente** ('virginity' and 'virtue in general'). **Vihuela** would not be properly alphabetized (that is, placed between **Vigilia o velada** and **Vil cosa**: 'vigil or wake' and 'vile thing') for another decade—but even then, the other **Vihuela** entry, after **Vituallas**, was maintained (and continued to appear at least until the 1610 Seville printing, where this study ends).[51]

The revised *Dictionarium* apparently sold well, for additional Granada printings appeared in 1540, 1543, 1545, 1550, 1552, 1554, and 1555. They can be divided into two groups. One series (1536, 1543, 1545, 1552, and 1555) is of large-format folio editions, their title pages centered on a woodcut portrait medallion of Nebrija. The other series (1540, 1550, 1554) is of smaller quarto volumes, derived from the folio editions and with title-page portraits of Nebrija at the top of a woodcut frame (compare fig. 1.6, the 1540 quarto edition, with fig. 1.7, the 1552 folio edition).

The volumes in the folio series introduced changes that were then copied by the volumes in the quarto series. The 1540 quarto printing is obviously based on the 1536 folio printing, as it contains the latter's expanded list of entries. At the same time, the 1540 printing also attempted to correct some alphabetic irregularities from 1536. The 1540 printing moved **Cabrituno** ('kid-like') ahead of **Cabron** and **Cabruno** ('large goat,' 'goat-like'), and **Margen del libro** ('margin of a book') was moved ahead of **Margomar** ('to feather'). Yet the 1540 printing also introduced alphabetization errors of its own, placing entries for **Ruego al ygual o menor** and **Ruego como quiera** ('request of an equal or lesser', 'request in general') after a string of entries related to **Rufian** ('ruffian')—out of order, and in contrast to the correct ordering of these entries in the 1536 printing.[52] The 1540 printing also modified the **Guiñar del ojo** of 1536 into **Guiñar hazer del ojo** (a small but telling adjustment for 'to wink', as we will see).

In contrast, these revised-order entries from 1540 do not appear in the 1543 folio version, which reverted to the 1536 printing as a source (revealed by the out-of-order **Cabrituno** and **Margen** sequences and correct-order **Ruego - Rufian** sequence). At the same time, the 1543 printing introduced its own alphabetic irregularities. The correctly ordered series of hair-related entries used in 1536 (**Guedeja de cabellos - Guedeja enhetrada - Guedejudo**) were shifted in 1543 to **Guedeja de cabellos - Guedejudo - Guedeja enhetrada** ('lock of hair', 'long-haired', 'curly lock of hair'). This irregularity was carried over to the 1545 folio printing, which was based on the 1543 folio version. In turn, the 1545 printing contained a number of spelling variations not shared with the previous versions of 1536 or 1540 or 1543. Two of these—important for their implications in the New World, as we will see in the next chapter—are the spellings **Xaraue para uomitar** and **Xenabe o mostaza** in 1545 ('syrup for vomiting' and 'mustard'), in contrast to **Xarafe para gomitar** and **Xenabe o mostaça** in 1536, 1540 and 1543.

The 1545 folio printing was the last to appear in Granada in the 1540s. In 1548, however, Adrián de Amberes published his own (possibly pirated) version in Estella, a town 45 kilometers southwest of Pamplona in the northeast corner of Iberia (map 2). The Alcalá printer Miguel de Eguía (who, as we saw, was involved in the 1520s and early 1530s editions of the *Dictionarium*) had published his last known work in Estella in 1546, so it is tempting to draw some connection between the two men. (Note that the name "de Amberes" means "of Antwerp," a major printing center we will travel to in the next section). The 1548 Estella printing includes the expanded list of entries introduced in 1536, and a number of smaller variations confirm that the 1536 folio from Granada (rather than the 1540, 1543, or 1545 versions) was Adrián's model. For example, the 1540 printing can be eliminated as a source because of the orderings of **Cabrituno, Margen del libro**, and **Ruego** in 1548; the 1543 and 1545 printings are also disqualified because of the placement of **Guedeja enhetrada**.

In 1550, a fifth Granada version appeared, a new printing of the quarto series begun in 1540. Both the 1540 and 1550 quarto printings have the same page layout (pages begin and end with the same terms), and they share the **Guiñar hazer del ojo** phrasing and ordering of **Cabrituno, Margen del libro,** and **Ruego** that sets them apart from the 1536, 1543, and 1545 Granada volumes.

Two years later, in 1552, a new and revised folio version was published in Granada. It was based on the earlier Granada folio printing from 1545, but contained some important transformations and innovations.[53] Up until 1552, the Granada editions of the *Dictionarium*—and indeed the 1548 Estella printing as well—included the same list of expanded entries introduced in 1536. Entry order was adjusted and spelling variations were introduced, as we have seen, but new terms were not added. In 1552, however, the core list was slightly modified (see appendix A, section 2). A handful of new entries was added (sixteen, all marked with asterisks) and two entries were dropped: **Basilisco este mesmo en Griego** ('basilisk, the same in Greek') and **Hoja o lamina** ('leaf or sheet'). The entries on a few pages were better alphabetized as well. A small but telling detail is, once again, the word for *lute,* whose spelling and placement had for so long been a source of trouble. The 1536 printing maintained the **Vihuela** spelling from its 1532 Alcalá model, but placed the entry in two different locations—neither of them in correct alphabetical order. With the 1552 folio version, however, only one **Vihuela** entry was included, and it was relocated (at long last) to correct alphabetical order: between **Vigilia o velada** and **Vil, cosa de poco precio** ('vigil or wake' and 'vile, thing of little value'). This revised 1552 version was then used in 1554 as the source for a new Granada quarto printing, which incorporated the expanded 1552 entry list and the correct placement of **Vihuela.** It also added one new term: **Caño** ('pipe'), placed out of order between **Ca[n]grejo pescado** ('crab, type of fish') and **Caña** ('reed'; see appendix A, section 3).

Another folio version was published in Granada one year later, in 1555. It was based on the 1552 printing, but with a slightly revised entry list (see appendix A, section 4). One of the new terms added in 1552 was dropped (**Desbaratar, o derribar:** 'to defeat, or throw down') and at least one new entry was added, **Cargo en officio** ('duty in office').

Exactly why both folio (1536, 1543, 1545, 1552, 1555) and quarto (1540, 1550, 1554) versions of the *Dictionarium* were being printed in southern Spain from 1536 to 1555 is unclear. Piracy is probably not at issue. The title pages of both sizes used the upper-case upsilon (Y, a Pythagorean

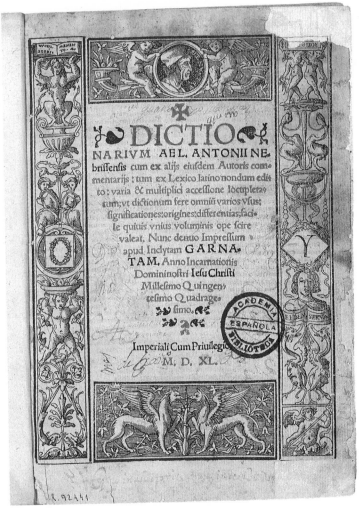

FIGURE 1.6. Title page of the 1540 Granada printing of the *Dictionarium*. Image courtesy of the Real Academia Española, Madrid, *2-B-6.

symbol) and laurel-wreath iconography emblematic of Nebrija's sons.[54] Because of their different page sizes, however, the same woodcut could not be used for both. In the folio volumes the upsilon is surrounded with a laurel wreath in the upper center of the title page (see fig. 1.7); the dolphin-adorned printer's mark at the end of the book also includes these two elements. The quarto editions display upsilon and wreath as separate elements on the left and right sides of the title's frame (see fig. 1.6). Other works by Antonio de

FIGURE 1.7. Title page of the 1552 Granada printing of the *Dictionarium*. © Biblioteca Nacional de España, Madrid, *R28932.

Nebrija were also printed by his sons, quarto-scale, during this period, and their title pages are framed with the same woodcuts used for the quarto editions of the *Dictionarium*.[55] In other words, it seems unlikely that any of these volumes was a pirated edition; their complicated opening woodcuts provide us with a kind of security stamp. Perhaps the simplest explanation for the quarto and folio versions is that the dictionaries were best sellers: so popular that Sancho and Sebastián could provide buyers with two sizes to

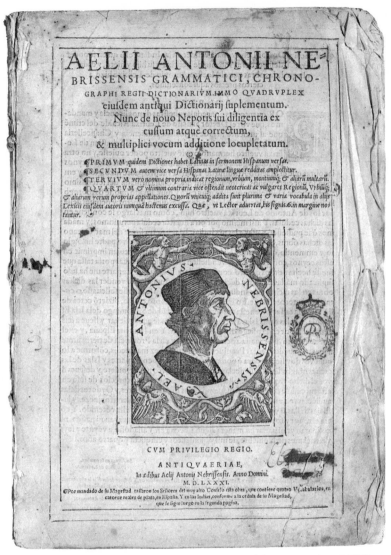

FIGURE 1.8. Title page of the 1581 Antequera printing of the *Dictionarium*. © Biblioteca Nacional de España, Madrid, *R28854.

choose from, the full-scale and the mini. Furthermore, the cover-enhancing woodcuts used for these editions would have a long life. As we will see, Sancho's son Antonio followed in his father's footsteps as a printer, and his folio versions of the *Dictionarium* from 1581 and 1585 reutilized the roundel portrait of Nebrija originally used for the folio frontispieces of 1545 and

1552 (figs. 0.1, 1.7, 1.8). In other words, this ancestral woodcut was passed down from father to son—and to grandson, for the block was reused on a *Dictionarium* title page as late as 1610 (see fig 1.10).

A final puzzle about the Granada dictionaries is that they name only Sancho de Nebrija as printer (and sometimes, no printer at all). But Sebastián's role is attested, if obliquely, by a signature in Cambridge University's copy of the 1550 version. Below the final printed line of text— "APVD INCLYTAM GRANATAM" ('in renowned Granada')—are the words "sebastianus nebriss," in a sixteenth-century hand. Does this inscription indicate the person from whom a buyer acquired the volume? Or is this a copy actually autographed by the man who oversaw its printing?

The 1555 folio *Dictionarium* would be the last complete Granada edition for over a decade.[56] Sancho de Nebrija died in 1556, and his brother Sebastián around 1560. Sancho's son Antonio took over the publication business of his father and uncle, and was printing books under his own name by 1563.[57] Four years later, in 1567, Antonio published his own Granada version, folio scale, of the *Dictionarium*. But although the title page of this volume featured a woodcut portrait of Nebrija first used on the 1555 folio, the lexical contents were not modeled on any previous edition from Granada.[58] Instead, entries for the 1567 version were based on a copy printed in Antwerp in 1553.[59] And so now we must leave Iberia, and travel back in time, to follow the translations of Nebrija to the Low Countries—lands which, owing to the tangled inheritances of Holy Roman Emperor Charles V, were ruled from Madrid for much of the sixteenth century.

Jan Steels and the Antwerp Expansions: 1545 to 1572

The renowned printer Jan Steels was born around 1500 in Brusthem, in the Duchy of Limbourg. He was publishing books in Antwerp by 1533, and in 1546 he inherited the publication business of his father-in-law, Michaël Hillen of Hoogstaten.[60] Steels was extremely prolific, putting his name to over three hundred volumes before his death in 1562. Three of these books were versions of Nebrija's *Dictionarium*, published in 1545, 1553, and 1560. A fourth Antwerp printing of the *Dictionarium* was overseen by Steels's widow in 1570.

At their core, the volumes in the Antwerp dictionary series are based on the 1540 Granada version. The 1545 Antwerp printing contains all the diagnostic traits of the 1540 volume outlined earlier: the phrasing of **Guiñar hazer del ojo**; the orderings of **Cabrituno**, **Margen del libro**, and **Ruego**. At the same time, the 1545 Antwerp printing marked another moment of expansion: 114 entries were added to the Castilian–Latin word list, additions that Steels flagged for interested buyers with marginal crosses (see appendix A, section 5). Steels also marked his pages with asterisks indicating terms that had been added in the 1536 Granada expansion. Steels's 1545 printing of the *Dictionarium* also expanded the Latin–Castilian section by around 2,500 entries.[61] Oddly, there seems to have been little overlap between the terms added to the Latin–Castilian and Castilian–Latin halves.[62] We know a lot more about the creation of the Latin–Castilian component of the 1545 Antwerp *Dictionarium,* and looking at its production history can help illuminate why multiple revisions of Nebrija's dictionary were printed in mid-sixteenth-century Antwerp.

During the 1500s Antwerp became, in the words of Fernand Braudel, "the center of the *entire* international economy."[63] Its dynamic port, and its status as a hub for trading companies, made it the richest city in Europe. As part of the Spanish crown, it also became a center for the publication of books in Castilian. From 1540 to 1560, 11 percent of all Spanish vernacular works printed in Europe were printed in Antwerp.[64] Many of these works were published by Jan Steels, who was well connected to pan-European intellectual and political circles. His father-in-law had known Erasmus, and Steels himself printed two editions of a Castilian translation of Homer's *Odyssey* by Gonzalo Pérez, personal secretary first to Charles V and then to Philip II.[65] All of this, of course, took place before 1566, when political and religious unrest plunged Antwerp and the Low Countries into forty years of war against Spanish rule.

Antwerp was also home to a large Jewish and Converso community, many of whose members had once lived in Iberia. The Nuñez, for example, were an important family of doctors, and one Luis Nuñez played a key role in bringing the 1545 Antwerp *Dictionarium* to press. Recall that in 1523, after the death of Antonio de Nebrija, his son Sebastián claimed from the University of Alcalá a number of his father's manuscripts. Among these was a "vocabulary of medicine bound in parchment"—apparently a collection of Latin terms from ancient and medieval authors that Antonio had been compiling since 1506.[66] Two decades later these handwritten pages found their way to Antwerp, and their entries were integrated by Jan Steels into the Latin–Castilian section of his 1545 *Dictionarium*. We don't know how the manuscript traveled to the Low Countries from Alcalá (or, more likely, from Granada). Perhaps Sancho and Sebastián sold it, short on funds after their father's death and unable for a decade to establish their own publication business. Or perhaps they made a copy for circulation. Whatever the case, it is not surprising that the text ended up in the hands of Steels, given his fame as a printer, his intellectual and political connections, and, more generally, the political ties linking the Low Countries to Iberia.

Steels decided not to publish the medical vocabulary as a stand-alone volume, but rather to integrate its Latin–Castilian entries into the Latin–Castilian word list of his own version of the *Dictionarium*. Unfortunately, because of either its physical condition or the nature of its entries, the far-traveled manuscript was difficult to read.[67] As a result—apparently after integrating entries *A* through *N* himself—Steels enlisted the help of Luis Nuñez, "philosopher and medical doctor," to complete the project.

Nuñez had been born in Santarem (just northeast of Lisbon) in the early 1500s (map 2). He attended the University of Salamanca, taught at the universities of Lisbon and Coimbra, and finally left Iberia (perhaps because of his Jewish ancestry) for Antwerp.[68] Once there, Nuñez kept in contact with his Portuguese colleagues; his letter of dedication printed at the beginning of the 1545 Antwerp *Dictionarium* is addressed to Jacques de Murça, rector at the University of Coimbra.[69] Nuñez was not involved in the subsequent 1553 Antwerp reprint, but was brought back for the 1560 version to correct and revise the *A* to *N* medical entries integrated in the 1540s, before he joined the project.[70] Nuñez's work in 1560 resulted in the reduction of the number of Latin–Castilian terms compared to the 1545 and 1553 printings; in particular, he removed Latin entries derived from Arabic words.

No such reduction afflicted the Castilian–Latin section of Steels's *Dictionarium*. Where the 1545 printing added 114 new terms not found in its 1540 source, the 1553 printing added 1,430 primary entries and 502 secondary entries (see appendix A, section 6).[71] As with the 1545 printing, new terms in 1553 were flagged with marginal crosses (fig. 1.9). The 1553 printing also added a fourth section of content. We saw earlier that starting with the 1512 Burgos / 1513 Salamanca expansion, Nebrija's dictionary was made up of three parts: Latin–Castilian and Castilian–Latin dictionaries, and a 'Names of towns' gazetteer. Another gazetteer was added in 1553: "Locorum neotericae ac vulgares appellationes" ('Modern and common names of places'). It

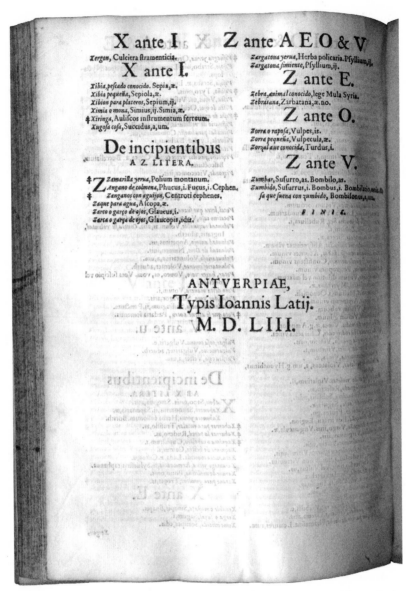

X ante I.

Xergon, Culcitra ſtramenticia.

X ante I.

Xibia, peſcado conocido. Sepia, æ.
Xibia pequeña, Sepiola, æ.
Xibion para plateros, Sepium, ij.
Ximia o mona, Simius, ij. Simia, æ.
‡ *Xiringa,* Auliſcos inſtrumentum ferreum.
Xugoſa coſa, Succidus, a, um.

De incipientibus
A Z LITERA.

‡ Z *Zamarilla yerua,* Polium montanum.
Zangano de colmena, Phucus, i. Fucus, i. Cephen.
‡ *Zanganos con aguijon,* Centroti cephenes.
Zaque para agua, Aſcopa, æ.
Zarco o garço de ojos, Glaucus, i.
Zarca o garça de ojos, Glaucopis, idis.

Z ante A E O & V

Zargatona yerua, Herba policaria. Pſyllium, ij.
Zargatona ſimiente, Pſyllium, ij.

Z ante E.

Zebra, animal conocido, lege Mula Syria.
Zebratana, Zarbatana, æ. no.

Z ante O.

Zorra o rapoſa, Vulpes, is.
Zorra pequeña, Vulpecula, æ.
Zorzal aue conocida, Turdus, i.

Z ante V.

Zumbar, Suſurro, as. Bombilo, as.
Zumbido, Suſurrus, i. Bombus, i. Bombilatio, æ. ſa que ſuena con zumbido, Bombiſonus, a, um.

F I N I S.

ANTVERPIAE,
Typis Ioannis Latij.
M. D. LIII.

FIGURE 1.9. Final page of the 1553 Antwerp printing of the *Dictionarium*, with marginal crosses used to mark new entries. Image courtesy of the Hispanic Society of America, New York.

provided the classical names for sixteenth-century places. An entry on the first folio, for example, reads "**Alcala de Henares,** villa del reyno de Toledo, donde ay estudio. Complutum"—that is, 'Alcala de Henares, town in the kingdom of Toledo, where there is scholarship,' followed by the town's name in Roman times, Complutum.

All of these expansions were carried over to the 1560 Antwerp printing.[72] As far as I can tell, no new Castilian–Latin entries were added to this version. This volume did, however, introduce a number of spelling variations, as well as a small alphabetization error: the **Zamarilla yerua - Zangano de colmena - Zanganos con aguijon** order of the 1553 printing ('poley, an herb,' 'buzzing of a beehive,' 'drones with stingers') became **Zangano de colmena - Zamarilla yerua - Zanganos con aguijon.** In turn, this ordering error and a few spelling variations introduced in 1560 were carried over to the 1570 printing.[73]

Published over the course of twenty-five years, the four Antwerp editions of the *Dictionarium* were made possible by a translation of the 1540 Granada version from southern Spain to the Low Countries. In the mid-1560s a countergift, as it were, made its way from the Low Countries south to Andalusia, as one of Steels's own volumes retraced in reverse the Antwerp-to-Granada journey of its ancestor.

Antonio's Grandson from Granada to Antequera: 1567, 1572, 1574, 1578, 1581

In 1567, three years before Jan Steels's widow published her 1570 Antwerp version of the *Dictionarium,* yet another printing was issued in Granada. But when Antonio de Nebrija's grandson (named Antonio after his grandfather) set out to publish his ancestor's famous dictionary, he used as his model a copy that had been printed in Antwerp over a decade before. Antonio's 1567 version includes the entries added to the 1553 Antwerp printing (entries not found in previous editions, including the 1545 Antwerp predecessor), and spelling variations of these added entries make clear the kinship between the 1553 Antwerp and 1567 Granada volumes, in contrast to the 1560 Antwerp version.[74]

In deciding to base his new edition on one from Antwerp, rather than one of the volumes printed in Granada by his father and uncle, Antonio was no doubt thinking of sales. We saw that Jan Steels added over a hundred new entries to his 1545 Antwerp version, and over fifteen hundred entries to the 1553 printing. In other words, the Antwerp versions were more robust than the contemporary editions printed by Antonio's kin. Indeed, Antonio's father and uncle had basically done the same thing back in 1536, when they used Miguel de Eguía's 1532 Alcalá dictionary as a model for their new Granada publication.

In 1572, the younger Antonio de Nebrija used his own 1567 volume as the model for yet another Granada edition.[75] But by the early 1570s Antonio had been working in Granada for almost a decade, and he apparently wanted a change. By 1573 he was publishing in Antequera, 100 kilometers to the west.[76] There he issued three different editions of the *Dictionarium*, each a different size: a quarto in 1574, a large folio (29 cm) in 1578, and a smaller folio (25.5 cm) in 1581. The covers from 1574 and 1578 feature a woodcut of the double-headed Habsburg eagle; the 1581 version used the round woodcut portrait of Antonio de Nebrija that had graced covers of the *Dictionarium* since the Granada printing of 1545 (see fig. 1.8).

In terms of content, the 1574 printing was *not* based on Antonio's earlier Granada volume from 1572. Rather, spelling variations match those of the Antwerp version published by Jan Steels's widow in 1570. The 1570 and 1574 volumes even share the same page and entry layouts.[77] In other words, once again a copy of the *Dictionarium* printed in the Low Countries retraced the steps of a distant ancestor back to southern Iberia. Four years later, in 1578, Antonio oversaw the concurrent production of yet another edition of his grandfather's dictionary, using presses in Antequera and Salamanca. This version includes a pre-frontispiece sheet with "Salmanticae, Apud Heredes Ioannis a Canoua" printed on the recto, and a printer's mark featuring an angel on the verso—both referring to the Salamanca-based Heirs of Juan de Canova printing house.[78] The reasons for Antonio's use of concurrent printing on this 1578 version are unclear, and equally unclear is exactly which previous edition was used as a model. On the one hand, the 1578 volume includes many features suggesting the Antwerp 1570 or Antequera 1574 printings—the ordering of **Guarda, en lugar de otro** before **Guarda, la persona que guarda** ('guard, in the place of another' and 'guard, the person who guards,' a revision first made in 1570) and of **Zangano de colmena** before **Zamarilla yerua**, as well as a number of spelling variations.[79] But other spelling variations separate the 1578 volume from the 1570 and 1574 versions, connecting it instead to much earlier editions, most closely the

Antwerp printing of 1553.[80] These patterns may suggest that different versions of the *Dictionarium* were being used as models for concurrent production by the printers in Antequera and Salamanca.

Despite this source ambiguity, one thing at least is certain about the 1578 volume: it included twenty-five new entries that had not appeared in any previous edition (see appendix A, section 7). These additions, oddly, were abandoned three years later, when Antonio de Nebrija published his grandfather's best seller yet again. This 1581 Granada printing reverted to the 1574 Antequera volume as a model, and it added three new entries of its own (see appendix A, section 8).[81]

Antonio's Grandson and the Granada Expansion: 1585, 1589

In 1582, after nearly a decade in Antequera, Antonio moved back to Granada.[82] In 1585 he published yet another version of the *Dictionarium*, based on the expanded-entry Antequera printing of 1578.[83] The 1585 version also included fifty-three new Castilian–Latin entries, a modest increase duly noted on the cover: "Only a few words have been added to [the Castilian–Latin section in] our latest edition, because in the first Latin[–Castilian] section many have been added" (fig. 0.1; see appendix A, section 9).[84] A fifth section was also added in 1585. The Latin–Castilian and Castilian–Latin dictionaries and "Oppidorum nomina" and "Locorum neotericae ac vulgares appellationes" gazetteers were now joined by a long list of Castilian loan words from Arabic.[85] Most were familiar terms, such as **Açucar,** **Açelgas,** and **Albur** ('sugar,' 'chard,' 'mullet'). But every third or fourth entry was followed by a brief definition, such as the opening folio's "**Alcaçar.** Es casa Real" and "**Alcaçaba.** Es fortaleza" ('Alcaçar. A royal house' and 'Alcaçaba. A fortress').

In turn, the 1585 Granada volume, including its fifty-three new entries, was used as a model for the Granada printing of 1589. This edition, once again, was the result of concurrent production, although in this case both publishers were located in Granada. Melchior Rodríguez Mercader oversaw the Latin–Castilian section, and Antonio de Nebrija oversaw the Castilian–Latin section. Although based on the 1585 printing and its expanded list of entries, at least one change was made in the new version: a glaring alphabetization error was (partially) corrected. In the 1578 and 1585 printings, the

DICCIO-
NARIO DE ROMAN-
CE EN LATIN. POR EL
MAESTRO ANTONIO DE NE-
BRISSA GRAMATICO, CORO-
NISTA DE LOS REYES
CATOLICOS.

☞ *VAN AÑADIDOS EN ESTA VLTIMA IMPRESSION POCOS vocablos, porque en el primero del Latin se an añadido muchos, y de Ambrosio Calepino, y otros muy importantes, que hasta oy no se an impresso en este Vocabulario; y à se enmendado de muchos vicios, y errores que tenia de la imprenta. Averiguase en el de Latin si es el vocablo de Ciceron, o no; y tambien de su Acento.*

¶ Pusose assi mesmo en el fin deste Vocabulario vn compendio de los vocablos Arabigos corruptos, de que comunmente vsamos en nuestra lengua Castellana.

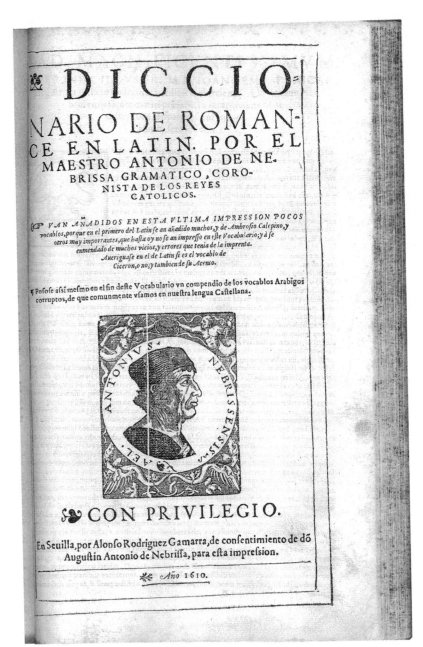

CON PRIVILEGIO.

En Seuilla, por Alonso Rodriguez Gamarra, de consentimiento de dõ Augustin Antonio de Nebrissa, para esta impression.

Año 1610.

FIGURE 1.10. Title page of the 1610 Seville printing of the *Dictionarium;* note the vertical break line in the woodcut portrait of Antonio de Nebrija, which also appears in figures 1.8 (1581) and 0.1 (1585). Image courtesy of the Real Academia Española, Madrid, *29-I-6 (3).

word for *syringe* had been spelled **Xeringa** (in contrast to the **Xiringa** of earlier editions). But this new *Xe-* word was left in the *Xi-* section, between **Ximia** and **Xugosa** ('she-ape' and 'juicy'). In 1589 the entry for **Xeringa** was moved up between **Xergon** and **Xerga, o sayal** ('straw bed' and 'sackcloth, or coarse stuff'). **Xeringa** was still out of alphabetical order, but at least it was included among other *Xer-* words.

For over two decades, Antonio de Nebrija had released a new version of his grandfather's dictionary every four years or so: in 1567, 1572, 1574, 1578, 1581, 1585, and 1589. At this rate, he was due for another printing around 1593, but his death in the early 1590s intervened. Yet the tradition continued, in a way. Antonio's son, Agustín Antonio, was also a printer, and after his father's death he moved the family publishing business back to Antequera, where Agustín had been born in 1580.[86]

Agustín, the Antequera Revision, and a Return to Seville: 1595, 1600, 1610

Agustín's 1595 Antequera printing of the *Dictionarium* was based on his father's five-part 1589 version, but it introduced a number of spelling variations, which were carried over to Agustín's second Antequera version of 1600.[87] A contract from 1602 shows Agustín working with Alonso Rodríguez Gamarra, an Antequeran printer. Rodríguez Gamarra moved to Seville around 1604, and there, in 1610, he released his own version of the *Dictionarium*—which was based, spelling variations reveal, on the Antequera printing of 1600.[88] This was an authorized edition. Its cover announced "the consent of don Agustín Antonio de Nebrija for this printing," and the title page was decorated with a Nebrija family heirloom: the round woodcut portrait that, as we have seen, was first used by Agustín's grandfather in Granada in 1545 (fig. 1.10).[89]

In the following year, 1611, Sebastián de Covarrubias Orozco published his famous *Tesoro de la lengua castellana, o española,* the world's first monolingual Castilian dictionary. We've seen that the entries in Nebrija's bilingual dictionaries were quite spare, with Castilian and Latin equivalents appearing on the same line of text. In contrast, Covarrubias followed each of his Castilian entries with a small paragraph of information, including definitions, etymologies, and sometimes quotations from classical and Castilian authors. The epigraphs on **Traduzir** and **Trasladar** that open this book are good examples of Covarrubias's style. As Thomas Smith-Stark has shown, these wordy entries have much in common with an older style of dictionary, the *Calepino* (named after Ambrogio Calepino, an Italian monk who published a massive and massively popular Latin dictionary in 1502), even as they point forward to the monolingual dictionaries we use today.[90] And so here, in the opening years of the seventeenth century, we conclude our survey of Nebrija's Castilian–Latin translations.

But our story is just beginning. The next chapter returns to the early sixteenth century, tracing how the Castilian word lists in these various translations of Nebrija were used, in turn, as frameworks for dictionaries translating Castilian into languages other than Latin. We will start in Granada, in southern Spain, just over a decade after that once-independent Muslim kingdom had fallen to the forces of King Ferdinand and Queen Isabella.

2
Arabic, Nahuatl, Tuscan, Tagalog . . .

Over the course of nearly a century, the list of Castilian–Latin entries first published in Nebrija's 1495 dictionary underwent constant changes: Salamanca in 1513, Granada in 1536, Antwerp in 1545 and 1553, and Granada again in 1552, 1554, 1555, 1578, 1581, and 1585. In turn, the volumes published in the wake of these ten metamorphoses had their own internal variations and peculiarities: changes in spelling, or in the alphabetization of particular entries. Against that backdrop of large- and small-scale transformations, this chapter explores how Castilian entries in these various printings were used as models for the creation of non-Latin translating dictionaries. We will focus on dictionaries organized by, or including a section with, Castilian terms as their leading categories. This means we will not consider some works clearly based on Nebrija, such as Gabriel Busa's 1507 Catalan–Latin / Latin–Catalan *Uocabularius,* or Cristóbal de Escobar's 1520 Latin–Sicilian–Castilian *Uocabularium.*[1] Only brief reference will be made to dictionaries that translate to Castilian from another languages, such as the Quechua–Castilian section of Domingo de Santo Tomás's 1560 *Lexicon,* the Tuscan–Castilian section of Cristóbal de las Casas's 1570 *Vocabulario,* or the French–Castilian–Latin structure of Heinrich Hornkens's 1599 *Recveil de dictionnaires francoys, espaignolz et latins* ('Collection of French, Spanish, and Latin dictionaries')—not to mention important manuscript dictionaries translating Mayan languages into Castilian.[2]

Even with these exclusions, we have dozens of titles to consider. And their connections—to one another, and to Nebrija—become ever more complicated over time (see fig. 0.3).[3] To trace these relations, this chapter is ordered chronologically, not geographically. As we move forward in time, we will shift back and forth across the Atlantic, from Europe to the Americas to Europe again and, finally, to Asia. As I will argue in this book's conclusion, such a back-and-forth movement has important implications for rethinking the relationship of "early modern" Europe to the "colonial" Philippines and Latin America.

1505: Castilian–Arabic

Pedro de Alcalá's *Arte para ligerame[n]te saber la le[n]gua arauiga* was printed in Granada in 1505. It was designed to help Catholic missionaries convert the many Muslims who still lived in that recently conquered kingdom. The volume includes a grammar, a section of catechistical texts in Arabic, and a Castilian–Arabic dictionary.[4] Arabic words are written with Latin characters throughout. Although each lettered section of the Castilian–Arabic dictionary is subdivided according to parts of speech (nouns, verbs, adverbs, and so forth), a quick comparison reveals that most entries were gathered from Nebrija. Indeed, Alcalá states in the prologue that he used as a model "one of the already existing compilations of words, translating it into Arabic," and that this compilation "was made by the honorable and prudent Master Antonio de Nebrija, to which I added various nouns and verbs and other parts of speech which occurred to me, and I left out some of those therein that lacked an Arabic translation."[5]

The *Arte*'s colophon reveals that "this work and vocabulary from Romance into Arabic" had been completed by 1501—which means that Alcalá must have used the 1495 Salamanca printing of Nebrija as a model.[6] At the same time (as his prologue makes clear) Alcalá was not bound by the limits of the 1495 *Vocabulario*. Although he didn't translate all of Nebrija's entries, he also added categories absent from his source, such as terms for *henna* (**Alheña**) and a special kind of silk cloth made by Muslim weavers (**Zarzahan**).[7]

1540s? Castilian–Latin–Nahuatl

The "Vocabulario trilingüe" is an unpublished manuscript housed at the Newberry Library in Chicago.[8] It is a fascinating document from sixteenth-century Central Mexico, blurring the boundaries of printing and writing. To create it, the authors first copied out, in full, the Castilian–Latin contents of a Nebrijan dictionary, entry by entry, in black ink. This Mediterranean framework in place, they then went back through the document, adding Nahuatl translations in red ink—at least in most cases.

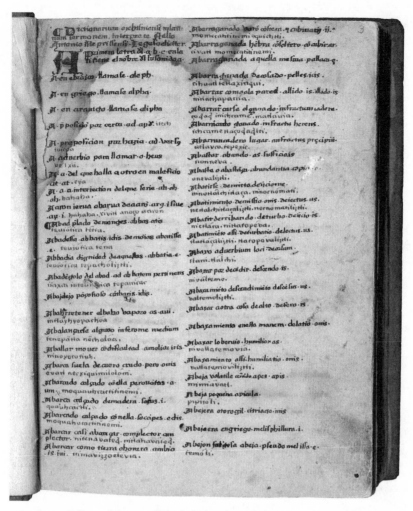

FIGURE 2.1. Folio 3r of the 1540s "Vocabulario trilingüe" (first page of entries). Image courtesy of the Newberry Library, Chicago, VAULT Ayer MS 1478.

Some Castilian–Latin entries are given no Nahuatl equivalent, and are simply followed by an empty space (fig. 2.1).[9]

Exactly when this manuscript was produced is unclear, but it probably dates to the 1540s.[10] Based on a careful analysis of the Nahuatl entries, Mary L. Clayton demonstrates that the text was produced by native Nahuatl speakers. For example, the Nahua authors were confused by the meaning of some of the Castilian–Latin entries. **Botilleria,** 'wine cellar or food storeroom,' is translated into Nahuatl as "cihuātl vinopixqui," 'a female wine-keeper.' **Cabra domestica et mansa**, 'a domestic and tame goat,' is followed by a comparative description: "maçācuācuauhtēntzoneh," 'a deer having horns and a beard.' **Almendro arbol conocido**, 'Almond, a well-known tree,' is translated by the more complicated explanation of "cē castillancuahuitl iuhqui cacahuatl ītech mochīhua," 'a Castile-place tree, [things] resembling peanuts grow from it.'[11]

But what was the original published source of this handmade vocabulary? For many years, scholars noted similarities between the Newberry manuscript and Gerald MacDonald's non-facsimile edition of the (first) 1516 *Dictionarium*. But they also noted discrepancies as well, such as the spelling of the title.[12] A splendid analysis by Heréndira Tellez Nieto, published in 2010, points out many additional differences between the spellings of entries in the Newberry manuscript and those in MacDonald's edition.[13] Thus where the Newberry manuscript has **Aceptar herencia** ('to accept an inheritance'), MacDonald has **Aceptar erencia**. Where the Newberry manuscript has **Ley de la manda del quarto** ('law of the fourth part of inherited goods'), MacDonald has **Ley de la manda del cuarto**. Where the Newberry manuscript has **Casas en la heredad** ('houses in inheritance'), MacDonald has **Casa en la eredad**. Where the Newberry manuscript has **Libre fecho de sieruo** ('free, made of a servant'), MacDonald has **Libre hecho de siervo**.

All of these divergences are deceptive. Each one is due to MacDonald's practice of standardizing and modernizing Nebrija's spelling. In the two printings of the *Dictionarium* dated 1516 (both legitimate and pirate copy), every one of these examples shares its spelling with the Newberry manuscript.[14] In these entries, at least, what seems at first to be a discrepancy between the Newberry manuscript and Nebrija is in fact a mirage, created by the interventions of a twentieth-century editor.

At the same time, Tellez Nieto's general point is valid. A number of Castilian spellings in the Newberry manuscript *are* different from the spellings in the *first* 1516 printing of Nebrija's dictionary. Thus where the Newberry manuscript has **Camara lo que assi se haze, Xaraue de medicina**, and **Xaraue para gomitar**, the first 1516 printing of the *Dictionarium* has **Camara lo q[ue] assi se faze, Xarafe de medicina**, and **Xarafe para gomitar**.

These variations are easily explained. As we saw in chapter 1, there were two slightly different "1516" versions of Nebrija's dictionary, one actually printed in 1516 and the other a pirated copy probably produced around 1520 (see figs. 1.3 and 1.4). A comparison of entries makes it clear that MacDonald used the "original" 1516 printing as his model (perhaps via a microfilm of the copy at the Hispanic Society of America in New York City).[15] In contrast, spelling variations in the Newberry manuscript match the variations of the pirated "1516" copy: **Camara lo que assi se haze, Xaraue de medicina, Xaraue para gomitar.** In other words, Castilian–Latin entries in the Newberry's "Vocabulario trilingüe" were copied out from the pirated "1516" Seville printing of Nebrija's *Dictionarium* (see fig. 0.3).[16]

1547: Castilian–Nahuatl

Our next example also comes from Central Mexico. Six manuscript copies of friar Andrés de Olmos's 1547 "Arte de la lengua mexicana" are known to exist. Only the version at Tulane University contains a vocabulary at the end.[17] It is divided into two parts, first Nahuatl–Castilian and then Castilian–Nahuatl. It is focused (but not exclusively so) on verbs. Karen Dakin has argued that the Nahuatl–Castilian section of this vocabulary is not actually the work of Olmos, but may instead be a list of verbs assembled by his students. Such a collaborative working model may explain the irregular structure of the Castilian–Nahuatl section as well.[18]

The Castilian–Nahuatl entries were gathered from several different sources. They are not listed in strict alphabetical order, and in several cases the same Castilian category is repeated on different pages. **Alegrar a otro** ('to make another happy') appears three times, once on 260r and twice on 260v. **Coronper virgen** ('to corrupt a virgin') appears on both 266r and 266v. **Enboluer algo** ('to wrap something') has separate entries on both 271r and 272v. One source for entries seems to be the Nahuatl–Castilian verb list that appears earlier in the manuscript. Esther Hernández argues that Olmos created and translated the list of indigenous verbs first, and then simply reordered it to generate the Castilian–Nahuatl entries.[19] But this reconstructed method does not explain all of the irregularities in the Castilian–Nahuatl section. Another source for the Castilian entries was clearly Nebrija's *Dictionarium*. Many *Z* entries in the Tulane manuscript are copied directly from Nebrija. Two entries for **Zunbar** appear out of alphabetical order: an error that also appears, as we saw in the last chapter, in the 1513 *Dictionarium*, and not corrected until the second Alcalá printing of 1520. The final three entries in the manuscript are actually Nebrijan *nouns*: **Zebratan[a]**, **Zora o raposa**, and **Zora pequeña**. Furthermore, it is not only in the *Z* section that traces of Nebrijan categories can be found. Complex multiword entries clearly drawn from Nebrija appear elsewhere in the manuscript: **Vender por menudo, Venir a la memoria, Visitar yr auer, Votar hazer el voto,** and **Votar dar el voto** ('to sell for a little,' 'to come to mind,' 'to visit, go to see,' 'to vote, make a vote,' 'to vote, cast a vote').[20]

Because the Tulane list focuses on verbs (thus limiting the number of entries), and is apparently transcribed from several sources, it is difficult to establish exactly which 1513-or-later printings of Nebrija were used as models. The out-of-order placement of the two **Zunbar** entries (before **Zebratan[a], Zora o raposa,** and **Zora pequeña**) suggests one parent: the 1513 Salamanca printing, the 1514 Zaragoza printing, one of the two "1516" Seville printings, or the first 1520 Alcalá printing. But it was not the only source. The spelling of the entry for **Visitar yr aver** is particularly noteworthy. The same spelling is found in the (pirated) "1516," 1532, and 1536-and-after printings, in contrast to the **Visitar ir auer** spelling used in 1513, 1520, and 1528. At least three entries echo categories added to the 1536 Granada expansion of the *Dictionarium:* **auer misericordia, saltar el macho sobre la hembra,** and **sobrepujar** ('to have mercy,' 'to mount, the male animal on the female,' and 'to excel') are paralleled in Olmos as **aber mi[sericordi]a, saltar el animal a la he[m]bra,** and **sebre pujar a otro.** Together, these verbs suggest that a second source used by Olmos and his collaborators was a copy of the *Dictionarium* from the Granada lineage of the 1530s and 1540s.

1555: Castilian–Nahuatl

As the two previous examples make clear, several Castilian–Nahuatl translating dictionaries were circulating as manuscripts in Central Mexico in the 1540s. A published Castilian–Nahuatl vocabulary did not appear until 1555: Alonso de Molina's *Vocabulario en la lengua castellana y mexicana* (fig. 2.2). It was the first dictionary to be printed in the Americas.[21]

Molina's debt to the word lists of Nebrija's *Dictionarium* is well known, but prior analyses have focused comparisons on the 1495 Salamanca printing or the 1516 Seville printing (or, more accurately, MacDonald's 1973 modernized edition of that work).[22] In fact, however, neither of these versions was the one used as a model by Molina and his indigenous collaborators. The 1555 *Vocabulario* contains a number of categories added to the *Dictionarium* in the 1536 Granada expansion, such as **Jazmin** and **Queso fresco.** At the same time, it does not incorporate entries from the 1545 or 1553 Antwerp expansions, or from the Granada expansions of 1552, 1554, or 1555.[23] And like the Granada printings of 1536, 1540, 1543, 1545, and 1550 (as

FIGURE 2.2. Title page of Alonso de Molina's 1555 Castilian–Nahuatl *Vocabulario*.
Image courtesy of the John Carter Brown Library at Brown University.

well as the Estella printing of 1548), Molina includes two separate entries
for *vihuela*, 'lute,' a redundancy that had been corrected in the 1552 Granada
version and its 1554 and 1555 descendants.

These basic features narrow the candidates for Molina's source to a version from Granada (1536, 1540, 1543, 1545, 1550) or Estella (1548). As we saw
in chapter 1, these printings contain a number of striking internal variations,
and they make it possible to identify exactly which version Molina used as

a model. Like the Granada folios of 1536, 1543, and 1545, as well as the 1548 Estella printing, but unlike the Granada quartos of 1540 and 1550, Molina's entries for **Ruego** come before the entries for **Rufian**—in correct alphabetical order. Like the 1543 and 1545 folios, but unlike the versions of 1536 and 1540 (as well as the 1548 Estella printing), Molina places **Guedijudo** ('long-haired') between the entries for **Guedija de cabellos** and **Guedija enhetrada**, not after them (an out-of-alphabetical order variation). Finally, in contrast to the 1543 folio, both Molina and the 1545 folio spell 'syrup' **Xaraue**, rather than—as in the printings from 1536, 1540, 1543, 1548, and 1550—**Xarafe**. Together, these details show that Molina used the 1545 Granada folio as his model.

At the same time—and unlike the Newberry manuscript discussed earlier—Molina and his collaborators did not limit themselves to the Castilian entries found in their Nebrijan source. They expanded existing categories, and even invented Castilian neologisms in order to capture the meanings of Nahuatl terms. A number of entries, for example, describe different types of maize (white, black, red, yellow, multicolored) and kinds of liquid foam (of chocolate, of water). The implications of this linguistic creativity will be explored further in the next two chapters.

Sixteen years later, in 1571, Molina published an expanded version of his vocabulary, which also added a reversed Nahuatl–Castilian section. Because this revised edition had such an important influence on subsequent indigenous-language vocabularies, it will be discussed on its own later in this chapter. First, however, we need to survey the immediate impact of the 1555 printing on Mesoamerican lexicography.

After 1555: Castilian–Nahuatl–Otomi

This trilingual dictionary—now in the library of the Museo Nacional de Antropología in Mexico City—is a published copy of Molina's 1555 *Vocabulario* to which Otomi equivalents have been added, by hand, after the Castilian–Nahuatl entries.[24] (Otomi, like Nahuatl, is a language spoken in Central Mexico.) This annotated volume (and several others like it, discussed in the pages to come) was never actually published as a separate Castilian–Otomi dictionary. But it gives us an idea of the method by which early modern linguists worked—and not only in the New World. That is, published dictionaries were brought to "the field" (which might be anywhere from Mexico to Tuscany to England). The margins around their printed entries (Castilian–Nahuatl entries, in this case) were then filled up with equivalent terms from a third language. This is the stage at which the authors of the Castilian–Nahuatl–Otomi volume ended their project. But other linguists went further. In some cases, they made clean copies, painstakingly transforming a chaos of printed and handwritten entries into a neat list. The Newberry's "Vocabulario trilingüe" is one example of this, and the same process seems to be behind a few of the Mayan dictionaries discussed later in this chapter. These clean copies might also incorporate notes from a number of different sources, which may explain the tangled mess of entries in Olmos's 1547 manuscript vocabulary.

In a few exceptional cases, the word lists generated by glossing published dictionaries were actually taken to printers for publication. Once bound and sold, these dictionaries-generated-from-dictionaries could prompt the whole word-gathering process once again, their clean margins inscribed with words from yet other languages. Such a multigenerational process is revealed by this trilingual Castilian–Nahuatl–Otomi volume. As we saw in the previous section, the 1545 Granada version of Nebrija's Castilian–Latin dictionary was used as a source for creating Molina's 1555 *Vocabulario*. That is, a copy of the Iberian publication was taken to Central Mexico, used to collect Nahuatl terms, and then those gathered words (perhaps recopied into a clean manuscript) were taken to a printer. A published copy of the resulting Castilian–Nahuatl dictionary then became the framework, in this case at least, for collecting words in Otomi. As we will see, such complex multisourced dictionaries—and the compilation processes their mixed entries imply—would become increasingly common, in both Europe and the Americas, over the course of the sixteenth and seventeenth centuries.

1557: Castilian–Nahuatl–Matlatzinca

Another copy of Molina's 1555 Castilian–Nahuatl *Vocabulario*, for example, is filled with handwritten marginal entries in Matlatzinca, a language also spoken in Central Mexico. The annotations were made by Molina's fellow Franciscan, Andrés de Castro, and are dated 1557. The volume is currently held by the Cornell University Library (see fig. 4.1).[25]

1559: Castilian–P'urhépecha

Friar Maturino Gilberti's 1559 *Vocabulario en lengua de Mechuacan* provides an example of a glossed dictionary that actually did make it to print.[26]

FIGURE 2.3. Internal title page of the Castilian–P'urhépecha section of Maturino Gilberti's 1559 *Vocabulario*, using the same woodcut seen in figure 2.2. Image courtesy of the John Carter Brown Library at Brown University.

Published in Mexico City in 1559, Gilberti's *Vocabulario* of P'urhépecha (a language spoken in western Mexico) has at its core a nearly perfect word-for-word copy of the Castilian entries in Molina's 1555 *Vocabulario*. Molina's Nahuatl entries have been left out, replaced by entries in P'urhépecha. Gilberti's text even includes the appendix of extra words Molina added at the end of his 1555 volume.

FIGURE 2.4. Mary placing a chasuble on Saint Ildefonso, in Maturino Gilberti's 1559 *Vocabulario*, printed from the same woodcut block used in figure 2.5. Image courtesy of the John Carter Brown Library at Brown University.

A small amount of editing relative to Molina's text has taken place. Gilberti includes only one entry for **Vihuela**, not two, and a number of categories in the final appendix have been cut as well.[27] The parallels between the works of Molina and Gilberti even extend to production and visual content. Gilberti's dictionary, like Molina's, was printed in Mexico City by Juan Pablos, who ornamented Gilberti's book with two woodcut

FIGURE 2.5. Mary placing a chasuble on Saint Ildefonso, in Alonso de Molina's 1555 Castilian–Nahuatl *Vocabulario*. Image courtesy of the John Carter Brown Library at Brown University.

images originally included in Molina: Saint Francis receiving the stigmata, and Saint Ildefonso (a seventh-century bishop who became the patron saint of Toledo) receiving a chasuble from the Virgin Mary (compare figs. 2.2 and 2.3, and 2.4 and 2.5).[28]

Gilberti's main innovation was to begin his volume with a P'urhépecha–Castilian dictionary. The *Vocabulario en lengua de Mechuacan* is the first bidirectional dictionary published in the Americas, and indeed is one of the earliest bidirectional non-Latin dictionaries published anywhere.

After 1559: Castilian–P'urhépecha–Otomi

Like its Castilian–Nahuatl printed source, Gilberti's *Vocabulario* would itself be used to generate dictionaries of yet other languages. For example, sometime after 1559 a copy of Gilberti's *Vocabulario en lengua de Mechuacan* was hand-glossed with Otomi translations (see fig. 4.2). This volume—now in the New York Public Library—records Otomi as spoken by a colony of miners working in Tzintzuntzan, the ancient Tarascan capital of west Mexico (map 1).[29] Once again, the margins of a published translating dictionary were filled with terms gathered from a third language—a practice whose implications we will explore further in chapter 4.

1560: Castilian–Quechua

One year after Gilberti's P'urhépecha–Castilian / Castilian–P'urhépecha *Vocabulario* appeared in Mexico City, Domingo de Santo Tomás (a Dominican friar serving as a missionary in Peru) published a Castilian–Quechua *Lexicon, o vocabulario de la lengua general del Perv*. But unlike dictionaries of indigenous languages from New Spain, which were printed in Mexico City, this Castilian–Quechua volume was printed across the ocean in Valladolid, in northwestern Spain (map 2).[30] It was the first American-language dictionary to be published in Europe.

Santo Tomás makes his debt to Nebrija clear in the introduction, writing that "this vocabulary goes by the same order as that of Antonio de Nebrija, alphabetically."[31] A number of details suggest that his work was based on the first, non-pirated 1516 Seville printing of Nebrija's *Dictionarium*. The *Lexicon* contains none of the entries added to the *Dictionarium* in the Granada expansions of 1536, 1552, 1554, or 1555, or in the Antwerp expansions of 1545 and 1553. The *Lexicon* also contains an alphabetization glitch found in the original 1495 Salamanca printing and not corrected until the 1536 Granada printing: *Gu-* entries are listed in two separate sections, first after *Gau-* (out of alphabetical order) and again after *Gru-*.

More specifically, the *Lexicon* contains at least four diagnostic spelling irregularities. The first two are shared by both 1516 printings of the *Dictionarium* but are not found in other versions. In the entry for **Casamiento el dote que**

se da ('marriage, the dowry which is given') the term *dote* ('dowry,' a feminine noun) is prefaced by *el* rather than the correct *la*. In the printings from 1513, 1514, 1520, 1528, 1532, and beyond, the entry reads correctly: **Casamiento la dote que se da**. The two 1516 printings, like Santo Tomás's *Lexicon*, also spell the word *honest* with an initial *h* in **Caridad amor honesto** ('charity, honest love'). That initial *h* is absent from other versions of the *Dictionarium*: 1503, 1506, 1513, 1514, 1520, 1528, 1532, and beyond.

Two other spelling glitches are shared only by the *Lexicon* and the first 1516 printing of the *Dictionarium*. They do not appear in the pirated "1516" Seville version (or indeed in any other early sixteenth-century printing). Both of these Castilian entries, significantly, are not given a Quechua equivalent. This strongly suggests they are entries copied (but never translated) from another printed source.[32] One is the entry for **Reprouar**, 'to condemn.' This -*uar* spelling is shared by the original 1516 Seville version, but the pirated "1516" copy uses a -*bar* spelling instead: **Reprobar**. Another untranslated category in the 1560 *Lexicon* is for 'setter of bones' (fig. 2.6). In most copies of Nebrija's *Dictionarium*—including the pirated Seville version—the word for *bones* is spelled *huessos*: **Concertador de huessos**. But in the original 1516 printing the word for *bones* is spelled *avessos*. In the 1560 Castilian–Quechua *Lexicon*, a similarly strange spelling is used: *vassos*.

To the Castilian entries selected from Nebrija, the *Lexicon* also added a few categories to accommodate the new things of the Americas, including chiles (**Axi, especias de Indios**), different types of maize (**Mayz, trigo de los Indios; Mayz tostado; Mayz cozido**), and even camelid bloodletting (**Sa[n]-grar la oueja, para comer la sangre**).[33]

1570, 1576, 1582, 1583, 1587, 1591, 1597, 1600, 1604, 1608: Castilian–Tuscan

Up until now, our survey of early modern Castilian dictionaries has involved only two other European languages, Latin and Arabic. In 1570, however, Cristóbal de las Casas published his bidirectional *Vocabvlario de las dos lengvas toscana y castellana*, with Tuscan–Castilian and Castilian–Tuscan sections. (Tuscan, of course, is a regional form of Italian). This Sevillan publication was followed by a 1576 printing (probably pirated) in Venice, and then another Venetian printing in 1582. The year after that, a

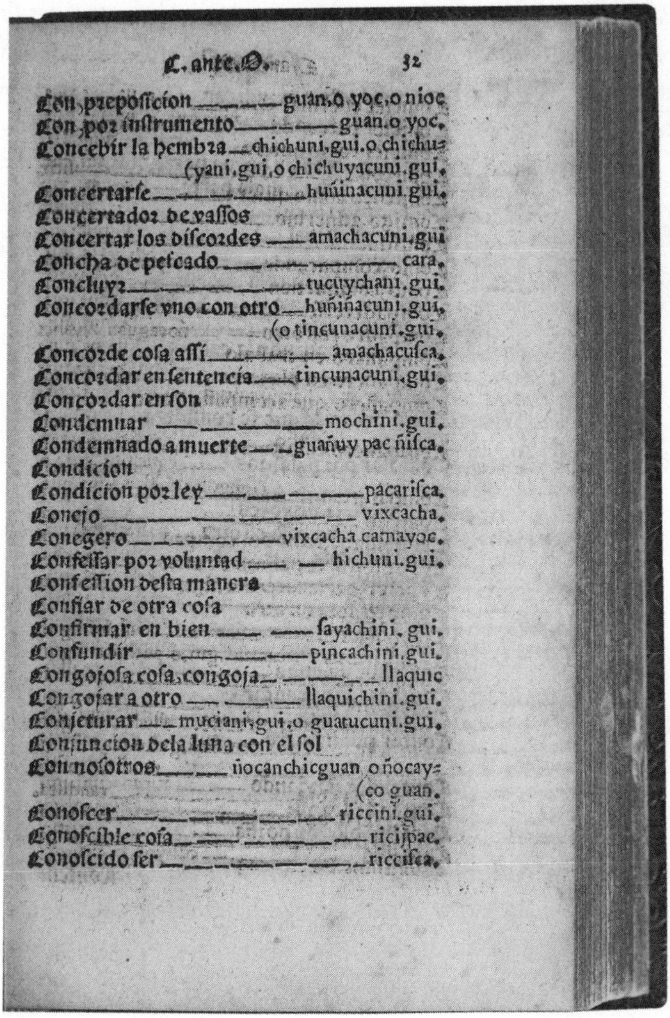
C. ante. O. 32

Con, prepoſicion ——— guan, o yoc, o nioc.
Con, por inſtrumento ——— guan, o yoc.
Concebir la hembra — chichuni, gui, o chichu-
(yani, gui, o chichuyacuni, gui.
Concertarſe ——— huñinacuni, gui.
Concertador de vaſſos
Concertar los diſcordes —— amachacuni, gui
Concha de peſcado ——— cara.
Concluyr ——— tucuychani, gui.
Concordarſe vno con otro — huñinacuni, gui,
(o tincunacuni, gui.
Concorde coſa aſſi ——— amachacuſca.
Concordar en ſentencia — tincunacuni, gui.
Concordar en ſon
Condemnar ——— mochini, gui.
Condemnado a muerte —— guañuy pac ñiſca.
Condicion
Condicion por ley ——— pacariſca.
Conejo ——— vixcacha.
Conegero ——— vixcacha camayoc.
Confeſſar por voluntad —— hichuni, gui.
Confeſſion deſta manera
Confiar de otra coſa
Confirmar en bien ——— ſayachini, gui.
Confundir ——— pincachini, gui.
Congojoſa coſa, congoja ——— llaquic
Congojar a otro ——— llaquichini, gui.
Conjecturar — muciani, gui, o guatucuni, gui.
Conjuncion dela luna con el ſol
Con noſotros ——— ñocanchicguan, o ñocay-
(co guan.
Conoſcer ——— riccini, gui.
Conoſcible coſa ——— ricijpac.
Conoſcido ſer ——— riccisca.

FIGURE 2.6. Folio 32r of Domingo de Santo Tomás's 1560 *Lexicon*, with untranslated entries (**Concertador de vassos, Concordar en son, Condicion, Confession desta manera, Confiar de otra cosa**). Image courtesy of the John Carter Brown Library at Brown University.

second Sevillan printing appeared, but after this all reprints were published in the city of canals: 1587, 1591, 1597, 1600, 1604, and 1608 (see fig. 0.3).

The original 1570 printing of the *Vocabulario* was based on one of the early Granada printings of Nebrija's *Dictionarium*. It contains a number of entries added in the 1536 Granada expansion, but none of the categories added to the

Granada printings of 1552, 1554, or 1555, nor from the Antwerp expansions of 1545 and 1553 (such as **Verenjena**, 'eggplant'—a truly strange omission if one of the Antwerp series printings had been used as a model). Casas's *Vocabulario* also contains an alphabetization glitch present in the Granada series (up until 1555) but corrected in the Antwerp series: *Agu-* entries are found in two places, first after *Agall-* entries (out of correct order) and again after *Agr-* entries. Thus in Casas the *Ag-* entries run **Agalla - Agallas - Agatas - Aguija menuda - Aguijar - Aguijonear - Aguila - Aguileño - Aguinaldo - Agora**, then continue with *Ago-* and *Agr-* entries, and then pick up the *Agu-* entries again after **Agro: Agua - Aguador - Aguador del real - Aguar**. Specifically, Casas probably used the 1545 Granada version as a model, since he uses the **Xaraue** spelling for *syrup* (unlike the **Xarafe** spelling of the printings from 1536, 1540, 1543, 1548, and 1550). This was the final clue, remember, that we also used to identify the 1545 Granada printing as source for Alonso de Molina's 1555 Castilian–Nahuatl dictionary.

The contents of Casas's *Vocabulario* were slowly expanded over time. A group of new *Z* entries was added to the Venetian printing of 1582: **Zanges, Zuane, Zuiza, Zufre, Zumbas**, and **Zurrator** ('water bottle,' 'swan,' 'sulfur,' 'buzzing,' 'currier'). New *X* entries were added in 1591: **Axara** ('vessel'), **Xener** (a verb of unclear meaning). From minor spelling variations, it is clear that the original 1570 Sevillan printing was used as a model for both the Venetian printing of 1576 and the Sevillan printing of 1583.[34] After the Venetian off-shoot began, however, this family of dictionaries developed independently, and small but telling errors built up over time. These reveal that the 1576 Venetian printing begat the 1582 Venetian printing, which begat the 1587 Venetian printing, which begat the 1591 Venetian printing, which begat the 1597 Venetian printing, which begat the 1600 Venetian printing, which begat the 1604 Venetian printing. This straightforward descent pattern was broken four years later: spelling variations show that the 1608 version was based on the earlier Venetian printing of 1597.[35] These ever-expanding microvariations are important, for they will allow us to trace with accuracy which printing of Casas was later used as a source for Castilian terms in Richard Percyvall's Castilian–English–Latin *Bibliotheca Hispanica* of 1591.

Finally, as we have also seen in the New World, and as we first saw for Muslim Granada, the borrowed lists of Nebrija's Castilian–Latin categories were used flexibly by Casas. Some entries were dropped, and new Castilian entries were added to accommodate Tuscan categories, such as **Copo de**

Nieve ('snowflake') for *fiocco,* and **Hauas verdes** ('green fava beans') for *baccielli.*

1571: Castilian–Nahuatl

Sixteen years after the appearance of his first Castilian–Nahuatl *Vocabulario en la lengua castellana y mexicana,* Alonso de Molina published an expansion, pairing it with a reversed Nahuatl–Castilian second half.[36] This work was far more comprehensive than its predecessor. Where the 1555 volume contained around 13,866 Castilian–Nahuatl entries, the 1571 version contained around 17,410 Castilian–Nahuatl and 23,625 Nahuatl–Castilian entries.[37] As these statistics make clear (and as we have seen before in the Latin–Castilian and Castilian–Latin sections of Nebrija's own dictionary), the two halves of Molina's 1571 volume were not perfectly symmetrical. Nahuatl words that appear as translations in the Castilian–Nahuatl section of 1571 do not always appear as main entries in the Nahuatl–Castilian section, and in turn many leading Nahuatl entries in the second section do not have equivalents in the first. Furthermore, the list of Castilian–Nahuatl entries from 1555 was not simply copied over and expanded; the spelling of words was often altered from 1555 to 1571, evidence of Molina's increased sophistication in Nahuatl.[38] As far as I can tell, however, no new edition of Nebrija was called into service to create Molina's 1571 expansion. It contains none of the telltale entries added to the Antwerp expansions of 1545 and 1553, or to the Granada expansions of 1552, 1554, and 1555.

After 1571: Castilian–Nahuatl–Otomi

Like the 1555 version before it, the Castilian–Nahuatl section of Molina's 1571 *Vocabulario* was used as a model for new dictionaries. We saw earlier how two first-edition copies of Molina's printed dictionary were hand-glossed in additional languages (Otomi and Matlatzinca). The 1571 printing was used in the same way: new words in Otomi were handwritten after printed Castilian–Nahuatl entries on several pages of a copy from the American Museum of Natural History in New York City (see fig. 4.3).

After 1571: Castilian–Cakchiquel

A manuscript titled "Vocabulario en lengua castellana y [guate]malteca que se llama Cak chequel chi," by the Franciscan friar Juan Alonso, represents another way Molina's 1571 dictionary was used to generate new research—in this case, a word list for the Mayan language Cakchiquel.[39] Compiled in what is now Guatemala, each page of Alonso's manuscript (copies are held by the Library of Congress, the Firestone Library at Princeton University, the Bibliothèque Nationale in Paris, and the Lilly Library of Indiana University at Bloomington) is divided into two columns. Castilian categories from Molina are copied down in the left-hand column, and their Cakchiquel translations are written in the right-hand column. Alonso's list includes entries added to the 1571 printing of Molina's *Vocabulario,* making it clear that the revised edition—and not the 1555 original—was used as a model.[40] Since Alonso's vocabulary is a multiply copied yet unpublished manuscript, its dating is unclear. It was obviously compiled after 1571, when the revised edition of Molina became available. Based on the handwriting of the Lilly Library copy, Esther Hernández places its creation in the late sixteenth century.[41]

Yet although the 1571 *Vocabulario* was used as a model, Alonso—like so many Nebrijan translators before him—occasionally departed from his printed source. He dropped some Castilian categories (among them, various **Echar** entries on 77v–78v), and added new ones, such as **Echar agua o espuma de cacao sobre otra cosa liquida,** 'to pour water or chocolate foam over another liquid.'

Before 1572: Castilian–Tzeltal

Another manuscript dictionary generated from the categories of Molina's 1571 *Vocabulario* is the "Vocabulario de la lengua española y tzeldal." Attributed to the Dominican friar Domingo de Ara, it provides our earliest records of a Mayan language spoken in what is now Chiapas.[42] Currently housed in the library of the University of Pennsylvania, the surviving copy was made—as its cover announces—in 1620 by a fellow Dominican, Alonso de Guzmán.[43] Friar Domingo de Ara is not actually mentioned as the author of this Castilian–Tzeltal manuscript, but four years earlier, in 1616, Guzmán copied a Tzeltal–Castilian vocabulary which he *did* attribute to Ara. Guzmán's copies (two volumes for the Tzeltal–Castilian section and two for the Castilian–Tzeltal section) remained together until the nineteenth century, when they were acquired by Étienne Brasseur de

Bourborg, a French scholar of Middle American history. Brasseur sold the two Tzeltal–Castilian volumes first (they ended up in the Bancroft Library of the University of California at Berkeley). The two Castilian–Tzeltal volumes were sold later, and ended up in Pennsylvania.[44]

Domingo de Ara died in 1572—that is, the year after Molina's *Vocabulario* was published.[45] It is of course possible that Ara began (and even finished) his own dictionary project before he died, working with indigenous collaborators and a copy of Molina, adding Tzeltal translations in the margins next to the Castilian–Nahuatl entries. The simplest reconstruction of how Ara created the manuscripts attributed to him would begin with the Castilian–Nahuatl half of the 1571 *Vocabulario*. Using Molina's Castilian–Nahuatl word list as a framework, Ara would have gathered Tzeltal entries. In turn, this Castilian–Tzeltal compilation would have been the point of departure for a reversed Tzeltal–Castilian dictionary.

But as we have seen many times before, reversing the entries of a Castilian-to-second-language dictionary was always a complex undertaking. The two halves of Ara's manuscript are by no means mirror images; many of the Castilian–Tzeltal categories are not matched by Tzeltal–Castilian categories. Nevertheless, there is some indication that Castilian–Tzeltal entries were incorporated into the Tzeltal–Castilian list, such as the Nebrijan–Molinan phrases found in "**Chavagh**. gota coral" ('falling sickness') and "**Chamibalton**. piedra sobre q[ue] sacrificaban" ('stone on which they sacrificed'), or the series "**Chupac**. xabon - **Chupaqui**. xabonar - **Chupaquibil**. xabonado" ('soap', 'to soap', 'soaped').[46] A systematic comparison of the Tzeltal–Castilian and Castilian–Tzeltal manuscripts is needed to understand how the two halves relate to one another (and, in turn, to Molina). Unfortunately, since Ara's research survived in a single seventeenth-century copy, we don't know what the original manuscripts looked like when Alonso de Guzmán sat down to transcribe the work of his predecessor in four massive volumes.

1578: Castilian–Zapotec

Up until now, we have considered dictionaries whose lineage is fairly straight-forward: a single parent was used to generate the core list of words for a single descendant. Our two exceptions have been the 1578 Antequera *Dictionarium* and the Castilian–Nahuatl vocabulary in the Olmos manuscript at Tulane. To be sure, descendant dictionaries usually modified their sources, deleting or adding entries as necessary. But the chain of influence from single source to single child has—so far—been a simple one. With the 1578 *Vocabulario en lengua çapoteca*—composed in the Valley of Oaxaca (some 490 kilometers southeast of Mexico City) by the Dominican friar Juan de Córdova—the genealogies of vocabularies become more complicated.[47]

Esther Hernández has argued that Córdova used the 1571 version of Molina's Castilian–Nahuatl *Vocabulario* as a source.[48] This is certainly true; among other things, Córdova's entries related to digging sticks, and to the creation of chocolate foam, follow variants introduced by Molina in 1571.[49] But Córdova also incorporated a number of entries from the 1553-and-after Antwerp series of Nebrija's *Dictionarium* (such as 'ash tree' and 'brown paper') that do not appear in either version of Molina's Nahuatl vocabularies. (Remember that Molina's 1555 *Vocabulario* drew its entries from the 1545 Granada printing of Nebrija, and so did not include categories from the 1545 or 1553 Antwerp expansions; see fig. 0.3).[50] But determining exactly which of the 1553-and-after Antwerp-inspired printings of the *Dictionarium* that Córdova used as a model (Antwerp 1553, 1560, 1570; Granada 1567, 1572; Antequera 1574) is difficult.

After 1585: Castilian–Yucatec

Yucatec is a Mayan language spoken in the Yucatan peninsula, and four Castilian–Yucatec manuscript dictionaries survive from the late sixteenth and early seventeenth centuries.[51] Only one, now at the Hispanic Society of America in New York City, carries a date on its eighteenth-century cover: 1580. The attribution is problematic, as we will soon see. This manuscript is often referred to as the Solana after the author named on its title page, the Franciscan friar Alonso de Solana. Another Castilian–Yucatec manuscript dictionary, sometimes called the Motul II, is in the John Carter Brown Library at Brown University. A third, the "Bocabulario de maya than," is in Vienna. And a fourth, the "Diccionario de San Francisco," is at Tulane University (with a photographic copy in the Newberry Library).[52]

All of these manuscripts are ultimately descended from a single lost source. All share the same core of Castilian terms, derived from one of the 1585-and-after versions of Nebrija's dictionary—which means that the cover date of 1580 given for the Solana is incorrect, as other researchers have already suggested.[53] Since Alonso de Solana died in 1600 or 1601 (and since his attributed authorship of the Hispanic Society's Solana manuscript is probably accurate), the Nebrijan model behind the common source of these four dictionaries would have been the Granada printings of 1585 or 1589 or the Antequera printing of 1595.[54] Nebrija was not the only published model for the lost prototype; all four dictionaries also incorporate a number of non-Nebrijan categories found in Molina's Castilian–Nahuatl *Vocabulario*. Some of these categories are found in both the 1555 and 1571 printings of Molina, including **Adular, busca lisongear; Breton de col; Bruñir lo encalado**; and **Cacarear la gallina** ('to flatter, see *lisongear*,' 'cabbage sprout,' 'to burnish something whitewashed,' and 'to cluck, the chicken').[55] Others, however, were added to Molina in 1571, such as **Batata, Buena voluntad, Batir huevos, Mal criado**, and **Mal de ojos** ('potato,' 'goodwill,' 'to beat eggs,' 'badly raised,' and 'evil eye').

By paying close attention to the similarities and differences of entries in these four manuscripts, we can start to untangle their relationships to one another. Tables 1 to 7 compare clusters of entries from all four vocabularies. Table 1 includes *Br*- entries from **Brasero** to **Brindar** ('brazier,' 'to drink a toast'); tables 2 to 7 present related sets of terms for **Chocolate**, **Espuma** ('foam'), **Mazorca** ('cob'), **Maiz** ('maize'), **Perro** ('dog'), and **Tortilla**. In terms of overall entries, the greatest similarity is between the Solana and Motul II: they share many terms which are not found in either in the "Bocabulario" or "Diccionario." At the same time, however, most of the entries found in the Solana and Motul II also appear in the "Diccionario," linking these three dictionaries together and separating them from the "Bocabulario"—which, in turn, contains a number of entries not found in the other three manuscripts.[56] For example, many of the unique entries in the "Bocabulario" are categories taken from a 1585-or-after printing of Nebrija, categories not included in the other three dictionaries.[57]

This patterning suggests that there once existed at least three other, now-lost manuscripts which filled out the transmission chains linking the four surviving texts. A hypothetical first-generation Castilian–Yucatec vocabulary (YucatecMsA) would have included entries shared by all four dictionaries (and, as we will see, probably terms shared by the "Bocabulario" and two of the three remaining dictionaries as well). From tables 2, 4, 5, and 7, then, we can posit that first-generation entries for *chocolate* were **Chocolate** and **Chocolatera** ('chocolate' and 'chocolate-pot'); for *cob* were **Maçorca** and **Maçorca quitado el grano** ('cob,' 'degrained cob'); for *maize* were **Maiz granado** and **Maiz saçonado** ('kerneled maize' and 'seasoned maize'); and for *tortilla* were **Tortilla** and **Tortilla hacer** ('tortilla,' 'to make tortillas').

TABLE 1. Br- entries in the four Castilian–Yucatec dictionaries

Italics indicate entries shared by all four dictionaries.

"BOCABULARIO"	"DICCIONARIO"	SOLANA	MOTUL II
brasero con brasas	Bracero	*brasero*	*brasero*
brasas o brasero que se pone debaxo de la cama		brasero o brasa que se pone de mano de la cama	brasero o brasa que se pone debajo de la cama
braba cosa no mansa	Brava cosa	*braua cosa*	*braua cosa*
brauo acerse asi			
braua cosas y furiosa			
braua cosa caganerina y huraña que no se deja tocar			
brauas bestias y fieras q[ue] muerden o pican			
braua y perbersa como el demonio			
	Brava andar la mar	brauesa	braueza
	Braveza	braua andar la mar	braua anda la mar
	Braza . . . medirla		
	Brazado como de leña		
	Brazo ó mano		
brauo de rostro			
breña o malicia			
breñoso lugar			
brea			
breton de coles	Breton de col	*breton de col*	*breton de col*
breton hechar			
breue cosa o corta	Breve cosa	*breue cosa*	*braua cosa*
breue haçerse			
breue cosa y momenta-nea que pasa presto			
brincar el niño	*Brincar el niño*	*brincar el niño*	*brincar el niño*
	Brincarse bailando	brincarse bailando	brincarse baylando
brindar	*Brindar*	*brindar*	*brindar*

TABLE 2. *Chocolate* entries in the four Castilian–Yucatec dictionaries
Italics indicate entries shared by all four dictionaries.

"BOCABULARIO"	"DICCIONARIO"	SOLANA	MOTUL II
chocolate	*Chocolate*	*chocolate*	*chocolate*
chocolate en paneçillos			
		chocolate haçer	chocolate hazer
chocolatera que haçe chocolate	*Chocolatera*	*chocolatera*	*chocolatera*

Table 3. *Espuma* entries in the four Castilian–Yucatec dictionaries
Italics indicate entries shared by all four dictionaries.

"BOCABULARIO"	"DICCIONARIO"	SOLANA	MOTUL II
espuma Del agua	*Espuma*	*espuma*	*espuma*
Del cacao			
espumajos que uno hecha por la boca			
espumar hacer y echar despuma de si			
espumar quetando la espuma			
espumosa cosa	*Espumosa cosa*	*espumosa cosa*	*espumosa cosa*
		espumar haçer espuma	espumar hazer espuma
	Espumar quitar espuma	*espumar quitar la espuma*	*espumar quitar la espuma*
	Espuma del palo que se quema	espuma del palo que se quema	espuma del palo que se quema
	Espumar levantarse la espuma		espumar levantarse la espuma

Table 4. *Maçorca* entries in the four Castilian–Yucatec dictionaries
Italics indicate entries shared by all four dictionaries.

"BOCABULARIO"	"DICCIONARIO"	SOLANA	MOTUL II
maçorca de cacao		maçorca de cacao	Maçorca de cacao
maçorca de maiz *mientras esta en la caña*	*Mazorca*	*maçorca de maiz*	*Maçorca de Mayz*
maçorca echar el maiz	Mazorcas echar	maçorcas hechar	
mazorca de maiz con grano en la caña . . .			
mazorcas de maiz sacando las secas y buenas			
mazorca de maiz mui granado			
mazorca con cascara y todo			
mazorca, quitada la cascara			
maçorca de maiz quitado los granos	*Mazorca quitado el grano*	*maçorca quitando el grano*	*Maçorca quitando el grano*
	Mazorca mal granada y granzar de maiz mal desgranado	maçorca mal granada y grانças	Maçorca mal granada y grانças del mayz
	Mazorca que tiene granos a manchar	maçorca que tiene granos a manchas	Maçorca que tiene granos amanchas
	Mazorca bien granada y de muchos granos	maçorca bien granada y de muchos granos	Maçorca bien granada y de muchos granos
maçorcas de maiz q[ue] guardan para semilla			
Ocho maçorcas de maiz tengo para sembrar			

Table 5. *Maiz* entries in the four Castilian–Yucatec dictionaries
Italics indicate entries shared by all four dictionaries.

"BOCABULARIO"	"DICCIONARIO"	SOLANA	MOTUL II
maiz en grano			
el maiz del pueblo			
maiz tostado			
maiz cocido con sal y frisoles			
maiz cosido			
maiz cocido en agua y cal preparado para hazer pan			
bengo a llebar maiz			
maiz tierno y nuebo			
maiz amarilo de pequeña			
maiz temprano que se sembra temprano			
[maiz que se sembra] tardio			
maiz espigado			
	maiz	maiz	Mayz
	blanco	maiz blanco	Mayz blanco
	Maiz que se haze y sazona en 90 dias	maiz que se hace y sasona en 90 dias	Mayz que se haze y saçona en 90 dias
			saçonarse el mayz
	Maiz preparado para pan	maiz preparado para pan	Mayz preparado
	Maiz preparar asi	maiz coser o preparar ansi	Mayz coçer o preparar anssi
	Maiz que no nace	maiz que no nace	Mayz que no naçe
	Maiz en cierne	maiz en cierna	Mayz en çierna
		maiz estar con las baruas blancas o negros	Mayz estar con las barbas blancas o negras
[maiz] granado	*Maiz granado*	*maiz granado*	*Mayz granado*
maiz ya saçonado	*Maiz sazonado, interpolado*	*maiz saçonado o interpolado*	*Mayz sazonado interpolado*
	Maiz que nace	maiz que nace	Mayz que naze
	Maiz crecido un poco	maiz mas cresido un poco	Mayz mas creçido
	Maiz que cubre las piedras	maiz que cubre las piedras	Mayz que cubre las piedras
maiz amarillo			

Table 6. *Perro* entries in the four Castilian–Yucatec dictionaries
Italics indicate entries shared by all four dictionaries.

"BOCABULARIO"	"DICCIONARIO"	SOLANA	MOTUL II
Perro	*Perro* ó perra	*perro* y perra	*perro*
			perra
Perrito de falda			
Perro sin pelo			
Perro de pelo corto y ygual			
Perro sanudo			
Perro manso criado en cassa			
Perro perdido q[ue] se entra en casa agena			
Perro de muestra			
	Perro domestico	perro domestico	perro de meztiço
		perro brauo	perro brauo
	Perro de la tierra	perro de la tierra	perro de la tierra
	Perro ó animal sin cola	perro o animal sin cola	perro o animal sin cola
			perro arremeter o açocar, vide arremeter: açocar

Table 7. *Tortilla–Tortuga* entries in the four Castilian–Yucatec dictionaries
Italics indicate entries shared by all four dictionaries.

"BOCABULARIO"	"DICCIONARIO"	SOLANA	MOTUL II
tortillas hacer	*tortilla*	*tortilla*	*tortilla*
tortilla	*tortilla hacer*	*tortilla haçer*	*tortilla hazer*
	tortilas hacer subcinericeas	tortillas haçer sub çinerias	tortillas hazer sub çeneriçias
		tortolilla	tortililla
tortuga o galapago	*tortuga*	*tortuga*	*tortuga*

This original source then gave birth to two main lines of descent. One is represented by the "Bocabulario," which (as we've seen) was expanded with a number of Castilian entries not found in the other three manuscripts, some invented by its authors and others copied from a 1585-or-after printing of Nebrija. The other line of descent is represented by the "Diccionario," the Solana, and the Motul II, since all three (as shown in tables 1–7) share many entries not found in the "Bocabulario." At least two lost manuscripts must have existed in this second line of descent. The earlier of these (YucatecMsB) was an expanded version of YucatecMsA. Added to its core list were all of the entries *not* found in the "Bocabulario" but shared by the "Diccionario" and (usually) both the Solana and the Motul II. The "Diccionario" was then copied from YucatecMsB, although sometimes categories were left out by the scribe (which explains why certain categories absent in the "Diccionario" are shared by the "Bocabulario," the Solana, and the Motul II, such as **Brasas o brasero que se pone debaxo de la cama** ('cinders or brazier which is put under the bed') and **Espumar hacer** ('to make foam'). In turn, YucatecMsB was also used to create a third lost manuscript, YucatecMsC, which included new entries not found in any of the earlier compilations. YucatecMsC was separately copied to create both the Solana and Motul II (which explains why both manuscripts contain many of the same additions not found in earlier manuscripts, as well as why some entries are shared by only one of these manuscripts and the "Diccionario": the Solana and Motul II are not directly related to one another as parent-child, but as siblings: independent copies of a third, missing source).[58]

The relationship between these four manuscripts has been the subject of some debate, and the conclusions reached here differ from those of prior researchers. A few illustrative examples will help clarify my arguments. First, consider the entries for *tortilla* (table 7). All four surviving dictionaries have entries for both **Tortilla** and **Tortilla hazer**, revealing that both terms were included in the originary YucatecMsA. Then, in YucatecMsB, a new entry, **Tortillas hacer subcinericeas** ('tortillas to make under ashes') was added. As a result, three *tortilla*-related entries were subsequently copied into the "Diccionario," on the one hand, and YucatecMsC, on the other. In turn, when the YucatecMsC was created, an entry for **Tortililla** was added as well—and so both that entry and variant spellings of **Tortilas hacer subcinericeas** were later copied from YucatecMsC into the Solana and the Motul II.

A similar process can be seen in table 6, with various entries for *perro,* 'dog.' This was the only entry included in YucatecMsA, and it was duly copied into the "Bocabulario"—whose authors also added a whole set of dog-related entries found in none of the other manuscripts. When YucatecMsB was created from YucatecMsA, the original **Perro** entry was expanded to include the female form (**Perra**) as well as three new variations: **Perro domestico, Perro de la tierra**, and **Perro o animal sin cola** ('domestic dog,' 'local dog,' 'dog or animal without a tail'). All of these were copied from YucatecMsB into the "Diccionario." They were also copied from YucatecMsB into YucatecMsC, to which yet another entry was added: **Perro brauo** ('fierce dog'). All six categories were then copied into the Solana. The transfer of canine entries from YucatecMsC to the Motul II was more complicated. The copyist transformed the entry for **Perro domestico** from YucatecMsC into **Perro de meztiço** ('mestizo dog'—perhaps he misread the source entry in YucatecMsC); he also added a new term not found in any of the other texts, **Perro arremeter o açocar, vide arremeter: açocar** ('dog, to assail or beat, see *to assail, to beat*').

As a final example, consider the *Br-* entries in table 1. The first entry is **Brasero** ('brazier'). Shared by all four vocabularies, it was one of the terms included in the YucatecMsA source. The authors of the "Bocabulario," however, expanded this entry slightly when they copied it as **Brasero con brasas** ('brazier with cinders'). The next item in table 1 has a somewhat curious distribution. **Brasas o brasero que se pone debaxo de la cama** ('brazier with cinders which is put below the bed') is present in the "Bocabulario," absent from the "Diccionario," present in the Motul II, and present in the Solana with a variant spelling: **Brasero o brasa que se pone de mano de la cama** ('brazier with cinders which is put beside the bed'). We can reconstruct the transmission history of this entry as follows. It was present in YucatecMsA, and was recopied into both the "Bocabulario" and YucatecMsB. When YucatecMsB was copied by later dictionary-makers, this particular entry was left out of the "Diccionario," but was carried over to YucatecMsC. In turn, when YucatecMsC was used as a source for both the Solana and Motul II, the entry was copied into those two manuscripts—although the scribe of the Solana misread **debajo** ('beneath') as **de mano** ('beside').[59]

1586, 1603, 1604, 1614: Castilian–Quechua

Antonio Ricardo lived in Mexico City during the 1570s; in 1578 he printed Córdova's Castillian-Zapotec *Vocabulario*. By 1586 he had moved to Lima, where he published a single-volume grammar and dictionary of Quechua, titled *Arte, y vocabvlario en la lengva general del Perv llamado Quichua, y en la lengua Española*. The actual author (or authors) of this text is unknown, and much debated.[60] The volume begins with a Quechua–Castilian vocabulary, followed by a Castilian–Quechua vocabulary in the second section. The volume's third and final section contains the Quechua grammar.

The Castilian–Quechua dictionary clearly draws from two different sources. The first is the 1560 *Lexicon* of Domingo de Santo Tomás, which was discussed earlier in this chapter. A number of entries from that printing are borrowed word for word, although occasionally the Quechua definition has been revised. For example, Castilian–Quechua entries copied exactly from the 1560 *Lexicon* include "**Maçorca de maiz** chocllo," "**Mayz tostado** camcha," and "**Mayz cozido** muti" ('maize cob,' 'toasted maize,' 'cooked maize'). The Quechua translation for **Maçorca de mayz seco** ('cob of dried maize'), however, is revised from "Morir o cazpa" in 1560 to simply "Murir" in 1586. The second source may have been the 1578 printing of Nebrija's *Dictionarium*. The Castilian–Quechua entries include three terms added to the 1578 Antequera expansion (**Añudar, dar ñudo**; **Bostezar**; and **Charlatan**: 'to knot, make a knot,' 'to gape or yawn,' 'prattler'), as well as fifteen terms that had been part of the *Dictionarium*'s core list since the 1553 Antwerp printing.[61] At the same time, the 1586 volume also added entirely new Castilian entries for Quechua categories, such as **Copa de plata** ('silver cup') for *aquilla* and **Copa de madera** ('wooden cup') for *quero*.

This vocabulary was reprinted three times, once in Seville (1603) and twice in Lima (1604, 1614). The Seville printing, although given a variant title (*Grammatica y vocabolario en la lengva general del Perv llamada Quichua, y en la lengua Española*) is an almost perfect copy of its 1586 parent, down to page layouts and word divisions. Some spelling errors were corrected, however, and at least one spelling variation was introduced: **Vestirse la India la manta de abajo** in 1586 ('to put on, the indigenous woman, the lower mantle') became **Vestirse la India la manta de abaxo** in 1603.[62] In contrast, the (second) version printed by Antonio Ricardo in 1604 Lima was "corrected and expanded" by Friar Juan Martínez, as its title declared: *Vocabvlario en la lengva general del Perv llamada Quichua, y en la lengua Española. Nvevamente emendado y añadido de algunas cosas que faltauan por el Padre Maestro Fray Iuan Martinez[,] Cathedratico de la Lengua*. Page layouts in 1604 are different from the 1586 and 1603 versions, and some spelling variations have emerged, although other spellings connect this version to its 1586 ancestor—such as **Vestirse la India la manta de abajo.** The Lima printing from 1614 (by Antonio Ricardo's successor Francisco del Canto) reverted to the 1586 version as a model: their page layouts are almost identical, and the changes in content and spelling introduced in 1604 are not present.[63]

1587: Castilian–Nahuatl–Otomi

This trilingual vocabulary—once owned by Eduard Seler, a German scholar of Middle America—is now lost, but it was a published copy of Molina's 1571 *Vocabulario* to which marginal translations in Otomi were added around 1587. In other words, this volume was akin to the Otomi-glossed copies of Molina from 1555 and 1571 that were discussed earlier. The original sixteenth-century volume was listed in the catalog of Seler's books prepared at his death in 1922. Most of Seler's library was passed on to his adopted son, Gustavo Stein, but was destroyed by Allied bombing during World War II.[64] Fortunately, Seler made a copy of the Castilian-Otomi entries, which still survives.[65]

1591: Castilian–English–Latin

Like many projects on languages from the New World—and as with Pedro de Alcalá's 1505 publication on Arabic—Richard Percyvall's 1591 *Bibliotheca Hispanica* consists of two parts: a grammar (of Castilian) and a vocabulary (Castilian–English–Latin). And like many missionary linguists, Percyvall drew on earlier, unpublished work: a grammar and dictionary project by Thomas D'Oylie. Mentioned on Percyvall's title page as well as in the preface, D'Oylie or Doyley was connected to a group of Spanish translators at Oxford.[66] Percyvall's preface also mentions two other lexicographers we have met before: "Christoval de las Casas, and Nebrissensis." Casas, of course, was the author of a Castilian–Tuscan / Tuscan–Castilian *Vocabulario* first published in 1570, and Nebrissensis is the Latin form of Nebrija.

As we've seen, the 1587 Venetian printing of Casas incorporated a number of new terms, such as **Zanges, Zuane, Zuiza, Zufre,** and **Zumbas.** Since all of these are included in the *Bibliotheca* (and since a new version of Casas would not be printed until 1591), we can assume that Percyvall used the 1587 printing of Casas as a model. In turn, recall that Casas probably used the 1545 Granada printing of Nebrija's *Dictionarium* as his original source in

1570. In contrast, Percyvall incorporates a number of Nebrijan terms not found in Casas that were added to the 1545 and 1553 Antwerp expansions of Nebrija—terms such as **Verengena** ('eggplant') from 1545 and **Xaharrar** and **Zamarilla** ('to whitewash,' 'poley, an herb') from 1553. Spelling variations confirm that Percyvall's specific Nebrijan model was the 1553 Antwerp printing.[67]

1593: Castilian–Mixtec

If two separate printed sources were used to create both Juan de Córdova's 1578 Castilian–Zapotec dictionary as well as Richard Percyvall's 1591 Castilian–English–Latin dictionary, no less than three parents can be detected in the pages of friar Francisco de Alvarado's *Vocabvlario en lengva misteca,* published in 1593 (see fig. 0.2). Alvarado's vocabulary compiled and coordinated the work of Dominican predecessors in what is now the Mexican state of Oaxaca. Specifically, Alvarado was connected with a Dominican monastery in the Mixtec town of Teposcolula (map 1). As Thomas Smith-Stark has pointed out, Alvarado acknowledges his debts in the work's full title: "Vocabulary of the Mixtec language, done by the fathers of the Order of Preachers [i.e., the Dominican order], who reside in the Mixtec region, and of late compiled, and finished by the father Friar Francisco de Alvarado."[68]

To begin, Alvarado's *Vocabvlario* incorporates Castilian categories that made their debut in Molina's 1571 Castilian–Nahuatl dictionary, such as terms for 'digging stick' (**Coa o pala para cauar**) and 'potato' (**Batata**).[69] The 1571 version of Molina was also, as we saw earlier, used as a model for Córdova's 1578 Castilian–Zapotec dictionary, but Córdova also added a number of new categories not found in Molina. Alvarado clearly drew on Córdova's *Vocabvlario* as well, because he incorporates categories created by Córdova and not found in Molina, such as entries for 'ballcourt' and different types of maize.[70] Remember that Molina (1571) was not Córdova's only lexical source; Córdova also incorporated Castilian categories from one of the Antwerp-series printings of Nebrija's Castilian–Latin *Dictionarium.* Alvarado seems to have independently drawn on an Antwerp-series *Dictionarium* as well, for he includes complex categories added in the 1553 Antwerp expansion that were not included by Córdova in his own *Vocabulario,* such as **Azul escuro** and **Muger soltera** ('dark blue' and 'single woman').[71] In contrast, there is no clear evidence that terms added to the 1578 and 1585 printings of Nebrija were borrowed by Alvarado, suggesting seven possible Nebrijan models: the Antwerp printings of 1553, 1560, and 1570; the Granada printings of 1567 and 1572; and the Antequera printings of 1574 and 1581.[72] At the same time, like so many lexicographers before him, Alvarado added categories of his own: terms for different kinds of capes (including 'a cape which the nobles used to wear, that looks like a jaguar pelt'), and for indigenous slaves.[73]

We can therefore imagine Alvarado compiling the manuscript he eventually published in Mexico City from (at least) three separate books, each bearing Mixtec glosses in their margins: a copy of Alonso de Molina's 1571 Castilian–Nahuatl *Vocabulario*, a copy of Juan de Córdova's 1578 Castilian–Zapotec *Vocabulario*, and one of seven 1553-and-after expansions of Antonio de Nebrija's Castilian–Latin *Dictionarium*. In turn—if this hypothetical situation is correct—we can imagine each Mixtec-annotated copy of these previously published books as having been prepared by a different Dominican colleague of Alvarado: "done by the fathers of the Order of Preachers, who reside in the Mixtec region, and of late compiled, and finished by the father Friar Francisco de Alvarado."

1599: Castilian–English

Eight years after Percyvall's Castilian–English *Bibliotheca Hispanica* was published in London, John Minsheu brought forth his own revised edition: *A Dictionarie in Spanish and English, first published into the English tongue by Ric. Perciuale Gent. Now enlarged and amplified with many thousand words, as by this marke * to each of them prefixed may appeere. . . .*[74] The *Dictionarie* included a Castilian–English vocabulary, an English–Castilian vocabulary, and a concluding "briefe Table of sundrie Arabian and Moorish words vsuall in the Spanish tongue"—a subsection inspired by a similar appendix first included in the 1585 printing of Nebrija's *Dictionarium*.

Minsheu makes reference to three previous authors in his introductory remarks: "*Nebrissensis, Cristóuall de Casas,* and M. *Perciuals.*" The 1591 Castilian–English dictionary of Richard Percyvall is clearly Minsheu's core text. As we saw earlier, Percyvall himself had drawn selectively from the 1553 Antwerp printing of Nebrija as well as the 1587 Venetian printing of Casas. In turn, Minsheu drew on newer printings of both Nebrija and Casas, incorporating their recently added categories into the *Dictionarie.* From Nebrija, Minsheu included terms first added to the 1585 Granada printing, such as

Abadejo, Peçe; Maestro de Campo; and **Xaral** ('poor Jack, a fish,' 'field master,' 'briar patch'). The "Table of sundrie Arabian and Moorish words" further indicates that he must have used either the Granada printings of 1585 or 1589, or the Antequera printing of 1595. From Casas, Minsheu included terms added to the 1591 Venice printing, such as **Viuienda** ('residence'). Spelling variations confirm that Minsheu's source was the 1591 printing of Casas, as opposed to the version from 1597.[75]

At the same time, Minsheu took advantage of the similarities of Castilian and Italian, and Castilian and Latin, to add new Castilian entries based on the contents of at least two dictionaries for translating English and Latin: Thomas Thomas's 1587 *Dictionarium Latinae et Anglicanae* (a unidirectional Latin–English dictionary) and John Florio's 1598 *A Worlde of Words* (a bidirectional Italian–English dictionary). Latin and Italian entries from these two sources were translated into Castilian, and their English definitions then copied into the manuscript of Minsheu's new compilation.[76] In sum, the 1599 *Dictionarie in Spanish and English* is the child of three main parents—Percyvall 1591, Casas 1591, and a 1585, 1589, or 1595 printing of Nebrija's *Dictionarium*—with two godparents, as it were, on the side—Florio 1598 and Thomas 1587.[77]

But Minsheu did not simply copy other entries blindly. In a number of cases he expanded their definitions, and these offer fascinating glimpses into the language of Shakespeare's time. The entry for **Abarraganamiénto** reads "leman keeping, loosenesse of life, wicked fleshly liuing togither betwixt two keeping togither in fleshie filthinesse at rack & manger." Or, for, **Zamarílla**: "an herbe called Poley (Inchanters saie) being cast into an armie, will cause the souldiers to be in feare." Or, for **Zébra**: "a kinde of beast most swifte, in Africa, his breath is smelling like muske."

Late 1500s: Castilian–P'urhépecha

The late sixteenth-century manuscript known as the "Diccionario grande de la lengua de Michoacan" was compiled in west Mexico. It is currently housed in the Latin American Library of Tulane University.[78] The anonymous author drew on two different sources for his Castilian entries: an earlier dictionary of P'urhépecha, Gilberti's 1559 *Vocabulario en lengua de Mechuacan* (which, as we saw earlier, was based closely on Molina's 1555 Castilian–Nahuatl *Vocabulario*) and the 1571 revised version of Molina.

Many of the Castilian–P'urhépecha entries in the "Diccionario grande" are (not surprisingly) identical to those in Gilberti. But other entries are borrowed from categories added to the Castilian–Nahuatl section of Molina's *Vocabulario* in 1571—terms absent from Molina's original 1555 version, and thus absent from Gilberti as well. For example, Molina added the category of **Mayz desgranado** ('loose maize kernels') to his list of maize-related terms in 1571, and this category also appears in the "Diccionario grande."

Late 1500s or early 1600s: Castilian–Tzotzil

This anonymous Castilian–Tzotzil manuscript dictionary was compiled in southern Mexico, in what is today Chiapas. Now housed at Princeton University, a transcription and photographic facsimile were published in 1988 by Robert M. Laughlin and John Haviland. Its list of Castilian entries, as Laughlin has shown, is based on a manuscript we met earlier: the "Vocabulario de la lengua española y tzeldal" attributed to Friar Domingo de Ara. (Tzeltal and Tzotzil, both Mayan languages, are closely related.) Ara's "Vocabulario," remember, was based on Molina's 1571 Castilian–Nahuatl dictionary. But since both Ara's "Vocabulario" and the anonymous Tzotzil dictionary *share* entries and alphabetization irregularities *not* found in Molina, it is clear that Molina was not an independent source for the Tzotzil work.[79]

1604, 1606: Castilian–French

In Paris in 1604, Jean Pallet published a French–Castilian / Castilian–French *Diccionario mvy copioso de la lengua española y françesa*. Two years later, a somewhat abridged edition was printed in Brussels (prefaced by a privilege for printing from the Archduke of Austria).[80]

As Louis Cooper has shown, about half of the entries in the French–Castilian section of the *Diccionario* were taken from Heinrich Hornkens's 1599 *Recveil de dictionnaires francoys, espaignolz et latins* ('Collection of French, Spanish, and Latin dictionaries') a dictionary in which leading entries in French were followed by translations into Castilian and Latin. That is, Pallet copied the French–Castilian sections of many of Hornkens's entries into his own book manuscript. Entries copied directly from Hornkens account for about half of the entries in the French–Castilian section of the *Diccionario*. In turn, many—but by no means all—of these

French–Castilian entries were reversed in order to create the Castilian–French section of Pallet's *Diccionario.*

But although the 1599 *Recveil* was a major source for Pallet, it was not the only one. Another seems to have been Minsheu's 1599 *Dictionarie in Spanish and English.* Pallet's *Diccionario* incorporates terms from Minsheu that Minsheu himself had copied from previous dictionaries, such as **Abadejo,** **Xaral,** and **Xarcia** (included in Nebrija's *Dictionarium* from the 1585 printing on), as well **Viuienda** and **Xara** (included in Casas's *Vocabulario de las dos lenguas toscana y castellana* from the 1591 printing on). Working backward, it is clear that these telling Castilian terms used by Pallet were not reverse-engineered out of Hornkens's French–Castilian entries. Nor were they reverse-engineered out of Pallet's own French–Castilian entries, since many of the Castilian–French pairs have no French–Castilian parallel in the second section of Pallet's *Diccionario.*[81]

That Minsheu was Pallet's singular source, rather than Nebrija and Casas independently, is suggested by his translation of *syrup* from French into Castilian. Pallet offers two possibilities for **Syrop** ("jaraue, xarope") and these match quite closely the paired entry forms we find in Minsheu: "**Xaráve, m. or Xarópe,** a sirrupe, a potion."[82] In contrast, entry forms in both Nebrija and Casas provide single options for *syrup,* not a pair of alternate spellings: **Xarabe de medicina** (Nebrija 1595, 1600, 1610); **Xaraua** (Casas 1600, 1604).

1605: Castilian–Nahuatl–Otomi

So far we have considered three printed copies of Molina's 1555 and 1571 Castilian–Nahuatl *Vocabularios* glossed with Otomi entries in their margins. In the early seventeenth century, the Franciscan friar Alonso Urbano composed—but never published—his own manuscript on Otomi. Currently housed at the Bibliothèque Nationale in Paris, it begins with a 15-folio grammar, followed by a massive 421-folio trilingual Castilian–Nahuatl–Otomi vocabulary.[83] Since the Castilian–Nahuatl entries are word for word the same as the entries in the 1555 printing of Molina's *Vocabulario,* Urbano's text probably represents a hand-copied transformation of a now-lost print/manuscript hybrid. This source would have looked a lot like the glossed 1555 copy of Molina in the library of Mexico's Museo Nacional de Antropología discussed earlier in this chapter. On each page, a printed Castilian–Nahuatl core would have been surrounded by Otomi translations hand-inked in the margins. Both printed and handwritten entries were then copied together into Urbano's new manuscript. Indeed, Urbano's handwritten tome even mimics some of the visual features in Molina's printed work. Like Molina, each page is crowned by an alphabetizing header (A. ante. D.; A. ante. D. et. F; H. ante. v.; and so forth) and a number of subsections begin with massive initial capital letters that mimic the decorative woodcuts used for section headings in Molina's printed version (for the letters *I, Q, X,* and *Z,* among others).

1607: Castilian–French

Following close on the heels of the 1604 and 1606 printings of Jean Pallet's Castilian–French / French–Castilian *Diccionario,* in 1607 César Oudin published his own two-way *Tesoro de las dos lengvas francesa y española* in Paris.[84] Oudin—later famous as the first French translator of *Don Quixote*—had published a Castilian grammar in 1597, a grammar that is even mentioned in the introduction to Pallet's dictionary. Like Molina and Córdova and other New World missionary linguists, and like Richard Percyvall in London, Oudin therefore paired his grammatical publication with a (separately published) vocabulary.

It is unclear, however, if this had always been his intention. The entries in Oudin's *Tesoro* are gathered from two published sources: the recently printed 1604 version of Pallet's *Diccionario,* and Minsheu's 1599 *Dictionarie in Spanish and English.*[85] This dual heritage can be clearly seen in the final pages of Oudin's Castilian–French section, which begin with **Zuane, Zuanete, Zufre, Zuin,** and **Zuiza** (all included, in the same order, in Minsheu), followed by **Zullon** and **Zullonear** (both copied from Pallet). The list returns to Minsheu for **Zumaque, Zumaya, Zumbar, Zumbido, Zumbre, Zumillo, Zumo;** then back to Pallet for **Zuñir, Zuñido;** then to Minsheu again for **Zuño, Zupia, Zurana paloma, Zurdo, Zurra;** then to **Zurrar** (included to redirect the reader to **Çurrar**); then back to Pallet for **Zurrado** and **Zurrador;** then **Zurradura** (redirecting the reader to **Çurradura**); then to Minsheu for **Zurrana palomo;** back to Pallet for **Zurrapa, Zurriar, Zurrio;** then **Zurron** and **Zurroncillo** (redirecting the reader to **Çurron** and **Çurroncillo**); and finally to Minsheu again for **Zurujano, Zurzir, Zutano, Zuzon.** Later printings of Oudin's *Tesoro* would incorporate words from yet more authors: most noteworthy is the expanded version printed in Paris in 1616, which included entries from the 1611 *Tesoro de la lengua castellana, o española* of Sebastián de Covarrubias Orozco.[86]

1608: Castilian–Quechua

Diego González Holguín's *Vocabvlario de la lengva general de todo el Perv llamada lengua Qquichua, o del Inca* was printed in Lima in 1608. It is an expansion of the Quechua *Arte, y vocabulario* first published in the same city some twenty years before, and reprinted there in 1604.[87] Spelling variations reveal that González Holguín used the more recent 1604 volume as his model.[88] At the same time—as we have come to expect in descendant-generation vocabularies—some inherited categories from 1604 were notably expanded in the 1608 volume. The three categories of **Maçorca** ('cob') in 1604 become ten in 1608.[89] The eight subcategories of **Mayz** in 1604 are repeated (with some slight modifications) and expanded to thirteen in 1608.[90] González Holguín also added entirely new categories, such as five delicious entries for types of potatoes.[91]

1609: Castilian–French–Italian

Girolamo Vittori's *Tesoro de las tres lengvas francesa, italiana, y española*, published in Geneva in 1609, is a two-part trilingual dictionary.[92] The first half translates Castilian entries into French and then Italian. The second half translates French entries into Castilian and Italian. Vittori's *Tesoro* is therefore different from the other trilingual vocabularies we have seen so far (the Newberry's Castilian–Latin–Nahuatl manuscript from the 1540s and Percyvall's Castilian–Latin–English publication from 1591) in that, although including terms in three languages, it allowed readers to choose between Castilian and French as the leading entry language. In other words, Vittori's two-part structure adapted the basic form of bidirectional dictionaries in order to provide readers access to three different tongues.

Vittori lifted the Castilian–French and French–Castilian sections of his work directly from Cesar Oudin's 1607 Castilian–French / French–Castilian *Tesoro de las dos lengvas francesa y española*. Following practices we have seen in the Americas, we can imagine Vittori acquiring a copy of Oudin's *Tesoro*, writing Italian translations in the margin after each entry in both the Castilian–French and French–Castilian sections, and then taking this glossed book to a printer as the "manuscript" of his own publication. The flagrancy of Vittori's appropriation did not go unnoticed: Oudin realized how his own work had been used, and included an accusation of piracy in the introductory "Advertissement aux lecteurs" of the revised 1616 printing of his *Tesoro*.[93]

At the same time, as Louis Cooper reveals, Vittori also added new Castilian categories not included in Oudin's list.[94] From the list of added terms provided by Cooper, we can see that Vittori used both Minsheu's 1599 *Dictionarie* as well as Nebrija's *Dictionarium* itself to expand his Castilian entries.[95] Specifically, Vittori used one of the late Nebrijan printings, from 1578, 1585, 1589, 1595, or 1600. Other terms added by Vittori, however, are not found in either Minsheu or Nebrija (such as **Fresas**, 'strawberries'), suggesting yet other sources, or contributions from his own linguistic knowledge.

1612: Castilian–Aymara

In 1612, Ludovico Bertonio published his *Vocabvlario de la lengva aymara* in Juli, a town on the shores of Lake Titicaca where the Jesuits had a school (map 1).[96] Aymara, like Quechua, was (and still is) spoken in the central Andes, and the two languages share many words. Bertonio was a Jesuit colleague of González Holguín, and this Castilian–Aymara dictionary was clearly modeled on González Holguín's 1608 Quechua vocabulary (which was in turn, as we have seen, modeled on the 1604 printing of an anonymous Quechua dictionary first published in 1586). As it happens, these various books are also connected to a single publishing house. Francisco del Canto printed the dictionaries of both González Holguín (1608) and Bertonio (1612), and in 1614 reprinted their distant ancestor, the anonymous Quechua dictionary of 1586. That is, Canto published three connected generations of Andean lexical scholarship, although in nonlinear order: parent first (González Holguín), then child (Bertonio), and then a new version of the child's great-grandparent (the anonymous *Arte, y vocabvlario* from 1586, which González Holguín borrowed from in its transformed 1604 printing; see fig. 0.3).

But where González Holguín typically expanded the contents of his dictionary model, Bertonio reduced and simplified the categories he borrowed from González Holguín. Where González Holguín increased the three entries for **Maçorca** from his 1604 model to eight, Bertonio cut González Holguín's **Maçorca** entries down to five.[97] González Holguín's entries for types of potatoes (**Papas**) were all removed by Bertonio. Where González Holguín borrowed the **Copa de plata** and **Copa de madera** categories from his predecessor (amending the former to read **Copa de plata, o oro**), Bertonio lists only a **Copa de oro** ('cup of gold'), dropping the category of **Copa de madera** (that is, the wooden *quero*) entirely.

1613: Castilian–Tagalog

Our final example leaves the Mediterratlantic world and crosses the Pacific to Asia. Pedro de San Buenaventura's *Vocabvlario de lengva tagala. El romance castellano pvesto primero* is a two part Castilian–Tagalog/Tagalog–Castilian dictionary. It was published in 1613 by the famous Tagalog printers Thomas Pinpin and Domingo Loay in the Philippine town of Pila (map 1).[98] In many ways, the structure of the entries in this *Vocabvlario* is quite distinct from the other translating dictionaries we have seen. Many of San Buenaventura's entries take up two or more lines of type. They typically begin with simple Castilian–Tagalog word pairs, but these are followed by whole phrases in Castilian translated into Tagalog, showing each word's use in context (and illustrating variations in the base term's meaning). The presence of these extensive Castilian phrases means that today San Buenaventura's *Vocabvlario* is as much a guide to the meaning of terms in early modern Castilian as it is a source of information on early modern Tagalog. For example, consider the entry for **Astilejos**—a constellation whose identification has caused some debate in Aztec studies. It is first translated into Tagalog as "Balatic." But then the entry continues, and switches back to Castilian, in order to specify what this constellation looks like and offer an alternative name: "o las marias que deçimos son tres estrellas juntas" ('or the Marys which we say are three stars together').[99] In other words, the Astilejos constellation was what we identify today as the three stars in Orion's belt—or, in Aztec cosmography, Mamalhuaztli, the Fire Drill.[100]

In his prologue, San Buenaventura writes that he worked on the project for seven years; on page 618 he specifies that he began on May 20, 1606 (fig. 2.7). Unfortunately—and in contrast other early modern lexicographers—he does not mention what sources, if any, were used to generate his base list of Castilian entries. Most of his leading entries are but a single

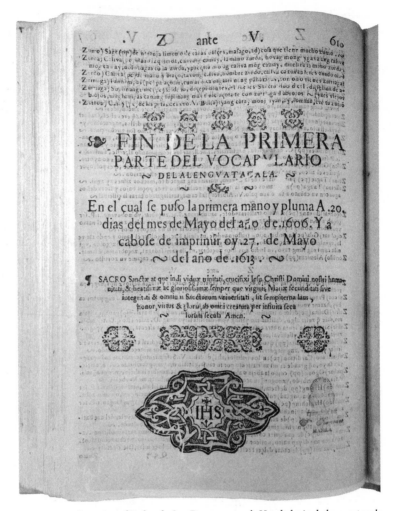

FIGURE 2.7. Page 610 of Pedro de San Buenaventura's *Vocabvlario de lengva tagala.* Image courtesy of the Archivo Franciscano Ibero-Oriental, Madrid.

word, unlike the longer phrases often used in Nebrijan translations. This stripped-down approach makes it difficult to trace the previous publications on which San Buenaventura may have drawn.

A few clues, however, suggest that Nebrija's *Dictionarium,* or a dictionary descended from it, was ancestor to San Buenaventura's opus. In his introduction, San Buenaventura warns the reader that his *Vocabvlario* has no separate section for the letter *X:* "This Vocabulary does not use the letter *X* for spelling **xabon, xeme, xerga**, etcetera, but they are instead placed under *I.*"[101] These *X*-initial words had long been included in Nebrija's dictionary and its descendants, starting with the Salamanca printings of 1495 (for **Xabon**, 'soap,' and **Xerga**, 'sackcloth') and 1513 (for **Xeme**, 'span'). If San Buenaventura did use a printed source as his model, chances are it was based on Nebrija, and included an *X* section with **Xabon, Xeme**, and **Xerga**. The Franciscan would have been conscious of departing from the traditional orthography of Castilian dictionaries, and may have felt it necessary to warn his readers, accustomed to looking for certain words under *X*, of the change. Moreover, Joaquín García-Medall's statistical analysis of San Buenaventura's entries for *A, B,* and *C* reveals a significant overlap with Nebrijan categories.[102]

Curiously, the early modern Castilian dictionary whose entries most resemble those of the *Vocabvlario de lengva tagala* is John Minsheu's 1599 *Dictionarie in Spanish and English*. Both texts share a number of *Z*-initial words not found in other early modern Castilian dictionaries (most not even present in Minsheu's Castilian–English source, Percyvall's 1591 *Bibliotheca Hispanica*).[103] Among these shared words are terms usually spelled with an initial *C* or *Ç*. For example, both Minsheu and San Buenaventura use **Zebolla** instead of **Cebolla** ('onion') and **Zedula** instead of **Cedula** ('decree').

If San Buenaventura did indeed begin his project around 1606, this would have certainly allowed a copy of Minsheu's 1599 *Dictionarie* to travel from London to the Philippines. We can even reconstruct the possible routes by which this hypothetical book journeyed. The English East India Company was established in 1599, and in December 1600 it received a royal charter from Queen Elizabeth I. The first Company voyage set sail the next year, and in 1602 a trading post was established at Bantam on the island of Java (map 1). Given the well-established presence of the Spaniards in the East Indies (the first Spanish settlement was founded in the Philippines in 1565; the islands themselves were named after prince Philip of Spain in 1542), and given the peace negotiations between England and Spain in the early years of the seventeenth century, it would not be surprising if copies of Minsheu's English–Castilian / Castilian–English dictionary were sailing to East Asia— and arriving in the Philippines—by the early 1600s.[104] Very little work has been done with San Buenaventura's *Vocabvlario*, in part because surviving copies of the original are extremely rare. Fortunately, future research on this amazing source has been made much easier by the publication of a facsimile version in 1994 by Librerías "París-Valencia."[105]

From Nebrija's Latin–Castilian *Lexicon* of 1492 to San Buenaventura's Castilian–Tagalog *Vocabvlario* of 1613, these first two chapters have surveyed over 120 years of dictionary making. We have followed the changes to Castilian–Latin word lists in different printings of Nebrija, and we have traced the increasingly tangled relations between those printings and the dictionaries of other languages that Nebrija's work inspired. Now, having mapped these complicated genealogies, we will focus in the next two chapters on the Americas—and on sixteenth-century New Spain in particular—to consider how the complex global history of dictionary making can help us better understand the visual and material legacies of prehispanic and early modern Mesoamerica.

3

From the Shores of Tripoli to the Halls of Montezuma

The translating dictionary is a deceptively simple genre. Its use requires little grammatical knowledge. The varied entries—for wooden cups and henna, for syrups and syringes—provide fascinating glimpses of lost cultural worlds. In the indigenous New World, such dictionaries are often our earliest—and our richest—records of Native American languages. For all of these reasons, translating dictionaries have long been used by art historians, epigraphers, and archaeologists to interpret art, writing, and material culture from the prehispanic past. But as the previous two chapters have shown, the formal simplicity and linguistic transparency of translating dictionaries are deeply deceptive. In many cases, their entries have nothing to do with Native American cultures—they are simply categories borrowed from a Castilian–Latin dictionary originally compiled to help early modern readers understand the pagan Mediterranean. But by knowing the complex backstory behind the entries included in, say, Alonso de Molina's 1555 Castilian–Nahuatl *Vocabulario,* or Domingo de Santo Tomás's 1560 Castilian–Quechua *Lexicon,* we are better able to appreciate when entries are included in a dictionary simply because they had already been included in Nebrija, and when—in significant contrast—they have been added to a core Nebrijan list in order to capture distinctive features of life in the New World.

Using the genealogy of vocabularies in figure 0.3 as a map, we can now navigate the tangled networks linking ancient Rome, prehispanic Mesoamerica, and the early modern Mediterratlantic world. This chapter uses that map to undertake three case studies, sample journeys through linguistic space and time. The first is a simple comparison of Juan de Córdova's 1578 Castilian–Zapotec dictionary with its Castilian–Latin source, an

Antwerp-series edition of Nebrija's *Dictionarium*. Reuniting parent and child uncovers how isolated readings of Córdova have led researchers astray in their reconstructions of prehispanic Zapotec society.

The second journey is more complex. It begins with an entry in Francisco de Alvarado's 1593 Castilian–Mixtec dictionary, one that has been used to interpret the imagery of prehispanic and viceregal Mixtec books. But by reading that entry—and its neglected companion—alongside Castilian–Latin, Castilian–Nahuatl, and Castilian–Zapotec dictionaries, a new interpretive horizon emerges for one aspect of Mixtec writing: what we have thought to be glyphs for altars are more likely depictions of archaeological ruins.

The final example begins by comparing the single entry for 'to shine or to glitter' found in all editions of Nebrija's Castilian–Latin dictionary with its multiple entries in Molina's 1571 Castilian–Nahuatl dictionary—an entry-expansion clearly meant to capture complex Nahua aesthetics of reflected light. This dictionary-attested richness is further supported by other sixteenth-century documents in Nahuatl, which allow us to reconstruct a conceptual map of Nahua visuality. And yet when we turn to the images of Nahua art and hieroglyphic writing, a very different landscape of reflectivity is recorded.

Overall, these case studies present three possible journeys into linguistic and cultural worlds. They show how the lexical entries in indigenous vocabularies can deceive, how they can offer resources to enrich our understanding of Native American visual and material culture, and how, in some cases, they preserve indigenous ways of understanding the world not even recorded by indigenous systems of communication.

Zapotec Augurs?

Since the sixteenth century, indigenous customs in the Americas have been compared to the pagan practices of ancient Greece and Rome.[1] Aztec gods and goddesses, for example, were interpreted through Greek and Roman analogies. Huitzilopochtli was "another Mars"; Tezcatlipoca was "another Jupiter"; Cihuacoatl was a New World Venus.[2] In an article from 1978, the archaeologist Joyce Marcus critiqued the ways in which these centuries-old analogies still shaped interpretations of the prehispanic past: "While the eyewitness accounts of the early Spanish chroniclers are invaluable, it must be remembered that many were priests whose assignment was to stamp out

Zapotec religion, not understand it. Many also had a Classical education, including knowledge of the ancient Greco-Roman pantheon which served as their model for an 'idolatrous' religion. Add to this the fact that they never fully comprehended Zapotec royal ancestor worship, and you have the makings of a serious misunderstanding."[3] One of the Catholic missionaries cited by Marcus is Juan de Córdova, author of the 1578 Castilian–Zapotec dictionary discussed in the previous chapter. Ironically, in a more recent study Marcus herself is unknowingly caught by Córdova's classical snares.

In the opening pages of *Women's Ritual in Formative Oaxaca*, Marcus writes that the Zapotec of prehispanic Oaxaca used the following fortune-telling techniques: "divination by water, by stars, by fire, by air, by birds, and by the sacrifice of animals and humans."[4] From this list, Marcus focuses on divination by water, translated in Córdova's dictionary as "tinijàaya niça." She uses this lexical nugget to aid in the interpretation of prehispanic archaeological remains, arguing that a pair of plaster depressions in the floors of a Formative-period house at San José Mogote (1150–700 BCE) were originally filled with water and used for divination (map 1). The two depressions were painted yellow and red; Marcus proposes that they originally formed part of a set of four, one for each of the cardinal directions.[5]

As it happens, however, Marcus's list of Zapotec divination techniques (presented without a citation) is not quite what it seems. It has been culled—of course—from the Castilian–Zapotec entries in Juan de Córdova's *Vocabvlario en lengva çapoteca*. Two types of divination-related entries are included in Córdova: for the act of divination itself (**Adiuinar, Diuinar**), and for the person of the diviner (**Adiuino, Diuino**). One list appears on folio 10r. It begins with 'to divine without auguries, or to prophesy' and then continues with categories for divination by water and by signs or dreams:

Adiuinar sin agueros, o profetizar. Tinñijàa.l.tinnijyaaya, coñnij.
Adiuinacion assi. Vide etiam adiuinar. Quela connijàa l. yaa.
Adiuino tal. Peni coñnijaa l.yaa.
Adiuinar por suertes o agueros. Tochillaya, tibeea. vel. tebeea pijci. col.
Adiuinacion assi. Vide diuinar. Quelahuechilla.
Adiuino assi. Peni huechilla. l. tiñnij niça. l. tònija niça.
Adiuinar por agua. Tinijàaya niça, tiñijaniçaya.
Adiuinacion assi. Quelahueñijniça, quela coñijaa niça.
Adiuino assi. Huènij niça, connijaa niça, connij niça.
Adiuinar por signos o sueños. Tebeea pecala, pe. vel. tibeea pecala, col.

Another list appears on folio 143v. It begins with 'to divine by dreams' and continues with entries for divination by auguries, stars, earth, fire, air, water, birds, and sacrifices:

> **Diuinar por los sueños.** Vide adeuinar. Tibèepecàlaya. l. tebèe, pe.
> **Diuinar por agueros.** Tibèepijzia. l. tebèe, pe.
> **Diuino por sueños.** Còlanij cobèepecàla.
> **Diuino por agueros.** Colanij còbèe pijzi.
> **Diuino por estrellas.** Colanij pèl le.
> **Por la tierra.** Colanijyòo.
> **Diuino por el fuego.** Colanij quij.
> **Diuino por el ayre.** Colanij pèe.
> **Diuino por el agua.** Colanij niça.
> **Por las aues.** Colanij mànizàbi.
> **Diuino por sacrificios.** Colanij pichijlla. **Por el rostro.** colanijlào peni.
> **Diuino grande por arte magica.** Colanijtào.

As we saw in chapter 2, Córdova's categories were based on entries in one of the 1553-and-after Antwerp editions of Nebrija's Castilian–Latin *Dictionarium*.[6] And if we turn to those European sources, we encounter the very same techniques listed by Córdova: divination by stars, earth, water, air, fire, birds, sacrifices:

> **Diuino por estrellas,** Mathematicus, i.
> **Diuinacion por estrellas,** Mathesis.
> **Diuino por la tierra,** Geomanticus, a, um.
> **Diuinacion por la tierra,** Geomantia, ae.
> **Diuino por el agua,** Hydromanticus, a.
> **Diuinacion assi,** Hydromantia, ae.
> **Diuinacion por el ayre,** Aeromantia, ae.
> **Diuino por el ayre,** Aeromanticus, a, um.
> **Diuino por el fuego,** Pyromanticus, a, um.
> **Diuinacion en esta manera,** Pyromantia, ae.
> **Diuino por bacines.** Engastromantes, u.
> **Diuinacion en esta manera,** Engastromantia, ae.
> **Diuino por las aues,** Augur, Auspex, icis.
> **Diuinacion en esta manera,** Auspicina, ae. Augurium, ij.
> **Diuino por sacrificios,** Haruspex, icis.

Diuinacion en esta manera, Haruspicina, ae.

Diuinacion por cuerpo muerto, Necromanticus, a. um.

Diuinacion assi, Necromantia, ae.

Diuino por las assaduras, Extipex, icis.

Diuinacion en esta manera, Extipicium, ij.

Diuino por la cara, Metoposcopus, i.

Diuinacion assi, Metoposcopice, es.

Diuino por las manos, Chiromanticus, a, um.

Diuinacion en esta manera, Chiromantia, ae.

Diuinar por coniecturas, Coniecto, as. Conijcio, is.

Diuino por los sueños, Coniector, oris.

Diuinar por los sueños, Coniecto, as.

Diuinacion en esta manera, Coniectus. us.

In other words, the divinatory techniques Marcus claims were used by Zapotecs in prehispanic Oaxaca are in fact divinatory techniques used by the ancient Romans. Lurking behind Córdova's Zapotec translations are Nebrija's Castilian translations of Latin terms for the antique practices of hydromancy, pyromancy, augury, and haruspicy.

The suspicious status of Córdova's Castilian entries for "Zapotec" forms of divination is heightened when we consider the Zapotec translations themselves. They present a complex combination of prehispanic terminology and viceregal neologism. Most of the forms for *diviner* (**Diuino**) listed on folio 143v begin with the word *Còlanij*. As Thomas C. Smith-Stark makes clear in a brilliant discussion of Zapotec religion, the term *Còlanij* appears throughout Córdova's *Vocabulario*, and in his 1578 Zapotec grammar as well. It is used to define such sixteenth-century Castilian categories as *agorero, divino, doctor en fiestas, echador de fiestas,* and *sortilego* ('augur,' 'diviner,' 'expert in festivals,' 'person who throws a festival,' 'sortilege-diviner'). The root of *Còlanij* is *lanìi,* 'fiesta' (that is, holy day), and Smith-Stark argues that the *Còlanij* was above all a daykeeper: a calendar specialist who used the sacred cycles of Mesoamerican time to look into the past and future, and to determine auspicious days for holding important events.[7]

When asked to provide Zapotec equivalents for Castilian translations of Latin diviniation experts, it seems that Córdova's obliging indigenous collaborators created literal translations of the Castilian phrases presented to them, using the term for a prehispanic calendar specialist as a base. Thus **Diuino por el fuego,** 'fire-augur' (the Castilian rendering of the Latin *pyromanticus*), is translated by following *Còlanij* with *quij* (the Zapotec word for fire). **Diuino por el ayre**, 'wind-augur' (the Castilian rendering of the Latin *aeromanticus*), is translated by following *Còlanij* with *pèe* (the Zapotec word for wind or spirit). **Diuino por el agua**, 'water-augur' (the Castilian rendering of the Latin *hydromanticus*), is translated by following *Còlanij* with *niça* (the Zapotec word for water). Completing these elemental techniques is the augur who uses earth (**Por la tierra**, the Castilian rendering of the Latin *geomanticus*), which follows *Còlanij* with *yòo* (the Zapotec word for earth). Most suspicious of all—as Smith-Stark recognizes—is the term offered for **Diuino por sacrificios** ('sacrifice-augur').[8] This Castilian category was originally Nebrija's translation of the Latin *haruspex*: someone who tells the future from the entrails of sacrificed animals. The Zapotec phrase offered as a translation for this term in Córdova contains no lexical reference to sacrifice at all. This is a striking absence, given the importance of human and animal sacrifice in prehispanic Zapotec religion. Rather, the translation given is "Còlanij pichijlla," which pairs the term for calendar specialist with *pichijlla*, the beans used to perform sortilege divination. The Zapotec *haruspex*, then, is a 'daykeeper who uses beans'—with no sacrificed entrails in sight. All of these entries reveal how purported Zapotec terms for many of the fortune-tellers listed on folio 143v of Córdova's *Vocabulario* are not actually words with prehispanic histories. Rather, they are neologisms, created when Córdova's no-doubt-puzzled Zapotec assistants were asked to translate the Latinate Castilian categories being read to them from a printed copy of Nebrija's *Dictionarium*.

If we return to Marcus's *tiniyaaya niça* (Córdova's "Tinijàaya niça"), the Zapotec phrase offered as a translation for 'to tell the future with water' (**Adiuinar por agua**—itself a translation of the Latin category *hydromantia*), we again encounter a fascinating mix of metaphor and literalness. As Smith-Stark observes, a well-attested translation for **Adiuinar** ('to prophesy') in the 1578 *Vocabulario* is "nijàa," which combines the word for to speak (*nnìi*) with the word for style or craft (*yàa*). That is, *nijàa* literally means 'to speak with style' or 'to speak artfully.'[9] As is common in sixteenth-century Mesoamerican vocabularies, the entry for **Adiuinar por agua** presents this verb in a conjugated first person form: *ti+nijàa+ya*, 'I speak artfully.'[10] It is then followed by an object: *niça*, or water. Read literally, "Tinijàaya niça" translates as 'I speak artfully of (or with) water.' Like the various Zapotec terms offered as translations for Latinate Castilian categories of fortune-teller, the Zapotec "Tinijàaya niça" is a (suspiciously) literal translation of the Castilian phrase that comes before it: **Adiuinar por** agua. "Tinijàaya niça" has been created by appending a clearly prehispanic metaphor (divination as artful speech) with a flat-footed specifying object (niça, 'water') in order to better match the multiword Castilian translation (**Adiuinar por agua**) of the single Latin word *hydromantia*.

The implications of these revelations for Marcus's archaeological claims are complex. Many Mediterranean cultural practices had surprisingly close parallels in Mesoamerica—even if those parallels concealed deeper differences, something James Lockhart calls "double mistaken identity."[11] For example, divination by looking into reflective surfaces (mirrors, liquids) is a practice shared across centuries of both Mediterranean and Mesoamerican history. Prehispanic images and archaeological remains make clear that such scrying techniques were not introduced by the Europeans. Marcus duly acknowledges this archaeological and art historical evidence in her citations.[12] In other words, Córdova's Castilian category of **Adiuinar por agua**, although ultimately derived from ancient Roman hydromancy, is not an essential piece of evidence for Marcus's archaeological interpretation—even though she repeatedly includes the Zapotec "translation" in order to enhance the reality effect of her statements about ancient Formative life: "One kind of women's divining, called *tiniyaaya niça*, involved kneeling on a mat while casting maize kernels onto the surface of a water-filled basin, then noting the number of kernels that remained floating."[13]

Marcus's use of historical and ethnographic materials has been discussed elsewhere.[14] The issue I want to raise here is the interpretive danger that arises when subsequent scholars cite her categories of "ancient Zapotec divination" as fact, or as a starting point for other analyses of prehispanic archaeological remains.[15] Pagan antiquity haunts interpretations of indigenous Mesoamerica today as it did in the sixteenth century. But with a critical difference: when sixteenth-century friars like Bernardino de Sahagún or Juan de Córdova remade the prehispanic past in the image of ancient Rome, they did so intentionally, openly.

Mixtec Altars?

Córdova's entries for different types of divination provide fascinating glimpses onto prehispanic practices (the idea of divination as artful speech) while at the same time they reveal how Mediterranean visions were exported to Mesoamerica (the Zapotec *haruspex* uses neither entrails nor sacrifice, but beans). A similar mix of tradition and invention is found in our second example,

FIGURE 3.1. A facsimile edition of the Mixtec Codex Nuttall, showing its screenfolded format.

which moves to a nearby region of Oaxaca and shifts from prehispanic archaeology to prehispanic iconography. Both before and after the arrival of the Europeans, the Mixtecs of northwestern Oaxaca created books from long strips of folded and gessoed deerskin (fig. 3.1). In these "codices" or "screenfolds," the Mixtecs painted images of people, places, and things to record their sacred political histories. Temples and palaces, for example, are usually depicted as two-part structures: a roofed building constructed atop a staircase-platform. These images are accurate reflections of most elite and sacred architecture, in which multiroomed houses and temples were built on artificial hills of earth and masonry. A number of place signs in the Mixtec screenfolds, however, feature architectural platforms *without* any building on top.

Several of these platforms are drawn on the pages of the late sixteenth-century Codex Muro.[16] A flowering tree grows out of them, and a royal husband and wife are drawn beside them (fig. 3.2). These visual signs for a ruling couple and their town of origin are provided with an alphabetic label, "yya chyo yuhu": 'Nobles (*yya*) of the *Chiyo* of the White Flowering Tree (*yuhndu*).'[17] Chiyoyuhu ('*Chiyo* of the White Flowering Tree') was the Mixtec name for Suchixtlan, a town in the Nochixtlan Valley (map 1). In order to interpret the meaning of the word *chiyo*, twentieth-century investigators turned to the pages of Francisco de Alvarado's 1593 *Vocabvlario en lengva misteca*. There, the word *chiyo* appears in a number of entries:

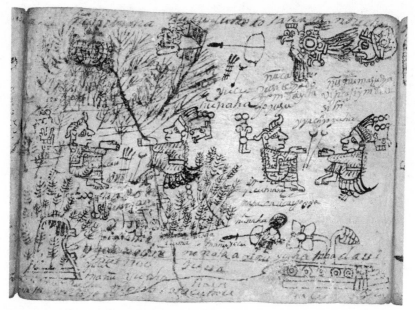

FIGURE 3.2. Page 6 of the Codex Muro, with a *chiyo* platform in the lower right corner. Reproduction authorized by the Instituto Nacional de Antropología e Historia, Mexico.

Altar. *chiyo.*

Antiguo lugar. chiyoyata.

Cimiento. chiyo huahi.

Fundar, poner fundamento. yodzahandi chiyo yodzamandi chiyondi, yotniño sitendi, yotnaandi site, yodzacaindi site, yodzacaindi yuu saha.

Sitio por asiento de casa o lugar. chiyo.[18]

Most of these entries refer to architecture. An 'ancient place' is an 'old *chiyo*' ("chiyoyata"). An architectural foundation (**Cimiento**) is 'the *chiyo* of a house' ("chiyo huahi"). 'To build a foundation' is rendered as 'I make a *chiyo*' ("yodzahandi chiyo"). The 'site for a house or place' is simply "chiyo." Yet—given longstanding interest in native religion on the part of Mesoamerican scholars—the interpretation usually used for the word *chiyo* today, as well as for images of architectural platforms in the Mixtec screenfolds, is *altar.*[19]

But if we turn to the dictionary page on which "chiyo" is given as a translation for **Altar**, things become more complicated. Alvarado's vocabulary provided its Dominican users with not one type of altar, but two. Each was given its own Mixtec-language translation. On folio 17v we find the following entry-pair:

> Altar. chiyo.
> **Altar de demonios** tayu quacu. tayu dzana

That is, an 'altar' is followed by an 'altar for demons.' Given these twinned categories, the use of *chiyo* as 'altar' in the first entry suggests that this translation was offered to Dominican readers as a sanitized term for referring to a *Catholic altar*. In contrast, an indigenous altar—as a place for sacrifice or contacting indigenous gods—is marked by demonic association. Significantly, the Mixtec terms offered to translate this 'altar for demons' are, first, "tayu quacu" ('throne for a god-image') and second, "tayu dzana" ('bad throne'). The idea of sacred locations as *thrones* where divinities are seated is prehispanic in origin, and continues to this day.[20] In other words, Alvarado's seemingly simple translation of **Altar** as "chiyo" may in fact be a Catholic innovation, the semantic extension of an extant word designed to separate Christian altars from their indigenous counterparts.

This interpretation becomes stronger if we turn to the other dictionaries Alvarado used to generate categories for his own vocabulary.[21] As we saw in the previous chapter, Alvarado drew on three sources for his Castilian categories: one of the 1553-and-after printings of Nebrija's Castilian–Latin dictionary, Alonso de Molina's 1571 Castilian–Nahuatl dictionary, and Juan de Córdova's 1578 Castilian–Zapotec dictionary. By itself, Nebrija's Castilian–Latin *Dictionarium* doesn't seem to be of much use. The 1553 printing, for example, has only one **Altar** entry—'Altar where they sacrifice' ("**Altar donde sacrifican.** Altare,is. Ara,ae.") But if we turn to Alvarado's New World sources, we quickly notice that Nebrija's singular entry was dynamically expanded to better fit the needs of Catholic missionaries.[22] Both Molina and Córdova provide multiple **Altar**- entries, and both are concerned with separating normal (that is, Catholic) altars from their demonic (that is, indigenous) counterparts. Molina (folio 9r) provides two Castilian categories: 'Altar' and 'Altar for demons':

> **Altar.** lo mismo. vel. mumuztli
> **Altar de demonios**, que ponian en los caminos hecho de tierra. mumuztli. tlalmumuztli.

Significantly, for the first entry Molina recommends that the Castilian term *altar* be loaned directly into Nahuatl, untranslated: "**Altar** lo mismo" ('altar, the same [word]'). He then follows this with an 'or' (*vel*) reference to the Nahuatl *mumuztli*, which leads to Molina's second altar category.[23] **Altar de demonios**, 'which they put in the roads made of earth' is translated by both "mumuztli" and the variant "tlalmumuztli" ('earth-*mumuztli*'). As in Alvarado, then—and remember that Alvarado was looking at Molina's categories when creating his own dictionary—we have two altar-categories, the second of which is specified as a demonic, non-Catholic site.[24]

Turning to Córdova's Castilian–Zapotec dictionary, published seven years after Molina, the concern to distinguish Christian from indigenous altars becomes even more explicit. Córdova includes three entries for altar (folio 24r):

> **Altar para Dios**. Pecógoláya nitaca missa
> **Altar qualquiera**. Pecógo.
> **Altar para el demonio**, vide cu, de los Indios. Pecógoxiténipezeeláo.

Córdova first lists an 'Altar for God,' then an 'Altar in general,' and finally an 'Altar for the demon.' Attention to the Zapotec equivalents given for these obviously Catholic Castilian categories is quite instructive. **Altar para Dios** is translated into Zapotec as "Pecógoláya nitaca missa," that is, 'throne where Mass is held' (using the Castilian *missa*, 'Mass,' as a loan word). The same base term for 'seat' or 'throne,' *pecógo*, is offered as a one-word definition for Córdova's second category: "**Altar qualquiera**. Pecógo." The term for 'throne' shows up again in Córdova's final category: an 'altar for the demon' is a "Pecógoxiténipezeeláo," a 'throne for the underworld god.'[25]

When Córdova's Zapotec collaborators were asked to provide him with translations of different types of altars, they—following prehispanic models—used the metaphor of the throne in all of them. In contrast, Alvarado's vocabulary only uses the prehispanic image of a throne (*tayu*) to define an indigenous altar, that is, what Catholic eyes saw as an 'altar for demons.' Thus when Alvarado uses *chiyo* to define the unmarked category of **Altar**, it seems likely—given the careful distinction of Christian and indigenous altars found in the categories of Molina and Córdova, Alvarado's New World sources—that the original meaning of *chiyo* as architectural foundation was extended by missionaries to encompass specifically Christian altars as well. What this means is that our interpretations of *chiyo* glyphs in prehispanic screenfold books should not read them as *altars*, with all of the sacred connotations that term implies. Instead, these *chiyo*, which look like architectural platforms on which no building has been constructed, should be described simply as *platforms*.[26]

We can push this identification further. These painted *chiyo* are probably meant to indicate what Alvarado calls *chiyoyata*: 'old foundations,' that is, archaeological sites already ancient in the 1400s and 1500s. For example, *chiyo* platforms on page 22 of the prehispanic screenfold known as the Codex Nuttall are used to represent the ruins of Monte Negro, or Black Hill—a city that had been abandoned for centuries when Mixtec artists painted it around 1500 (fig. 3.3).[27] Another example is found on page 23 of the Codex Vienna, which depicts the First Sunrise at the beginning of time (fig. 3.4).[28] Throughout Mesoamerica, archaeological remains are associated with First Sunrises. The Aztecs even believed that the Fifth Sun of their age of creation rose out of the ruined buildings at Teotihuacan, a city built long before the Aztecs came to power. Given these pan-Mesoamerican associations, it makes sense that page 23 of the Codex Vienna shows the dawning sun rising up out of a *chiyo* platform—that is, out of an archaeological ruin.[29]

The translated lives of "altars" in New Spain reveal how Franciscan and Dominican friars expanded a singular category from Nebrija (**Altar donde sacrifican**) in order to respond to the linguistic needs of their missionary situation. The indigenous terms offered as translations for these altered Nebrijan categories involved both linguistic extension (*chiyo* from 'foundation' to 'altar') and neologism (*Pecógoláya nitaca missa* as a 'throne where Mass is held'). But these altar-terms also preserved prehispanic models and categories, as when the image of a throne was used to refer to altars both Zapotec (*pecógo*) and Mixtec (*tayu*).

Nahua Bling!

We have now traced how Nebrijan categories were uncritically transferred to Mesoamerica (Córdova on divination), as well how Nebrijan categories were expanded in order to meet the linguistic needs of missionaries (Alvarado, Molina, and Córdova on altars). In both cases, we have seen how attention to the indigenous translations given for Castilian terms, even when clearly neologisms, can reveal cultural specificities that point beyond the procrustean beds of Mediterranean categories. Our third example

FIGURE 3.3. Page 22 of the Codex Nuttall, showing *chiyo* ruins on the summit of Monte Negro. Image courtesy of Akademische Druck- und Verlagsanstalt, Graz, Austria.

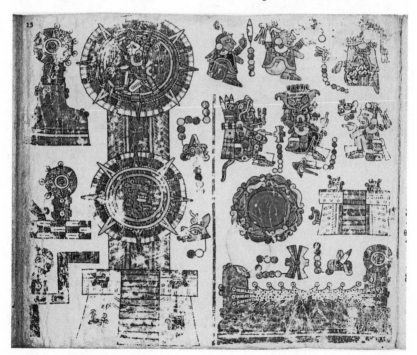

FIGURE 3.4. Page 23 of the Codex Vienna, showing the First Sunrise rising up from a *chiyo* platform. Image courtesy of Akademische Druck- und Verlagsanstalt, Graz, Austria.

further considers how Nebrijan entries were modified by New World situations. But in this case, transformations were made to Castilian categories in order to better capture the subtleties of indigenous words—here, in Nahuatl. These linguistic explorations will, once again, have important implications for our understanding of New World art and writing.

Ideas about seeing and vision were, and are, extremely important to Mesoamerican theories of knowledge, writing, and history.[30] This interest in the visual is reflected by the entries in Molina's 1571 vocabulary for **Relumbar o reluzir**, 'to shine or to glitter.' In Molina's original Nebrijan source—the 1545 Granada *Dictionarium*—this basic category (as was also the case for Nebrija's **Altar**) takes only one form:

> **Relumbrar, o reluzir.** luceo.es, luxi.

Molina duly copies this entry into his dictionary. But he then follows it with a number of variations, variations clearly meant to capture specific Nahua categories of reflected light (103v):

> **Relumbrar o reluzir.** ni, tlanextia.ni, pepetlaca.ni.pepetzca. ni, tzotzotlaca.
> **Relumbrar el agua con el sol o los campos.** pepeyoca.
> **Reluzir las piedras preciosas o los peces de[n]tro del agua con el moviemiento que hazen, o el ayuntamiento de las hormigas o las lagunas y campos, o las gentes ayuntadas por el mouimiento que hazen.** cuecueyoca.
> **Reluzir la seda o la pluma.** pepetzca.
> **Reluzir la grassa de la olla.** momotzca.

Translating the Castilian portion of these entries into English, we have:

> To shine or to glitter.
> To shine, as with sun on the water or on the fields.
> To glitter, as with precious stones or fish within the water with the movement that they make, or the anthill, or the lagoons and fields, or people joined by the movement that they make.
> To glitter, as with silk or feathers.
> To glitter, as with grease in the pot.

A whole world of visual distinctions is opened up by these definitions: the luster of silk and feathers is distinguished from the sun glittering on the water and the sparkle of precious stones.[31] Turning to the Nahuatl translations of these complex descriptions, we see that four Nahuatl terms are initially given for 'to shine or glitter': *tlanextia, pepetlaca, pepetzca, tzotzotlaca*. Two additional words, *pepeyoca* and *cuecueyoca,* are used in the following two entries to define more specific styles of reflection. The next type of reflection ('to glitter, as with silk or feathers') is defined by *pepetzca,* a term already introduced in the initial list of terms following **Relumbrar o reluzir**. The final example ("to glitter, as with grease in the pot") introduces a new word, *momotzca.*

Nahuatl is unique in the New World for the scale of its sixteenth-century alphabetic record. Thousands of pages in Nahuatl were written before 1600, and so with this case study we can go beyond dictionary entries and consider how these different terms for reflectiveness were actually used in practice, in the phrases of literary texts.[32] These literary sources confirm what is suggested by Molina's expansions of Nebrija's base category: sixteenth-century Nahuatl consistently used different terms to describe different kinds of reflectiveness.

Anthropologists and literary scholars have long been interested in the cultural construction of color.[33] Different languages parse the visual spectrum in different ways; *azul* is different from *teal* or *turquoise* or *navy* or *yax*. In a splendid essay from 1985, Umberto Eco explored the curious fields of color categories in Latin. He focused on Aulus Gellius' *Noctes Atticae* (*Attic Nights*) a second-century CE Latin miscellany. A dialogue in one of its chapters discusses the poetic—and seemingly quite strange—use of color terms. *Fulvus* (said by one of the speakers to be a mixture of red and green) characterizes such yellowish things as sand, gold, eagles, and lions, but also reddish jasper, and even air. *Flavus* (described in the *Noctes* as a mixture of red, green, and white) is used for blond hair, olive leaves, marble, and (in Virgil) the muddied yellowish-gray waters of the river Tiber. Virgil's use of *glaucus* for gray horses is debated by the speakers; in other contexts Virgil uses the word for willow trees, sea lettuce, and water. Gray horses are also described with the term *caeruleus,* which in turn is used for the sea and the sky and (elsewhere in Latin literature) watermelons, cucumbers, and a type of rye bread. *Luteus* (a "diluted red," says one of the participants) is used by Pliny for egg yolks and by Catullus for poppies.[34] Inspired by Marshall Sahlins's classic essay "Colors and Cultures," Eco argues that these Latin color categories should not be considered as abstract and absolute visual values.

mμ	Average English	Latin	Hanunóo Level 1	Hanunóo Level 2
800–650	Red	*Fulvus* / *Flavus*	Marara (dry) / Malagti (light)	
640–590	Orange		Marara (*Indelible*) / Malagti (*Weak*)	
580–550	Yellow		Malatuy (fresh)	
540–490	Green	*Glaucus*		
480–460	Blue		Mabi:ru (rotten) / Mabi:ru (dark) & Mabi:ru & Malatuy	
450–440	Indigo	*Caerullus*		
430–390	Violet			

FIGURE 3.5. Comparative color categories in Umberto Eco's "How Culture Conditions the Colours We See."

Rather, these categories were evoked as the properties of specific objects in particular visual and social contexts: "Latin poets were less sensitive to clear-cut spectral oppositions or gradations, and more sensitive to slight mixtures of spectrally distant hues. In other words, they were not interested in pigments but in perceptual effects due to the combined action of light, surfaces, the nature and purposes of objects."[35] Based on these verbal mappings, Eco created a visual chart graphing the relations between Latin terms, the color categories of twentieth-century English and Hanunóo (a Filipino language), and numbered wavelengths within the visual spectrum (fig. 3.5).

Figure 3.6 presents a parallel mapping, one focused on the categories of glittering light in sixteenth-century Nahuatl. By comparing how Molina's Nahuatl entries are used in other sixteenth-century texts, we find seven basic realms of signification, four of them overlapping. On its own is *tlanextia,* a term used for cool luminescence: the moon, Venus, glowworms.[36] *Pepetzca* is used for the soft reflectivity of silk, the wings of a smoky yellow butterfly, the sun, widgeon and quetzal feathers, the iridescent scarab, and gold.[37] Quetzal feathers, scarabs, and gold are also described by the term *pepetlaca,* which seems to have been used for metallic or lapidary reflections, including golden eagle feathers, pearls, a mineral called "mirror stone earth," indigo-dyed hair, the metal shields and lances of the Europeans, and turquoise and jade.[38] In turn, turquoise and jade overlap with *cuecueyoca,* which evokes the bright liquid reflectivity of yellow maize, the wood of the *tlaculolquauitl* tree, cherries, frogs' eggs, anthills, a shimmering desert, splashing fish, and sunlit fields and lagoons.[39] Sunlit fields and lagoons are also—following Molina—described by the term *pepeyoca,* along with

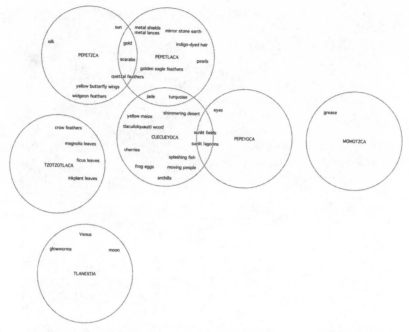

FIGURE 3.6. A map of Nahuatl categories for reflected light.

human eyes (apparently this was a kind of liquid reflectivity distinct from that of *cuecueyoca*).[40] Yet another kind of liquid luster was described by *momotzca*, whose use seems to have been limited to the shimmer of hot grease.[41] Finally, in contrast to the cool luminescence of *tlanextia* and the bright liquid reflectivity of *cuecueyoca* is the black-green glitter of *tzotzotlaca*, which captured the dark iridescence of raven feathers and the leaves of particular trees and plants: magnolia, ficus, inkplant.[42]

Jeanette Peterson first demonstrated that the Nahuas used a specific visual convention to indicate shining, reflective things: an eye. Splashing water, butterfly wings, featherwork, European metal helmets, even stars, were all marked with disembodied round eyeballs in order to highlight their glittering surfaces. These were eye-catching or eye-popping things.[43] Eyes are used to mark splashing water on a prehispanic calendar stone (fig. 3.7), a butterfly-patterned textile in the mid-sixteenth-century Codex Magliabechiano (fig. 3.8), a steel helmet flashing in the light of a burning temple on the circa 1552 Lienzo de Tlaxcala (fig. 3.9), and a featherwork image of a saint in the circa 1580 "General History of the Things of New Spain" (fig. 3.10).[44]

FIGURE 3.7. A Central Mexican calendar stone, with the Year 4 Water glyph in the upper right corner marked by two disembodied round eyes and one teardrop-shaped shell. Image courtesy of the Peabody Museum of Natural History, Yale University, YPM ANT.19231.

Eye glyphs were used to indicate reflectivity because Nahuatl used the same word for *eye* and *face* and *surface: ixtli*.[45] Disembodied eyes (*ixtli*) provided an ideal symbol to indicate that the surface (*ixtli*) they mark is eye-like, shining. Dana Leibsohn pushes this argument further, suggesting that the attraction of eyes and glittering surfaces involves a kind of sympathetic resonance: *ixtli* ('surfaces') attract *ixtli* ('eyes').[46] This kind of attraction is strikingly depicted in a small vignette from the 1540s Codex Mendoza (figs. 3.11 and 3.12).[47] An astronomer sits on a woven reed seat and looks up at the night sky, represented by a dark half-circle filled with round star-eyes. A

manta æ çinco Rosas

manta æmaij posa

manta æl sol

manta æ culebra

FIGURE 3.8. Folio 8v of the Codex Magliabechiano, with a disembodied eye marking a butterfly-patterned textile (upper right), as reproduced in *Codex Magliabecchiano XIII. Manuscrit mexicain post-Colombien de la Bibliothèque nationale de Florence; reproduit en photochromographie aux frais du duc de Loubat.*

dotted line projects outward from the astronomer's face; it traces the path of a disembodied eyeball, floating between the man and the sky. The glittering surface of the sky literally draws the human gaze toward it.

According to the categories mapped out in figure 3.6, the eyeball glyph was used to mark a number of *linguistically distinguished reflective properties:* butterflies and textiles (*pepetzca*), metal helmets (*pepetlaca*), splashing water (*cuecueyoca* or *pepeyoca*). What the images in figures 3.7 to 3.10 reveal is that in Central Mexican pictorial writing, specific linguistic variations were ignored in favor of a more general linguistic-conceptual reference. The disembodied eye indicated shininess in general; it did not distinguish the reflectivites of feathers, eyes, and pools of water.

The lesson here is that visual and verbal art may not always overlap—which makes the lexical riches of translating dictionaries all the more precious. Ever since Erwin Panofsky proposed his iconological method for the interpretation of visual culture, art historians and anthropologists have repeatedly subjugated visual materials to the requirements of linguistic

FIGURE 3.9. Cell 16 of the Lienzo de Tlaxcala, with disembodied eyes used to show light reflecting off a steel helmet (lower right; the head of the helmet-wearing and bearded Spaniard appears below an upward-thrusting spear and between two tall feather-topped battle standards). Image courtesy of wwww.mesolore.org.

evidence. Even among twenty-first-century art historians, arguments about visual meaning are viewed suspiciously if not backed up with alphabetic support.[48] But in the case of Nahua visual aesthetics, the visual archive and the linguistic archive do not align. Nahua artists used only one visual-linguistic convention to indicate reflectivity (the *ixtli*-eye), and in so doing they ignored the other kinds of visual attractiveness that they could apparently see, and talk about.[49]

This flattening out of Nahuatl's reflective categories is a mirror-image of Derrida's *différance*.[50] Derrida coined this term (based on the French *différence*) as part of his investigations into the denigration of writing and elevation of speech in Western philosophy. The newly coined *différance* was pronounced in the same way as *différence*, and thus the two words could

FIGURE 3.10. Folio 373r of Bernardino de Sahagún's "General History of the Things of New Spain" manuscript, with a disembodied eye used to indicate the shining reflectivity of feather mosaic (third vignette from the top; the eye marks a featherwork saint's image at bottom center). Florence, Biblioteca Medicea Laurenziana, Ms. Med. Palat. 219, c. 373r. Image courtesy of MiBACT.

FIGURE 3.11. Aztec stargazer (upper right corner) from the Nahua Codex Mendoza, as reproduced in volume 1 of Kingsborough's *Antiquities of Mexico* (1831). Image courtesy of Beinecke Rare Book and Manuscript Library, Yale University.

FIGURE 3.12. Aztec stargazer (detail) from the Nahua Codex Mendoza, as reproduced in volume 1 of Kingsborough's *Antiquities of Mexico*. Image courtesy of
Beinecke Rare Book and Manuscript Library, Yale University.

only be distinguished *through writing*. In contrast, the rich field of Nahuatl
categories for reflectivity—*tlanextia* versus *pepetzca* versus *pepetlaca* versus *cuecueyoca* versus *tzotzotlaca*—created a set of experiential distinctions
that could be rendered in speech, but not represented using the indigenous
system of hieroglyphic script. With the coming of the alphabet, however, all
that changed. Alphabetic records from five centuries ago allow us, now, to
reconstruct linguistically a complex terrain of visual experience.

4
Margins of Vocabularies

Zapotec divination, Mixtec ruins, Nahua surfaces: we have just seen how the linguistic riches of translating dictionaries can be used to interpret—or misinterpret—the material world. Intersections of language and materiality are central to this chapter as well, but here we explore the physical materiality of translating dictionaries themselves. Historians of the book have made clear that books and scrolls and tablets are more than just relays for information. They are also physical things, and in many cases their material properties transform the textual data recorded on their surfaces.[1] This chapter considers how one physical property of early modern books—ample blank margins, luxurious real estate in an era when paper was expensive and precious—played a key role in the very production of translating dictionaries.[2]

The vast majority of translating dictionaries created in the sixteenth and early seventeenth centuries were based on the entries of already published dictionaries. As we saw in chapter 1, internal variations enable us to trace new versions of Nebrija's *Dictionarium* to specific earlier printings. When language researchers in the sixteenth and early seventeenth centuries set out to create Castilian translating dictionaries for languages other than Latin, they also seem to have started by annotating the printed pages of existing books.[3]

Records of this practice survive in four published dictionaries from New Spain, their margins filled with translating glosses. They include a copy of Molina's 1555 Castilian–Nahuatl *Vocabulario* glossed with Otomi (in the library of the Museo Nacional de Antropología in Mexico City), a copy of the same *Vocabulario* glossed with Matlatzinca (in the Cornell University Library; fig. 4.1), a copy of Gilberti's 1559 Castilian–P'urhépecha *Vocabulario* glossed with Otomi (in the New York Public Library; fig. 4.2), and a copy

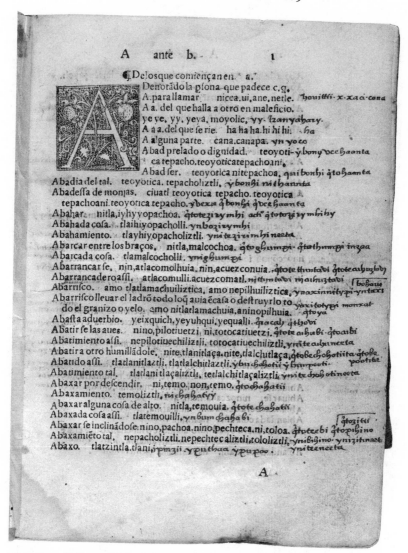

FIGURE 4.1. Folio 1r of Molina's 1555 Castilian–Nahuatl *Vocabulario*, with glosses in Matlatzinca. Image courtesy of Cornell University Library, Ithaca.

of Molina's 1571 Castilian–Nahuatl / Nahuatl–Castilian *Vocabulario* also glossed with Otomi (in the American Museum of Natural History in New York; fig. 4.3). A fifth example, this one a manuscript, is also relevant here: the Newberry Library's "Vocabulario trilingüe." As we saw in chapter 2, this was created by hand-copying in black ink the Castilian–Latin entries from a

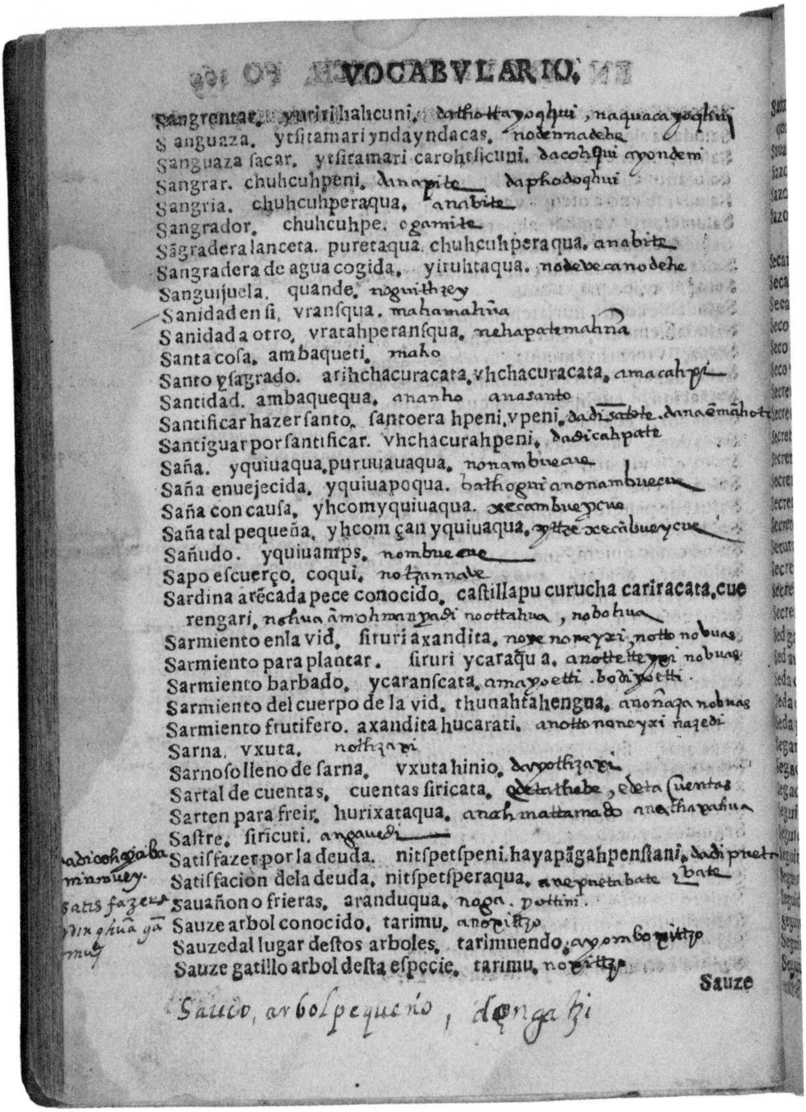

VOCABVLARIO. EN

Sangrentar. yuriri hahcuni.
Sanguaza. ytsitamari yndayndacas.
Sanguaza sacar. ytsitamari carohtsicuni.
Sangrar. chuhcuhpeni.
Sangria. chuhcuhperaqua.
Sangrador. chuhcuhpe.
Sãgradera lanceta. puretaqua. chuhcuhperaqua.
Sangradera de agua cogida. yiruhtaqua.
Sanguijuela. quande.
Sanidad en si. vransqua.
Sanidad a otro. vratahperansqua.
Santa cosa. ambaqueti.
Santo y sagrado. arihchacuracata. vhchacuracata.
Santidad. ambaquequa.
Santificar hazer santo. santoera hpeni. vpeni.
Santiguar por santificar. vhchacurahpeni.
Saña. yquiuaqua. puruuauaqua.
Saña enuejecida. yquiuapoqua.
Saña con causa. yhcomyquiuaqua.
Saña tal pequeña. yhcom çan yquiuaqua.
Sañudo. yquiuamps.
Sapo escuerço. coqui.
Sardina arẽcada pece conocido. castillapu curucha cariracata. cue rengari.
Sarmiento en la vid. siruri axandita.
Sarmiento para plantar. siruri ycaraq̃u a.
Sarmiento barbado. ycaranscata.
Sarmiento del cuerpo de la vid. thuuahtahengua.
Sarmiento frutifero. axandita hucarati.
Sarna. vxuta.
Sarnoso lleno de sarna. vxuta hinio.
Sartal de cuentas. cuentas siricata.
Sarten para freir. hurixataqua.
Sastre. siricuti.
Satisfazer por la deuda. nitspetspeni. hayapãgahpenstani.
Satisfacion de la deuda. nitspetsperaqua.
Sauañon o frieras. aranduqua.
Sauze arbol conocido. tarimu.
Sauzedal lugar destos arboles. tarimuendo.
Sauze gatillo arbol desta especie. tarimu.
Sauze

FIGURE 4.2. Folio 159v of Gilberti's 1559 Castilian–P'urhépecha *Vocabulario*, with glosses in Otomi. Image courtesy of Rare Books Division, The New York Public Library, Astor, Lenox, and Tilden Foundations, *KE1559.

"1516" printing of the *Dictionarium*, and then adding Nahuatl translations in red. But that volume's story did not end here, for after the main manuscript was completed yet more Castilian–Nahuatl entries were added to the margins by different hands in different inks (figs. 4.4, 4.5).[4]

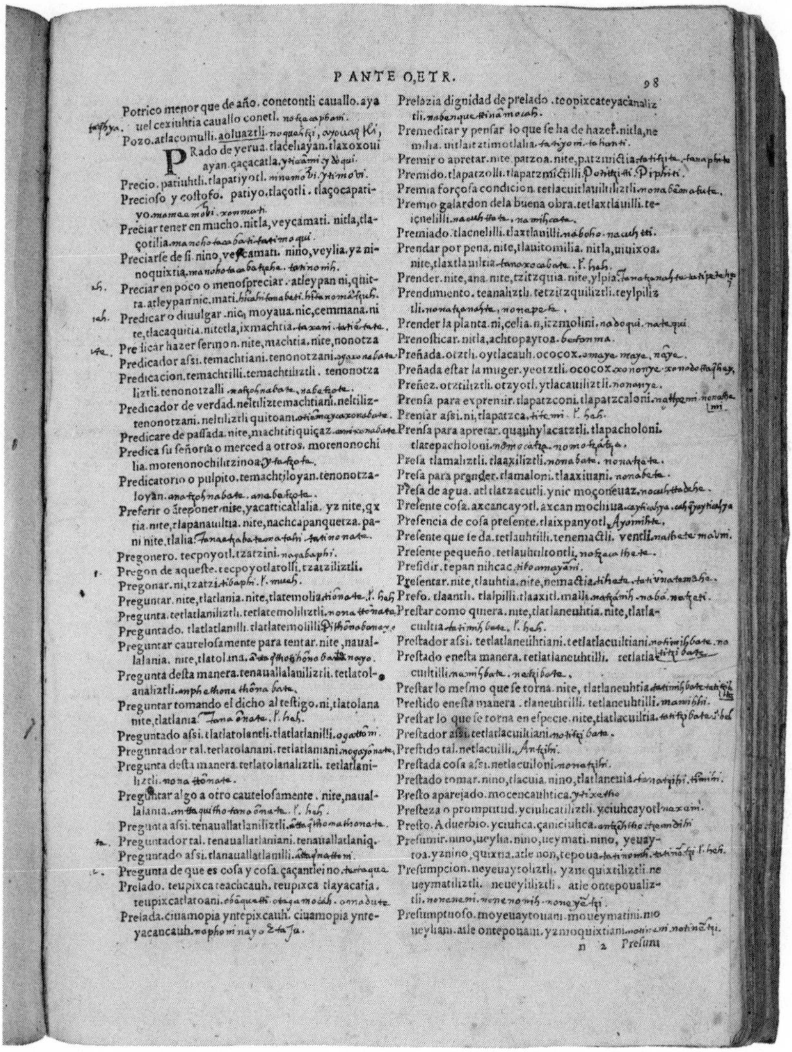

FIGURE 4.3. Folio 98r of Molina's 1571 Castilian–Nahuatl / Nahuatl–Castilian *Vocabulario*, with glosses in Otomi. Image courtesy of the American Museum of Natural History Library, New York, Rare Book Collection, J-4.

Such handwritten annotations have been of great interest to historians of reading.[5] One popular conceit for interpreting marginal notes is to see them as records of centuries-old conversations, conversations between reader and author. Yet the idea of marginalia as conversation is, in many cases, problematic. There is an important difference, Heather Jackson insists, "between

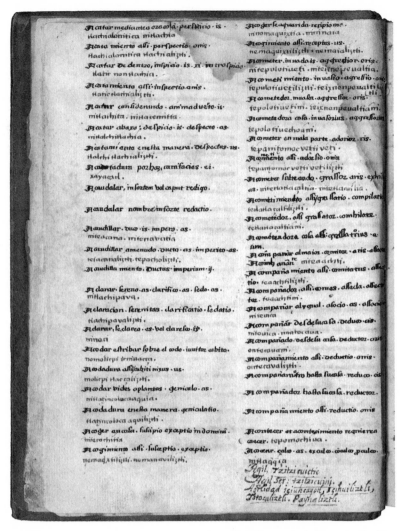

FIGURE 4.4. Folio 5v of the "Vocabulario trilingüe," with marginal glosses in Castilian and Nahuatl (for **Agil**, **Agil ser**, and **Agilidad**). Image courtesy of The Newberry Library, Chicago, VAULT Ayer MS 1478.

live social engagement and the enchanted mental space of reading." "For one thing," William Slights adds, "authors seldom have an opportunity to respond to annotators. Regardless of whether an annotator is speaking to himself, the author, or future readers, he is formulating his own ideas about himself as he reacts to what he is reading."[6]

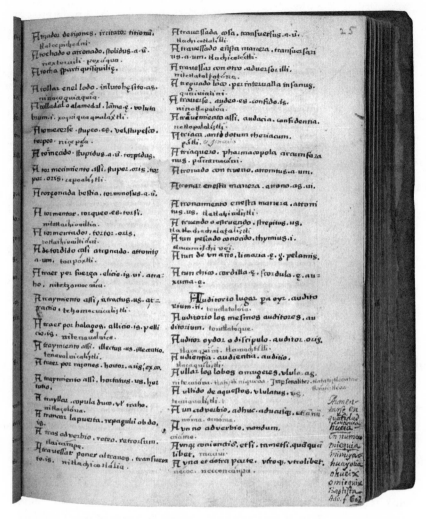

FIGURE 4.5. Folio 25r of the "Vocabulario trilingüe," with marginal glosses in Castilian and Nahuatl (for **Aumentarse en calidad continua** and **en numero**). Image courtesy of The Newberry Library, Chicago, VAULT Ayer MS 1478.

Yet there are significant exceptions. Anthony Grafton argues that early sixteenth-century notes in Guillaume Budé's copy of Vitruvius' *De archi-tectura* suggest Budé read the book together with Giovanni Giocondo, an Italian architect who was in Paris building the bridge of Notre Dame between 1500 and 1505.[7] In this case, marginalia record a sort of three-way conversation: between Budé and Giocondo, in person, and prompted by Vitruvius as a silent third. But perhaps the clearest examples of marginalia fossilizing long-silent conversations are the lists of translated words scribbled into the margins of printed dictionaries.

Precisely because they were physical things, made of ink and paper, translating dictionaries were capable of *generating social space*. Time and again throughout the early modern world, the speaker of one language sat down with the speaker of another language, opened a published dictionary, and then asked for translations of its entries, item by item, line by line. Once delivered (or invented), each new entry would be written down in the blank marginal space of the printed text.[8] Lexical glosses in the margins of translating dictionaries are in many cases residues of actual conversations long ago, conversations dedicated to generating those very lexical glosses. The verbal exchanges enabled by this book-centered social space were recursively inscribed on the pages of the book itself.

These social spaces of translation would have taken very different forms were it not for the global circulation not only of people, but of printed texts as well. Historians of the book have often revealed the ways in which reading can be a social act, showing how groups of readers form *interpretive communities* whose members "share the same reading styles and the same strategies of interpretation."[9] By extension, the practice of using published dictionaries to structure dialogues on language suggests an even more intimate kind of text-centered sociality: the *interpretive conversation*, generated around a core text by a small number of interlocutors.[10]

And yet when we are dealing with the interpretive conversations created by and for translating dictionaries—especially translating dictionaries undertaken by missionaries—we must remember that these book-centered interactions could be deeply hierarchical, riven by inequality and coercion. This brings us to the tympan.

In 1972, Jacques Derrida published *Marges de la philosophie*, translated into English as *Margins of Philosophy* in 1982. "Tympan" is the title of his opening essay. The margins which it tympanizes are conceptual and metaphysical, and relate to the limits of philosophy as a discipline and a way of thinking. But they offer a productive foundation (as they should, as a tympan) for thinking about the visual, social, and conceptual margins implicated by the glossed dictionaries illustrated on the preceding pages— and, by extension, about the glossed surfaces of now-lost copies of Nebrija's

Dictionarium, copies we know were essential to the creation of early modern translating dictionaries throughout the world.

Even as Derrida insists that "beyond the philosophical text there is not a blank, virgin, empty margin, but another text, a weave of differences of forces," he is skeptical about the ability of that *beyond* to disrupt philosophy. "Exteriority and alterity are concepts which by themselves have never surprised philosophical discourse. *Philosophy by itself has always been concerned with them.*" And so even when "borrowing its categories from the logos of the other," a philosophical author still speaks only of himself; as regards the other, "one reappropriates it for oneself, one disposes of it, one misses it, or rather one misses (the) missing (of) it, which, as concerns the other, always amounts to the same."[11]

> Can one violently puncture philosophy's field of listening without its immediately—even pretending in advance, by hearing what is said of it, by decoding the statement—making the penetration resonate within itself, appropriating the emission for itself, familiarly communicating it to itself between the inner and middle ear, following the path of a tube or inner opening, be it round or oval? In other words, can one puncture the tympanum of a philosopher and still be heard and understood by him? . . .
>
> In order effectively, practically to transform what one decries (tympanizes), must one still be heard and understood within it, henceforth subjecting oneself to the law of the inner hammer? In relaying the inner hammer, one risks permitting the noisiest discourse to participate in the most serene, least disturbed, best served economy of philosophical irony. Which is to say, and examples of this metaphysical drumming are not lacking today, that in taking this risk, one risks nothing.[12]

If we replace *philosophy* with *missionary linguistics,* Derrida's text is provocatively resonant—as it should be, as a tympan. Printed translating dictionaries also borrow "categories from the logos of the other," fitting them into preexisting structures (of phonetic transcription, of paginal order). Even when new terms are added, or even when Castilian neologisms are created, the basic structure of the printed page remains undisturbed. New terms are integrated alphabetically. Each Castilian entry is followed by its translation into a second language. There were of course vast lexical worlds that existed beyond the pages of these dictionaries—and this was as true for Castilian and Latin as it was for Mayan and Mixtec—but only a small part of that world ("another text, a weave of differences of forces") could ever be incorporated into printed dictionary space. And of course it goes without saying that the spoken word was always only translated into an *alphabetic* system. Translating dictionaries for the New World did not allow prehispanic traditions of glyphic writing to disturb their surfaces.

Issues of constraint and transformation and partiality should never be ignored when we study these printed and handwritten texts. At the same time, however, relocating Derrida's comments on the metaphysical margins of philosophy to the physical margins of the printed page raises a whole series of important issues, and reveals—as Derrida would appreciate—how binary models of inclusion and exclusion, even text and margin, fail to capture the complex geography of the marked-up printed page. "Like every limus, the limes, the short cut, signifies the oblique."[13]

In the Americas, at least, the social space created by word lists in printed dictionaries was profoundly unequal. Catholic missionaries set the terms, literally, of these conversations about language.[14] But they did not control them entirely. They might be met with silence, when terms could not be translated. These silences were sometimes transferred to print, as with the Castilian entries followed by blank space in the pages of Domingo de Santo Tomás's Castilian–Quechua *Lexicon* (see fig. 2.6).[15] At the same time, indigenous speakers—who of course understood the subtleties of their own languages far better than their friar-interviewers—could pursue a number of different strategies when they decided to offer up a translation for posterity. Indigenous-language translations of Castilian categories were not all the same, or of the same kind—and so what appears on the surface to be a tranquil field of neatly ordered alphabetic print is instead an unstable and treacherous juxtaposition of meanings and misunderstandings. Incorporation is not always domination.

The simplest kind of translation is what we might call a transparent translation—as when the Castilian *agua*, 'water,' was rendered as the Nahuatl *atl*, or when the Castilian *casa*, 'house,' was rendered as the Aymara *uta*. But even simple translations are rarely simple. Consider the Castilian word for rain, *lluvia*, which was translated into Mixtec as *dzavui*. *Dzavui* certainly means rain, even today, but it was also the name for the Mixtec rain god. To speak of rain was to speak of divinity. This is why *dzavui*, 'rain,' was also used to translate the Castilian word *idolo*, 'idol.'

In some cases, however, the complicated contours of a word's meaning in one language actually found a close parallel to the complicated contours of a word's meaning in another. A good example of this is when the Castilian **Viento y espiritu vital** ('wind and vital spirit') was translated in the Yucatan. This entry-form (included in the Hispanic Society of America's Solana manuscript) was derived from the Nebrijan category **Viento anima**, 'wind soul,' which was itself a translation of the Latin *spiritus*. In the Solana manuscript, the Castilian **Viento y espiritu vital** is translated into Yucatec Mayan as "ik"—a word that also indicates both wind and soul.[16] In other words, a Castilian bridge ('wind and vital spirit') connected surprisingly parallel concepts of animating force in both Latin (*spiritus*) and Yucatec (*ik*).

Another translation strategy, especially when faced with a strange foreign concept, was simply to render the meaning of that concept literally, creating a translation that was more like a descriptive definition. This probably explains the translation for *mosque* offered in Molina's 1555 Castilian–Nahuatl dictionary. **Mezquita** is defined as both "mahoma tlatlatlauhtilizcalli" ('Muhammed's house of oratory') and "mahoma calli" ('house of Muhammed').[17] This descriptive strategy is also behind the Zapotec neologisms for pagan Roman divination described in the previous chapter. As we saw, this descriptive method was sometimes crudely successful—as when **Diuino por el agua**, 'water-augur,' was translated into Zapotec as "Colanij niça" ('daykeeper who uses water'). But in other cases it caused a total misfire—as when **Diuino por sacrificios**, 'sacrifice-augur,' was translated into Zapotec as "Còlanij pichijlla," 'daykeeper who uses beans.'[18] And sometimes highly descriptive translations of Castilian words were not created-on-the-spot neologisms, but established indigenous terms for Old World things. James Lockhart describes several amazing examples in Nahuatl: the European candle as a 'beeswax torch' (*xicocuitlaocotl*), the European firearm as a 'fire trumpet' (*tlequiquiztli*).[19]

But when important local concepts had no Castilian equivalent, they could actually (as we saw many times in chapter 2) expand the Nebrijan core. This was the case with the Nahuatl terms for reflectivity discussed in chapter 3. Long and descriptive Castilian phrases were assembled in order to capture the precise connotations of a single Nahuatl term. To define *pepeyoca*, Molina offered **Relumbrar el agua con el sol o los campos**: 'to shine, as with sun on the water or on the fields.' To define *cuecueyoca*, Molina offered **Reluzir las piedras preciosas o los peces de[n]tro del agua con el moviemiento que hazen, o el ayuntamiento de las hormigas o las lagunas**

y campos, o las gentes ayuntadas por el mouimiento que hazen: 'to glitter, as with precious stones or fish within the water with the movement that they make, or the anthill, or the lagoons and fields, or people joined by the movement that they make.' Such Castilian translations of new Amerindian categories were not always so complicated; in 1560 the Andean *quero* was rendered simply as **Copa de madera**—'wooden cup.'

Finally, in a few rare cases an extant indigenous term actually prompted the creation of a *Castilian neologism*. Alonso de Molina confesses doing this in the introduction to his 1555 *Vocabulario*. He invented the Castilianesque *abaxador* (building on the existing Castilian verb *abajar*, 'to lower') in order to translate the Nahuatl *tlatemouiani*:

> In this vocabulary appear certain Romance terms which don't really belong in our Castilian, or which are seldom used: and this is done to better explain the qualities of the language of the Indians, and so we include *Abaxador*, even though it is not used in our Romance language, in order to explain the word *tlatemouiani*, which in good Romance means he who takes something down.[20]

This varied range of responses to translation demands, responses preserved in the lexical contents of translating dictionaries, finds a striking parallel in the visual layouts of glossed vocabularies. If we pay close attention to these records of ancient interviews, we can see how the pages of early modern printed dictionaries cannot easily be divided into a text/margin binary. Instead, glossing reveals how each page contains a complex landscape of *different marginal spaces*. Studied carefully, these varied kinds of glosses, and their relative placement on the printed page, reveal much about the social and conceptual negotiations involved in the creation of early modern translating dictionaries.

In most cases, new translations were added as *extensions of the printed line*, written down in the fjords of a ragged-right marginal space. This can be seen clearly on folio 1r of Cornell's 1555 *Vocabulario*, as well as on folio 98r of the American Museum of Natural History's 1571 *Vocabulario* (see figs. 4.1 and 4.3; note how the two-column format of the latter creates "margins" not simply on the edges of the page, but in a central fissure as well: a core margin, as it were). It is clear, with this style of glossing, how the words gathered in an interview were determined by what had already been printed. The 1571 *Vocabulario* also demonstrates that word-gatherings were not always successful: a number of its printed entries are not followed by Otomi glosses, a failure of translation we have seen before (see fig. 4.3; compare with fig. 2.6).

The marginal space created after the end of a printed line was but one kind of marginal topography. The margins at the top and the bottom of dictionary pages—and sometimes the left and right page-edges as well— were spaces in which *new* terms could be added, words not included in the linguistic architecture of the printed page. It was here, in the paper ocean surrounding the main printed text, that entries for demonic altar, or Nahuatl reflectivity, would have been added. For example, folio 159v of the New York Public Library's Gilberti includes a new entry for **Sauco, arbol pequeño** ('elder, small tree') added to the bottom margin, as well as a new entry for **Satisfazer** ('to satisfy') added to the left page-edge margin (see fig. 4.2). Folio 5v of the Newberry's handwritten "Vocabularo trilingüe" includes new entries for **Agil**, **Agil ser**, and **Agilidad** ('agile,' 'to be agile,' 'agility') at the bottom margin (see fig. 4.4). On folio 25r of the same manuscript, new entries for **Aumentarse en calidad continua** and **en numero** ('to increase in a continuous quality' and 'in number') have been entered into the right page-edge margin (see fig. 4.5).

We can therefore imagine how different kinds of translated terms would have been written into different kinds of marginal space. Transparent or less than transparent translations, as well as descriptive definitions (whether precise or confused, made up on the spot or already incorporated into everyday speech) would have been added to the page's *central margins:* the blank spaces created after a preexisting entry's line of type had ended. In contrast, when an indigenous concept prompted the addition of a new Castilian category—or even triggered the creation of a Castilian neologism—those kinds of additions would have been written in a page's *outer margins:* above and below, left and right. "Can this text become the margin of a margin? Where has the body of the text gone when the margin is no longer a secondary virginity but an inexhaustible reserve, the stereographic activity of an entirely other ear?"[21]

What these printed words and annotated pages reveal, then, is that the physical and conceptual spaces of early modern translation are poorly explained by binary logics. Contrasts of text versus margin, or radical exteriority versus appropriated incorporation, totally fail to capture the subtleties of translation in practice. Just as each page of a printed dictionary presented not a simple text/margin dichotomy, but a complex geography of printed and marginal spaces, so too did the terms offered as translations by indigenous experts vary widely in their focus, inventiveness, and critique—to say nothing of sheer refusals. Extensions, incorporations, interventions, absences: as Derrida would appreciate, the graphics and glosses of dictionary pages do indeed "blur the line which separates a text from its controlled margin."

Conclusions

When we open the translations of Nebrija, we open doorways. The rendering of Castilian into Latin cannot be separated from the rendering of Castilian into Arabic or English or Cakchiquel. These translations form a single corpus, and if we cut off branches from this family tree in our scholarship (by claiming they deal with peripheral areas or idioms), we violate the Nebrijan legacy. Thus in the Americas, Nebrijan translations reveal how deeply our understandings of the prehispanic past are bound up with the culture of early modern Europe, and its antique heritage. Paying attention to how Latin-derived categories were, and were not, translated into Zapotec and Mixtec and Nahuatl presents us with new vistas for understanding archaeological ruins and painted manuscripts. Paradoxically, it is only by taking the Renaissance foundations of our prehispanic knowledge seriously that we can *avoid* forever remaking native society into the image of ancient Rome.[1]

But this does not mean that the Nebrijan corpus requires American history to be always dominated by European evidence. These translations also show how our visions of early modern Europe can be enriched by drawing on New World archives. By studying how indigenous-language dictionaries printed in Spanish America were glossed with terms from yet other indigenous languages, we can reconstruct how dictionaries printed in Europe would have been glossed to create translating tools for European vernaculars as well.

Above all, dictionary translations—both linguistic and spatial—offer important lessons for thinking about the geographies and temporalities of the early modern world. The production of Castilian translating dictionaries based on Nebrija, the fitting of foreign terms into a core list of Castilian categories, was not a practice that respected the divisions of Old World versus New, or that distinguished a European center from a marginal Philippines and Latin America.

Bruno Latour's critique of clichéd binaries in science studies (in which "cultures, minds, methods, or societies" are either "prescientific" or "scientific") is also relevant for mapping the early modern world: "the 'grand dichotomy' with its self-righteous certainty should be replaced by many *uncertain* and *unexpected* divides. . . . All such dichotomous distinctions can be convincing only as long as they are enforced by a strong asymmetrical bias that treats the two sides of the divide or border very differently."[2] Dichotomous assumptions about language or geography (European versus non-European, the West versus the Rest) do not explain the translations of Nebrija linguistically or spatially. English and Tuscan and French and Arabic were molded into a Nebrijan frame as much as were Nahuatl and Quechua and Mixtec and Tagalog. The 1545 Granada printing of Nebrija's *Dictionarium* was used as a model both in Mexico (to translate Nahuatl, in 1555) and in Italy (to translate Tuscan, in 1570). John Minsheu's 1599 Castilian–English dictionary was published in London, but it soon traveled to Paris (where it inspired a Castilian–French dictionary in 1604) and to the Philippines, to Pila (where it inspired a Castilian–Tagalog dictionary in 1613). The translations of dictionaries—both linguistic and spatial—do not obey a concentric logic by which metropoles radiate their influence outward to peripheries. Instead, these translations reveal complex networks in a profoundly interconnected world, where Castilian–Nahuatl and Castilian–P'urhépecha vocabularies were printed decades before Castilian–English and Castilian–French ones.

The translations of Nebrija do not tell a transparently "first in Europe, then elsewhere" kind of story.[3] They challenge the flattening of "Europe" into a single, homogenous terrain, and replace the grand dichotomy of Europe and Elsewhere with constellations of printing workshops mapped across the globe. They undermine our denials of coevalness in the era after 1492, denials by which the same centuries are temporally described as "early modern" in Europe, but "colonial" in America and Asia.[4] By studying these far-flung genealogies, we are able—as Frederick Cooper and Bruno Latour would appreciate—to avoid vague discussions of early modern globalizations, and talk instead about specific connections, particular paths: routes across land and sea, which we can reconstruct at the level of the printed page, and so reveal the movement of books (and people, and ideas) from Granada to Antwerp to Mexico City to Teposcolula, or from Venice to London to Pila.[5]

Appendix A

The Transformation of Entries in Nebrija's *Dictionarium,* 1536–1585

1. CHANGES TO THE 1536 GRANADA PRINTING

Entries added (300)

Abeto arbol peregrino
Abocados
A buen tiempo o a sazon
Acuchilladas
Aduar o aldea de los Alarbes
A empuxones, o a toques
Agujerada cosa
A la sazon
Alcahuete de cosas turpes
Alcarauia siluestre
Alcuña o linaje
Aldeas o aduares de los Arabes
Aleche pece
Alimentar: o mantener
Alimento: o mantenimiento
Al presente
Alquilar alguna cosa
Alquiler o arrendamiento
Alquimista
Amanderecha
Amanizquierda
Amoladuras de hierro en griego
Andar de combite en combite
Assentarse sobre las piernas o cuclillas
A tiempo o sazon
Aunque te pese
Auer mucha verguença
Auer mucho miedo o temor
Auer misericordia
Bastaje o ganapan
Bastaje o ganapan en griego
Berça perruna

Betonica yerua nota
Bragas estas mesmas [as *subligaculum* . . .]
Bragas estas mesmas [as *succinctoriu[m]* . . .]
Bragas aquestas mesmas [as *tigillum* . . .]
Bruñir para que reluza
Brusco o jusbarba mata conocida
Buua o boja
Carcarear el gallo
Cal por regar
Cala o tienta de curujano
Can sobre que cargan las vigas
Cantaro en que echan las suertes
Cara a cara
Cara cosa que vale mucho
Cara por hazia alguna parte
Cardenillo, que se haze del cobre
Carestia, o careza
Carmel yerua conocida
Carne mola en los varones
Caruoncol piedra preciosa
Cauallo siluestre y brauo
Cauallo de caña
Cauar horadando
Cocadriz serpiente proprio del nilo
Collado del monte o cerro
Collado el mesmo
Comedor de galapagos
Comoquiera
Con sazon y tiempo
Contenterse de los deleites
Continencia la obra de contenerse
Continentemente en esta manera
Continua cosa o tierra firme
Conuiene a saber, declarando
Cortadura de vñas

Cosa generalmente
Cosa sin prouecho
Cosa no de fiesta
Cubillo, o abadejo escarauajo po[n]-
    çoñoso
Cuchara de hierro para sacar carne
Çapatero de viejo, o reme[n]don
Çarça perruna
Ceatica enfermedad
Cedaço blanco de seda
Cera colorada
Cerco o corrillo de ombres
Cerrado el cielo qua[n]do esta nublado
Cerrado el camino aspero no bien
    hallado
Cinquipil de los judios
Cintoria yerua
Cisterna o algibe de agua
Dearrebatado
De coraçon
De corillo en corillo
De era en era
Demasiadamente
Denegar no conceder, o no otorgar
Depunta o con punta
Derecha cosa que no es izquierda
Desamparo
Desamparada o desierta cosa
Desamparador de persona o lugar
Desamparo de persona o lugar
Despachar
Despacho
Despendedor el que gasta
Destroncar arrancar de tronco
De todo punto
Deuiesso
De uilla en villa
Dientes los que mostramos quando
    reymos
Dientes los quatro delanteros con que
    recebimos el bocado
Diocesis administracion o juridicion
Dissimular que no se vee lo que se vee
Dolada cosa
Dolor generalmente
Dolorosa cosa
Dormidor con los ojos abiertos

Dura por dificil y cruelmente
Duramente vn poquillo
Duro lo dificil y cruel
Duro por el escasso cerca de auariento
Ebeno arbor peregrina de Etiopia
Ebeno madera negra deste arbol
Ebeno de la india negra y blanco
Edad ygual con otro
Embuelta vna cosa co[n] otra
Encontinente o luego
Encorporar o mezclar vna cosa co[n]
    otro
Enfrente de otro lugar
Enseuada cosa
Entesamiento obra de entesar o extender
Escuela de dançar, o baylar
Escusada cosa que no es menester
Esparraguera de donde sale el tallo
Espelunca o cueua
Esquadra de cantero que labra piedra
Fistigo o alhocigo arbol
Fistigo o alhocigo fruto del
Flor como de cardos o cerraja yerua
Fragosa cosa o aspera de piedras
Frechadura como de arco
Gajo donde se juntan las vuas
Garruuia vayna de qualquier legumbre
Gauilan flor seca q[ue] buela de algu-
    [n]as yeruas
Gobi pece
Guardador de cabras
Guardador de ganado mayor
Guiar la dança
Guia del que guia la dança
Guia la mesma obra de guiar
Guirnalda de flores
Harina lo sotil della
Harma o ruda siluestre
Hauarraz yerua y simiente della
Hauarraz la mesma en griego
Hazer como siluo entre las menos
Higado de puerco mo[n]tes
Higado de asno
Hoja o lamina
Huerfano de padre
Hueste gente de guerra
Iazmin

Iazmin de los vergeles
Iusbarba o brusco mata conocida
Ierua lombriguera
Ijares
Ijada e[n]fermedad
Illustre cosa famosa o esclarecida
Incontinente en cosa de passion
Incontinencia aquella obra de no se
   contener
Inconueniente cosa que no conuiene
Ladrar los cachorros [as *baubo . . .*]
Lamina o hoja
Lapidario de piedras preciosas
Librero que vende libros
Librero que escriue libros
Linaloe
Listada cosa de diuersos colores
Ludir o fregar vna cosa con otra
Llamar o traer de lexos
Llamar o tocar con la mano
Llamar a la puerta
Maçonadura, obra de maçar
Mala y falsamente
Malhechora cosa
Mançanilla yerua nota
Mançanilla en griego
Mancebo aun no barbado
Mampesada
Marhojo o moho de los arboles
Marquesita piedra de que se funde el
   cobre
Marsopa genero de vallena
Mente la parte de la anima appetetiua
Mercaduria de esclauos
Mezereon
Mirar altraues o de trauersia
Mirar al cielo
Moneda falsa
Muy mucho o con veheme[n]tia
Mula que anda de andadura
Mular cosa de mula o mulo
Mular cosa o azemilar
Mulatero o azemilero
Musgaño
Neruio de los compañones
Ofrenda que sacrificamos
Ondear de onda en onda

Oro reduzido en riel
Oro guañin
Padrastro o repelo cerca de la vña
Palma de la mano coruada
Palmada co[n] la mano o bofetada
Pan de cierta manera p[ar]a luchadores
Pan vizcocho como turron
Papo de las aues
Pared de texbique
Parte dar
Patear o hollar o pisar
Peyne de box p[ar]a peynar
Pelador o descortezador
Peladura o descortezadura
Pelear la capa al braço
Pelear en[e]sta ma[n]era
Pelear en esta manera
Pellejeria lugar do[nde] se venden
   pellejos
Pellico palabras dichas en p[er]juyzio
   de otro
Perder la verguença
Perpetuar o continuar
Perpetua o continuamente
Perpetua o continua cosa
Perpetuidad o continuidad
Persuadir o induzir con razones
Peruetano
Pesador en qualquier manera
Piedra esta mesma enfermedad
Piñon mondado
Piñones con cascara
Poblar cibdad o lugar
Poblador assi
Poblazon obra de poblar assi
Preferir o anteponer
Prelacia dignidad de prelado
Premio galardon de buena obra
Prestamente
Puercas estas mismas
Quebrar el espinazo
Queso generalmente
Queso de vacas
Queso fresco o cerrion
Quixones yerua nota
Rabo de puerco o erbatu yerua
Rauano gagisco

Rebatada cosa
Rebusca despues de la vendimia
Repelo o padrastro cerca de la vña
Rufian o alcaguete
Rufianeria o alcagueteria
Rufianear o alcaguetear
Rugimiento de las tripas
Sachar o escardar la tierra
Sachadura o escardadura
Sachador o escardador
Salmorejo de vinagre y sal
Saltar el macho sobre la hembra
Saltear con lanças
Sauañon o frieras
Semola o acemit
Sentarse
Sentarse en cuclillas
Siluo hecho con las manos
Siluo en esta manera
Sinzelar labrar de sinzel
Sobrepujar
Socolor
Solicitar poner en cuydado
Solicito estar y congoxoso
Solicita cosa o cuydadosa co[n] co[n]goxa
Solicitamente y con congoxa
Sorze raton pequeño
Sudor de las ingles de la yegua
Tabique pared
Texbique pared
Topar topetando con cuerno
Tortella yerua conocida
Traer o llamar de lexos
Trastrocar
Trastrocamiento
Trementina
Tremielga pece
Triaquero
Turron o pan vizcocho
Vaguido enfermedad
Vaguida cosa
Vaporosa cosa que echa baho o vapor
Vela para hazer sombra
Venero o minero de algun metal
Veril piedra preciosa
Vestidura de chamelote
Vientre
Vientre de muger

Vientre intestino ciego
Vinniebla yerua conocida
Virtud generalmente
Virtud por la fortaleza o esfuerço
Virtuoso
Vituperio
Zargatona yerua

2. CHANGES TO THE 1552 GRANADA PRINTING

Entries removed (2)

Basilisco este mesmo en Griego
Hoja o lamina

Entries added (16)

Barra, o banco en la mar
Bastida este mesmo engeño
Coruina, pescado conocido
Culpar a menudo
Curador dado al menor de xxv años
Curador de arboles
Desbaratar, o derribar
Granillo de higo
Hijo, q[ue] tiene abuelo, muerto el padre
Izquierda cosa de mal aguero
Letra grande, o capital
Ondeando, de onda en onda
Pelear assi
Vrce, o breço, mata conocida
Venino, podre
Vino, que llaman de tintin

3. CHANGES TO THE 1554 GRANADA PRINTING

Entries added (1)

Caño

4. CHANGES TO THE 1555 GRANADA PRINTING

Entries removed (1)

Desbaratar, o derribar

Entries added (1)

Cargo en officio

5. CHANGES TO THE 1545 ANTWERP PRINTING

Entries added (114)

Abadejo aue
Abutarda
Agua miel
Agua rosada
Aiuda cristel [as *infusum . . .*]
Alarguez
Albahaquilla de rio
Alcanfor goma
Aleda o hiez de colmena
Algarroua
Almisque
Almoradux yerua
Ambargris
Amoladura de barbero
Araña que llaman, aguazil de mosca
Armoniaque goma
Atramuzes legumbre
Barua de cabron yerua
Bemena
Bretonica yerua
Cabra de almiscle
Cambronera mata
Cogujada aue galerita
Cubebas fruto
Çamarilla yerua
Datil azedo de la india
Empeine de piedra
Epithimo yerua
Epilepsia enfermedad
Escambrones
Espiga romana
Esquinante paja
Estinco pecezillo
Eufragia yerua
Fistola dolencia
Flor de cobre
Gacela o raueço
Gallillo o campanilla
Gallocresta yerua
Gamo animal
Gama o corça
Garco raez como hongo
Goruion goma de cierta yerua
Gualdas yerua

Habubilla
Haua marina
Hortiga yerua
Hortiguilla muerta
Huesso qualquiera
Huesso del espinazo
Huessos de que se este co[m]pone
Iuiuba acofeifa
Yerua artetica
Yerua almisclera
Yerua buena morisca
Yerua de tunez
Yerua piñuela
Yerua gatera
Lacargama
Leche de trigo
Macias
Malagueta
Mana roçio del cielo
Miel y agoa
Mielgas yerua
Mirabolanos
Mirra goma
Momia carne de cuerpo humano
    embalsamado
Muerdago de roble
Murezillo del brazo
Neguilla simiente
Nuca de la cabeça hasta baxo
Ojo de buey yerua
Opio çumo de dormideras negras
Palo del balsamo
Pan porcino
Pan y queso
Passa vua [as *vua insolata*]
Pelleja primera del ojo
Pelleja segunda
Pera olorosa
Perlesia dolencia
Rebeço o gazela animal
Ruda yerua siluestre
Ruiponces raiz
Sagre halcon
Sanamunda yerua
Sandalos
Scamonea medicina purgatiua
Sen yerua medicinal
Serapino goma

Sorua fruta
Soruo arbol
Tagarote halcon
Taragoncia yerua
Termentina
Tierra sellada
Tigeretas de vid
Tiro animal
Tolondron o tumor
Tomillo salsero
Torpigo pescado q[ue] quita el sentido
Toruisco yerua
Triguero paxaro
Turbitraiz
Tutano de huesso
Vbrera en la boca de los niños
Vua de raposa
Valeriana yerua
Vellota fruta
Verenjena
Vinagre y azeite rosado
Vino aguado
Visnaga yerua

6. CHANGES TO THE 1553 ANTWERP PRINTING

Entries removed (7)

Abutarda [as *otis, idos*]
Almisque
Cinta o cinto en griego
Logrero en griego
Passa vua [as *vua insolata*]
Sagre halcon
Tutano de huesso

Entries added (1,430 primary entries and 502 entry expansions; entry expansions are enclosed in parentheses)

Abarraganamiento
Abaxar la cabeça
Abaxar los parpados de los ojos
Abrir o tender hazia fuera
    (Cosa que se puede abrir y cerrar)
Aclarar lo escuro
Aclarar lo turuio
    (Aquella obra de acocear)

(Aquella obra de acossar)
Acostar hazia otra cosa
Acostarse con otro
    (Cosa para assi acusar)
Açada de dos dientes para cauar
Acelga siluestre
Acidente de la enfermedad
    (Aquella obra de achacar)
Adalid, guia
Administrar la hazienda
Adolecer otra vez
Adulterio de casados
Afearlo hermoso (Afeamiento assi,
    Afeador assi)
Afeitar lo q[ue] se ve[n]de (Afeye assi)
Agora a cabo de tanto tiempo
    (Cargo quien tiene de los aguaduchos)
    (El que adeuina por agueros de aues,
        Cosa pertenesciente a aquellos
        agueros)
    (Agujetas sin cabo)
Aguzadera a la qual conuiene agua
Aguzadera con azeite
Ahogar de antes
Ahogamiento de vrina
Ahornagarse la tierra (Aquel
    ahornagamiento)
Ahorrar el esclauo (Ahorradura assi)
Aire hazer con moscador
Aiuntar vna cosa a otra (Cosa que se
    puede aiuntar, Aiuntablemente)
Aiuntamiento de humor corrupto
Aiuntamiento con parienta
Ala con que nada el pece
Alabar juntame[n]te (Aquella alabança)
Albança vana
Alabanciosa cosa de si
    (De albañar en albañar)
Albardar asno
Alcançar con lisonjas (Alcanse assi)
Alcaparal de alcaparras
Alcauci del cardo que se come
Alçar el real
Alçar hazia arriba
    (Cosa de alerze, Pinpollo de alerze,
        Vino adobado con resina de alerze)
Alexarse de algun lugar
Algunos poquillos mas

Alheli blanco
  (Cosa de alheña, Azeyte de alheña)
Alimpiar otra vez
Aljongero blanco yerua
Aljongera negro yerua
Allegarse con otro
Allegamiento assi
  (Pescador de almadrauas)
Almeaja pescado de concha
Almeja de los rios
Almeja o caracol de la mar
Almizquera genero de raton
Almohada para debajo los pies
  (Cosa pertenesciente a almoneda, El
  que haze almoneda)
Alquilar de otro
Alquilador que alquila de otro
Alquiladiza cosa
Alquitran
Alta cosa en despeñadero
  (Salario del ama)
Amansar juntamente (Aquella obra de
  amansar)
Amansarse lo fiero
Amar juntamente con otros
Amar perdidamente
Amar otra vez
Amenazar con otro
Amonestar antes
Amontonada cosa
  (Requirir de amores)
Andar en puterias
Andadura assi (Andador en esta manera)
Andas en que se lleua algo
Anduares, aldeas de Alarabes
  (Platero que haze los anillos, Caxa de
  los anillos)
Animal que biue vn dia
Animales ceñidos
Antes este que estotro
Añadir encima de otro
  (Cosa de vn año, Cosa de vno, dos,
  tres, años, Cada vn año, Cosa que
  trae dos vezes en el año, Cosa de
  espacio de des años, Aquel espacio
  de dos años)
Año peligroso en la vida (Cosa pertene-
  scie[n]te a aquel año)

Apacentar con otros
  (Sobremesa del aparador)
Aparcero, o quiñonero
  (Apartamiento)
  (Apartamiento en esta manera,
  Apartador enesta manera)
Apartar de lugar
A pedaços
Apercibimiento para pelear
Aplacar
Aplacar otra vez
Apoplexia enfermedad
  (Apretar mucho, Cosa que aprieta
  mucho)
  (Sulco que ha el arado, Cama del arado)
Arbol o viga que cae en el rio
Arder otra vez
  (Lugar donde se saca arena)
Armar con yelmo o capacete
Armar çancadilla
Armazon, o cama de madera
Armiños
  (Azeite de arraihan)
Arrancar debaxo
Arrancando de raiz
Arrebatar antes
Arroyarse el rio
Asarabacar especie de nardo
Asno de albarda o de ensalma
Asno de atahona
Asno montes
  (Caxco o suelo del asno)
Aspera cosa con sedas
  (El que por las assaduras dezia lo
  venidero)
Assentarse otra vez
Assiento del diente, o de la muela
Assiento hazer en el hondon
Assiento pequeño
Assistente que se da al censor
Assistente en la ciudad
Assonar el canto
Assonador de tal canto (Aquella obra de
  assonar el canto, Assonadas de guerra)
Assossegar lo turbado
  (Co[n] astucia)
Atadura de cuerdas
  (Cosa de atajo)

Atañer, o pertenecer algo
Atar en derredor
Atar otra vez
Atar con vimbres
Atauiar juntamente
Atauio assi
    (Lugar donde atormentan los hombres)
Atormentar juntamente
Atormentar haziendo sangre
Atreudia cosa y osada
Atreuida, y osadamente
Auarraz yerua
Aunque, coniunction
    (Lugar donde se crian aues, El que
        cria o guarda las aues)
Aue que biue de los mosquitos
Aues que de su natural buelan por baxo
Autor que primero inuenta alguna cosa
    (Cosa que tiene autoridad, Autores
    ruynes, Autores principales)
Axaqueca, dolor de cabeça
Axorcas para las piernas
Azedarse
Azeitunas coger ordeñando
Azeytera, o cangilon de azeite
    (Trassegador de azeyte)
Azeite de huego de alquitran
Azre arbol
Azul escuro (Mar de tal color)
Azul para pintar
Baga de laurel
Balança para pesar (Cosa de dos balancas)
Balsa de maderos trauados
    (Azeyte de Balsamo, Cosa vntada
        con balsamo, Yerua q[ue] hueue a
        balsamo)
Bambaneandose
    (Cosa del baño, Lugar donde ay baños)
Bañedor, y Bañedora
Baño de mugeres
Banquero publico
Barrer de lugar
Baruas de cabras o cabrones
Batir los dientes regañando
Berça de la llanta
Berriondez de puerca
Besar o ser besado (Beso assi)
Beso a boca medio abierta

(Cosa llena de bestias, Mayoral de
    bestias)
(Cosa de betun, Cosa trauada con
    betun)
Beuedor, que mucho beue (Aquella
    grande beuesia)
    (Cuello de la bexiga)
    (Cosa que haze bienauenturado,
    Bienaue[n]turado hazer)
Biendezir (Aquella obra de biendezir)
Bienhechora cosa (Aquella obra de
    bienhazer)
Bienquista y amigablemente
Bistorta yerua
Blanca cosa con lustre (Cosa vestido con
    veste blanca)
Boca del horno
Boca de leon yerua
Bolar de algun lugar
Bolar cerca
Bolar delante
Bolar encima de otra cosa
Bolarmenico
Boluer en retorno
Bonança en la mar, o calma
Bocellar de caxa, o de otra vasija
Bordadura de la vestidura (Cosa de vesti-
    dura bordada)
Borujo de oliuas
Bosque que se corta, o puede cortar
Botas para ir por la ciudad
Botas de camino
    (Cosa hecha de boueda, Cosa para
        boueda)
Bouear hazer a otro
    (Cosa de madera o de color de box)
Bozes dar a las bozes de otro (Cosa q[ue]
    da gra[n]des bozes)
Braço del monte
Bramar retumbando la boz
Bramido en esta manera
Brocal del pozo
Brozna, cosa y aspera
    (Cosa de buey o de vaca, A manera o
        costu[m]bre de buey)
    (Cantar el buho aue)
Bullir mucho como hiruiendo
Buscar razones para me[n]tir

Buscar con engaños
Buxeta de olor
    (Cosa de dos, o tres cabeças,
        Empadronado por cabeça, Cosa
        de cient cabeças)
Cabeça de perro yerua
Cabello curado, y no curado
    (Copete de los cabellos, Cosa que
        pertenesce a los cabellos, Cosa de
        luengos cabellos)
    (Cosa en que mucho cabe, Aq[ue]lla
        capacidad)
    (Cosa de aquel cabildo)
Cabron morueco
    (Ordeñador de las cabras, Cosa que
        tiene pies de cabras)
Caer lexos
Caer muchos en vna cosa
Caer el flueco de lo velloso
Caer en algo o acontescer
    (Auer gana de cagar)
    (Maestro de cayados, o bordones)
Caida de los cabellos
Caida del yelo o elada
Calças arrugadas
Calçon de fieltro
Caldo adobado con miel
Caldo de la carne o pescado
Calilla, o mecha para prouocar camara
Caluo hazer, o encaluar
Callar el nombre
Callar despues de hablar
    (El que mucho tiempo esta en la
        cama)
    (Estada en la cama)
Camara ante de la camara
Camara fresca para resfriar
    (Lo que gana el combiador con el
        cambio)
    (Cosa de camellos)
    (Lugar donde se encuentran dos
        caminos)
    (Cosa perteneciente al campo que se
        labra)
Campo que se labra y siembra (Cosa de
    aquel campo)
    (Cosa de can o perro)
    (Teja de aquella tal canal)

Canal entre dos alturas
Canastillo texido de vimbres
Cancion pequeña
Candado para las bragas
Candeda, flor de castaños
Canez de los cabellos
Canilla del braço
Cantar el cuclillo
Cantar el contrario
Cantero de escoda
Canteria de escoda
Canto acordado
Canto de cosas tristes
Canto para incitar la pelea
    (Cosa de materia de cañas)
Caña de lagunas
Caño pequeño (Cosa de caño, Acanalada
    cosa)
    (El que tañe con cañutos)
    (Cosa armada assi, Paje que lo lleua)
Capitan de la guarda del rey
Capitan de cient armados
Capitania de ciento
Capitania de la guarda del rey
    (Cosa de aquel tal capitel)
Carabo especie de naue
    (Cosa de carcel)
Carcel de esclauos para vender (Casa o
    lugar q[ue] se da por carcel)
Cardencha de peraile yerua
Carena parte de la naue
    (Dar carena al lado de la naue)
Cargar sobre si deuda
Cargar sobre si enemistades
Caridad que se da por los muertos
Carmesi dos vezes teñido
    (Cosa de mucha carne)
Carnero desmochado sin cuernos
Carnero morueco
Carnicera cosa y cruel
    (Cosa de madera de carpe)
    (El que rige el carro, Regir o gouernar
        carro, La obra de regir carro, Cosa
        de carro)
    (Contencion de correr con carros)
Carro texido de vimbres o varas
    (El que lleua a firmar las cartas al rey)
Cartilla que enseña a leer

Casa que se puede andar al derredor
Casarse fuera de su estado
Casera, muger que guarda la casa
Cassar y anullar la ley
Cassador, y aniquilador de la ley
Cassadora cosa para cassar la ley
　　(Lo que no responde a su casta, No
　　　responder a su casta)
Castillejo, juego de niños
　　(Cosa de castillo o de villa)
Cauadiza cosa
Cauadura, obra de cauar
　　(Varo[n] o muger a cauallo)
　　(Cosa de aquel tal cauallo)
Cauallo pequeño [as *asturco* . . .]
　　(Yunta de dos o quatro cauallos)
Cauallo garañon
Cauallo de alquiler
Cauallo que anda de tranco
Caualleriza, o establo de cauallos
Cauallero de la vanda
Cauallero de la garrotea
Cauar de antes
Cauadiza cosa
Cauar como piedra o madera (Cauadura
　　assi)
Caxa de punçones para debuxar
Clara cosa con muchos ojos
Clauo del gouernallo de la naue
Cobrir de moho, o marhojo
Cocle para asir de alguna cosa
Codicioso de herencia
Codo de tres dedos, mayor que el comun
　　(De medida de vn codo, Armadura del
　　codo)
Cogediza cosa
Cogombrillo amargo
Coladero de nieues
Colcedra de plumas
Colera ruuia
　　(Colgada cosa assi)
　　(Medicina para la colica passion)
Collaço hermano de leche
Coloquintida yerua
Color como de oro (Cosa de dos o tres
　　colores, Colorar de algu[n] color)
Colusion, hazer en el pleyto (Aquella

colusion, El que haze aquella colusion,
　　Cosa de aquella colusion)
　　(El que come y biue con otro junta-
　　me[n]te)
　　(Los que comen y no escotan)
Comer como en boda o confradia
　　(Aquella tal comida)
Comer debaxo
Començar a ser moço
　　(Cosa para cometer)
Cometer a la fe de otro
Cometimiento assi
　　(Comezon que haze materia)
Comida, ante de la cena
Comino
Comino de Guinea
Compadecerse
Compañero con otro
Competidor de alguna dignidad
Competicion odiosa entre dos
　　(Señal de compra)
Comprar junto (Co[m]pra juntamente)
Comprar para vender
Comprada cosa en esta manera
Concebimiento
　　(Pescador de aquellas)
Concierto de vender solo (Concertador
　　en esta manera)
Condenar por justicia al aduersario
　　(Cosa para co[n]denar)
Conferir, cotejar
Confacionador de cosas diuersas
Confacionadura assi
Confederar o hazer alidanças
Confessar ser le deudor
Conformar vna cosa con otra
Conformidad y semejança
Conformacion assi
Conforme y semejantemente
　　(Cosa de conjetura)
Conocedor de algun pleyto
Conocer de antes
Consagrada cosa con otra
Consagrar otra vez
　　(Cosa llena de consejo, Dador o
　　　demandador de co[n]sejo, Aquel
　　　de quien se demanda co[n]sejo)

Consistorio de senadores (Varon del
co[n]sistorio)
(Consolando con palabras)
Consumirse cosa de fuego
Contar con contantes (Cuenta en aquella
manera, Cosa para contar, Cosa para
aquella cuenta)
Contar multiplicando de diez en diez
(Contador assi, Cue[n]ta en aq[ue]lla
manera)
Contar relatando
Contador por numeros (Cuenta assi,
Cosa para contar con numeros)
Conte[n]der disputando (Contendedor
assi, Contencion, Cosa que assi
contiende)
Contrario ser en voto
(Escriuano de contratos)
(Cosa assi contribuida)
Copa o vaso de oro
Copa embuelto en la rueca
(Temblor de coraçon)
Coraxa entre dos muros
Cordero que siguen los otros
Cornerina piedra preciosa
(El que haze o vende coronas, Cosa
perteneciente a corona, La obra de
coronar)
Corona de oro
(Cosa de corral)
Corral donde se crian aues
(Corredor assi)
(Corrimie[n]to assi)
Corriente cosa en esta manera
Correr assi en derredor (Cosa que corre
en aquella manera)
Correr el campo los enemigos
(Corremie[n]to assi)
(El que anda de corrillo en corrillo,
De corrillo, en corrillo, Andar en
corrillos)
Cortar y gastar
Cortador de bolsas
Cortar el muslo o la pierna
Cortar miembro antes
Cosa no digna de ser oyda
Cosa rata y grata

Cosa señalada mas que otra
Coser vna cosa con otra
Cosida cosa con otra
Coser otra vez
(Armada cosa de cota de malla)
Cozimiento de muchas cosas
Crecer sobre otra cosa
Crecer en yerua
Crecida cosa que dexo de crecer
Crecer a otro (El que mucho y de ligero
cree)
Criarse juntamente vna cosa con otra
Criança de pollos
Criatura mal parida
Crines o cernejas de los animales
(Crinada cosa assi)
Cuadrar vna cosa con otra
Cuadra figura como dado
(Aquella obra de cuajar)
Cuantidad como piedra
Cuantidad como dinero
Cuanto mas
Cuartilla, doblegadura de la bestia
Cuatrega de cuatro cauallos
Cubrir de costras o encalar
Cuchillo coruo como cimitarra
(Acuchilladas)
Cuchillo de sierra
Cuello de la madre
(Cargo quie[n] tiene de las cuentas
del rey)
Cuerda que empareja los cauallos
Cuerda con que se guinda la vela
(Cosa de dos cuernos, De linaje de
cuernos, Que hiere con cuernos)
Cuerno para tener azeyte
(Lo que no tiene cuerpo, Cosa de dos
cuerpos)
(Cosa llena de cueuas, De cueua en
cueua)
(Con mucho cuidado)
(Cosa que trae culebra, Cosa pertene-
ciente a culebras)
Culpadame[n]te (Cosa digna de ser
culpada)
Cuñada muger de hermano
Curar con otros

Curar diligentemente
  (Çapatillo)
Çaraguelles, muslos de calças
Cecina de vaca
Cedaço para harina
  (Espacio entre ceja y ceja)
Celda del patron en la naue
  (Cosa que sostiene el cielo, Varon o
    muger que ho[n]rra el cielo, Cosa
    poderoso en el cielo)
Celidonia yerua
Cena quien pide como truhan
  (Auer gana de cenar, Cosa ordenada
    para cenar, Cosa de cena)
  (Resoluerse alguna cosa en ceniza)
  (El que fue y ya no lo es)
Centaurea yerua
Centella muerta
Ceñir por debaxo
Ceñidero de hilo colorado o cordon
Cerca, y quasi con las manos
Cercar de emprenta o texbique
Cercar de palizada o baluarte
Cercar de seto
  (Cercenadura)
Cerco poner a algun lugar
Cereza tiesta o dura
Cerrar con candado (Cerradura assi)
Cerrar la pierta con aldaua
Cerueza, pocion de trigo, o ceuada
  (Aquella dureza de ceruiz)
Ceuada sin hollejo
Ceuada tresmesina
Ceuada de cauallos
Ceuar para tomar las aues o peces
  (Contrahazer algun ciego)
Ciennudillos yerua
Cient vezes tanto
  (Multiplicar ciento tanto)
Cieruo que tiene la hiel en la cola
Cilindro relox del sol
  (Cosa de cilla)
Cimiento, o pared de piedra manpuesta
  (Cosa para tal manpuesta)
Cinta para ceñir debaxo
Cirio candela de cera
Cirial, en que lleuan los cirios (El

acolyte que lleua los ciriales)
Ciruela enxerida en serual
  (Cosa de cisterna o algibe)
Charlatar o chocarrear
Chamelote
Chillar el raton
Chiminea (Cosa de chiminea)
Chirriar la golondrina
Dança de hombres armados
Dañosa cosa como de enemigo
Dar a menudo
  (Cosas que se dan en retorno)
Dar priuilegio de templo
Dar el culpado por el daño que hizo
Dar en denuesto injurioso
Dar la prenda al vsurario por lo que da
Dar cuenta de lo recebido
Dar a otro caucion y fianças
Dar señal por la compra
Dar allarma
  (Dando a vezes)
Dar occasion de reñir
Dar buelta deshazie[n]do ya lo pe[n]-
sado
Darte lugar libre
De aqui a poco
De buena gana, sin ser requerido
De camino, De passada
Decendimiento cuesta ayuso
Decendendo cuesta abaxo
Decendientes en el linaje
Dedicacion de la iglesia
Dedo y medio
Delibrar el padre al hijo de su poder
  (Delibracion assi, Padre que assi deli-
    bra al hijo, Hijo assi delibrado por el
    padre)
Demandar muger para casar
Demandar otra vez
Dende entonces
Dentadura salida a fuera
Dentada cosa de pequeños dientes
Dentar la hez para segar
Denunciar por mensaje
Denunciacion assi
Denunciar en persona
Denunciacion assi

Denunciar en contrario
De parte de fuera
Deprender juntamente
  (Lugar donde se responde de derecho)
Derecho riguroso
Derramar lo liquido en cerco (Aquel
  derramamiento)
Derramar en derredor
Derramar antes
Derribar por deyuso
Derribar por el suelo
Derribar hazia otra cosa
Derribar mucho
Derrocar lagrimas (Lloro assi)
Desabahar
Desacostumbrarse
Desacostumbrar a otro
Desafio de vno por vno
Desafiador assi
Desarraigar en cerco
Desarraigamiento assi
Desastrada cosa
Desatar otra vez
  (Cosa descomulgada)
Descortezador assi (Aquel descortezar)
Descostumbre, o desuso
Descrecer
Descrecimiento, o menoscabo
Desde nueuo (Desde aqui a pocos dias)
Descubridor del secreto
Deselar o regalar
Desembarrar lo embarrado
Desembuchar
Desencassamiento del carnicol
Desensenar, sacar del seno (Aquella obra
  de sacar del seno)
Desfauorecer con las manos
Desfauor en esta manera
  (Desfigurada cosa)
Desflorar, quitar flores
Desfrutar, coger la fruta
Deshazer la venta por tachas
Deshojar las pampanas
Deshojador de pampanas
Desjarretar bestias
Desmenuzando en pieças
Desnudar lo vestido

Desnudez en esta manera
Despedaçado
Despegadura entre vña y carne
Despernar o desjarretar
  (Lugar puesto en despeñadero)
Desperar de la vida de alguno
Despertar otra vez
Despoblada cosa por seco
Despojar de armas
Despojar a otro de dignidad
Despoluorizar quebrando
Despojada cosa de su pegujal
Despuchar
  (Muy desseadamente)
Dessemejança de cosas
Desterronada tierra
  (Desterrado assi)
Destruir los argumentos de otro
  (Respuesta de aquellos argumentos)
Destruyr como apedreando (Destrucion
  assi, Destruydor assi)
Desuariar en vanas palabras (Desuario
  assi)
Desuentura
Desuenturadamente
Determinar en antes
  (Aquella obra de deuanar)
Dexar de venir en la razon y lo cierto
Dexar la possession
Dexarlo a su juramento
Dexar su officio o ley
Dezir mal al maldiziente
Dia mayor del año
Dia menor del año
Dia primero de qualquier mes
Dia en que es licito hazer toda cosa
Dia en que se entrepone en el bissiesto
  (Aquella doctrina con otro)
Diente crescido demasiadamente
Dientes en que se conoce la edad
Dientes del puerco jauali (Cosa que tiene
  dientes)
  (Cosa de dos dientes)
Diestro de entrambas las manos
Dilatar o estender el tiempo
Discordar en sentencia
Discordia en la sentencia

Distribuir y dar al que ruega
Distribucion en esta manera
Diuino por bacines
Diuinacion en esta manera [as *engastro-
mantes* . . .]
Diuinar por coniecturas
Diuulgar por fama y gloria
Diuulgado ser por fama y gloria
Doblar juntamente
Dobladura assi
Dolerse con otro
    (Cosa que assi se pega)
Dolencia que viene por los colostros
Dolencia de los lomos
Donzella casadera
Do[nde] quiera que
Dorar por parte de fuera (Cosa dorada
    por parte de fuera, Aquella doradura
    por de fuera)
Dormir al medio dia
Dormir aparte
Echar de si rayos de luz
Echar candado para cerrar
Echar en derredor (Echado estar en
    derredor)
Echar de si vapor o baho
Echar de si llamas de huego
Echar hojas el arbol
Echadiza cosa o que buela afuera
Echar hollejo la legumbre
Edificar de piedra manpuesta
Edificada cosa de tal manera
Edificar juntamente
Edificio de piedra marmol
Elegido para ser consul
Elegido para ser corregidor
    (Vara del embaxador)
Embiadiza cosa
Embiar socorro
    (Cosa sin embidia y malicia, Aquella
        limpieza de embidia)
Emelga entre dos sulcos
Empanada de pan y queso
Empandar o encoruar
Empeçer los enemigos
Empedrar calle
Empedrador assi
Emperezar a otro

Empobrecer a otro
Empulgueras del arco o ballesta
Empuxar de lugar
Empuchar en contrario
Enaspar todo el cuerpo
Encaladura de marmol
Encantar las venas
Encantar enderredor
En cerco, o en redondez
    (Encerrador de mantenimiento)
Encerrar por fuerça
Encerrar enderredor (Encerramiento
    assi)
Enclauijando los dedos
Encomendado a algun abogado
Encontinente o luego
Encontradiza cosa
Encontrar muchas vezes
Encontrado, o al encuentro
Encordio
Encoruada cosa hazia baxo
Encrespada cosa assi
Encruzijada de dos, tres, cuatro vias
Endechadera de muertos
Endentecer los niños (Aquella obra de
    endentecer)
Endurescer juntamente
En el mismo lugar
Enessar otra vez
Enfamada cosa (Cosa que puede ser bien
    enfamada)
Enfermo estar en cama
Enflaquecer a otra cosa
Enfrenar en contrario
Engañar halagando (Halago assi para
    engañar)
    (Cosa tomada con engaño, Cosa
        engañosa con assechança)
Engordada cosa
Engendrara cosa a dentro
Engeño para sacar agua de pozo
Enhetrar lo peynado
Enlazamiento de vnas vides con otras
Enlodadura de lodo
Enmagrecerse
Enmagrecer otra cosa
Enmagrecida cosa
Enredar enderredor (Enredado assi)

Ensañarse contra otro
Ensensios yerua (Vino adobado con
  ensensios)
Enseñar cria[n]ça a los niños (Aquella
  criança de niños, Ayo que assi los cria)
Ensuziar lo consagrado
Ensuziar juntamente
Ensuziamiento assi
Ensuziar con estiercol
Ensuziar vna cosa con otra
  (Ensuziamiento assi)
Ensuziar lo sagrado
Entibiar cosa fria
Entregar otra vez
Entremes de la tarasca
Entreoir, o oir de secreto
Entresacar los ramos
Entresijo en el animal
Enuernar temprano
Enues contrario de la haz
  (Quando no enxambran las abejas)
Enxerir vna cosa en otra
Epitaphio de la sepultura
Eredad en poblado
Eredad en el campo
  (El que con engaño trabaja heredar
    a otro)
Eredero de quien se confia la erencia
Ermanos de vn vientre
Eruecer
Equinoctial ygualdad del dia y de la
  noche (Los que biuen allende del
  equinoctial)
Escalador nocturno de casa
  (Ser escalentado)
Escandia para puchas
Escarauajo que verdeguea vn poco
Escoria de cobre hierro &c
Escote de qualquier comida
Escriuir lo que otro dize
Escriuir en vno (Escritura assi)
Escriuir con diligencia
Escriuir encima
  (El que tiene aquella escritura)
Escriptura truncar o cassar
Escuchador o velador
  (Manilla del escudo)

Escudilla para puchas
  (El que lleua el libro a la escuela)
Escupir tossiendo
Escuridad de la fama
Escurecida cosa
Esforçar otra vez
Espacio entre ceja y ceja
Espacio entre remo y remo
Espacio de tiempo lugar
Espacio de cinco años
Espantar a otro
Espanto sin causa manifiesta
Espeluzarse con otro
  (Cosa sin esperança)
Espiga del arbol para enxerir
Espinazo de animales
Espirar otra vez
  (Esportilla de esparto)
Esquadra o esquadron de gente
Esquilmar vacas y ouejas
Establo de bueyes
Establecer de antes
Establecida cosa assi
Estar ausente
Estar el aue sobre hueuos
Estar lexos
  (Aquel estar assi)
Estar juntamente (Estança assi)
Estender lo encogido (Estendimie[n]-
  to assi)
Estender la generacion
Estender los terminos del imperio
Estiercol liquido y ralo
Estiercol de los ratones
Estilo tragico (Cosa de aquel estilo)
Estimar en nada
  (Hazer estrellas)
Estrella de la tarde
Estrellas dos que reluzen en la tempestad
  (Cosa que reluze en las estrellas, Cosa
    que habla de las Estrellas)
  (Estribando con todas fuerças)
Excelente cosa
Excelencia tener en algo
  (Vnto para vntar exes)
Ezquerdear del camino
Facultad o poder de cada vno

Faltar el que murio en la pelea
Fama diuulgar o derramar
Fator de algun mercader
Fatoria cosa de fator
Fauorable hazer a otro
Feno que se siega en el otoño
Fiesta guardar sin obra
Fiestas del dios Baco
Fiestas situadas en el calendario
Fiestas del año que no se mudan
Fiestas voluntarias
Fiestas proprias de cada vno
Fin o salida de lo incierto
Fin tomado en mala parte
Fingir juntamente con otro
Fingida cosa juntamente
Fingir lo que no es
Flamenco aue conocida
Flete que dan las animas q[ue] van al
    infierno
Flete que se paga al barquero
Flor de romero yerua
Flor de mançanilla yerua
Florecer (Florida cosa)
Florecer otra vez
    (El que gouierna la flota)
Floxamente hazer alguna cosa (Cosa que
    haze algo assi floxamente)
Fluxo de sangre (Hombre o muger que
    lo tiene)
Forjada cosa en la yunque
Fornicar, andar en puterias
Fortalecer de antes
    (Fregar mucho)
    (Cosa que tiene dos frentes, Hombre
       de grande frente)
    (Antiguamente) [as orea . . .]
Fresno arbol (Cosa de fresno)
Fruto pequeño como de azetuña
    (Cosa que se puede fundir como
       metal)
Fundicion de metales (Vaso o lugar para
    fundir)
Furor por la locura (Furioso assi)
Gallochas, çapatos de paño
Gamonito, y flor della
Ganado mocho sin cuernos
    (Aquella conquista o vencimiento)

Gañir en derredor
Gañon con que tragamos
    (Gastada cosa)
Gastar comiendo
Gasto poco, o espensa
Gemir mucho
    (Cosa de vn mesmo genero y linaje)
Gente de frontera
Gente de pie puesta en ordenança
    (Hazedor de gestos)
    (Hombre perdido por glonias)
    (Vendedor de golosinas, Plaça donde
       venden golosinas)
Goteada cosa manchada a gotas
Gouernar gente de guerra
    (Cosa de grana, Vestido de grana)
Granada, cosa de muchos granos
Grandeza de animo
Granito del higo
    (Cosa vntada con greda, De materia
       de greda, Minero donde sacan
       greda)
Grita de los que acometen pelea
Grossura en la barriga
Guarda en lugar de otro
Guarda real
Guardar en vno (Aquella guarda)
Gudañeador, que siega feno
    (Cosa mucho guerreadora, Cosa que
       haze o trae guerra)
Guisada cosa con su çumo
Gusano de la seda imperfecto
    (Cosa aspera en lo que toca el gusto,
       Aquella aspereza al gusto)
    (El hablar mucho)
Habla abreuiada
Hablar osadamente
Hablador assi
Hablar vanidades (Habla desta manera)
Hablar despues de callar
    (Cosa que trae aquella hacha)
Hadada cosa
Halagar juntamente
Halagar otra vez
Halagueñamente
Hallar
Hallar, camino para la verdad
Hallar lo perdido

Harina de trigo
Harina todo de trigo
Harina de ceuada
Haronia y floxura
   (Cosa desta arte)
Hazer turpe pacto
Hazer buena la venta
Hazer alarde (Aquella obra de hazer alarde)
Hazer voto so[bre] cierta forma
Hazer, o señalar alguna nouedad
Hazedor de alguna nouedad (Aquella
   obra de hazer nouedad)
Hazer cada vno su officio
   (Estimador de las haziendas)
   (Cosa llena de habras)
Hechos grandes de reyes y principes
Hembras de los corchetes
Hendida cosa en muchas partes
Hermano, vide Ermano
Hermoso hazer
Hermosear con alguna gracia
Hermosa cosa con gracia
Hermosa y graciosamente
Herir con aguijon (Herida assi)
   (Cosa de hierro q[ue] sueña)
Herrar de fuego
   (Herreria, lugar donde se labra hierro)
Heruera con que tragamos
Heruer otra vez
Heuilla de la malla
Hiel de la tierra yerua o Cintoria
Higado de pato ceuado con higos
   (Codegor de higos)
Hilazas del lienço
Hincar los inojos o rodillas
Hincar juntamente
   (Dexar de hincharse)
Hincharse las yemas en el arbol
Hinchazon del veintre
Hinchazon tras las orejas
Hiscal cuerda de tres ramales de esparto
Historas que proceden de año en año
Hoce donde se ahocina el rio
Hoce para cortar vimbres
Hocino para leña
Hoja de berça
Hojas coger de los arboles
Hollin de la hornaza de cobre

Horadar mucho, o antes
   (Cosa de dos horcas)
   (Cosa comida de hormigas, Llena de
   hormigas)
Hornaza donde se funde el oro
Hueuo (Clara del hueuo)
Huyr mucho
Huyr a lugar (Lugar donde huymos por
   guarin)
   (Lugar donde se recogen los huydizos)
Huyr de alguna cosa
Huyr de vn peligro, y caer en otro
Huyr los desbaratados
   (Arte de hundir letras de molde)
Hundidor y hundidora
Hurto secreto y escondido
Iaezes de cauallos
Iassar enderredor
Iaula para las aues
   (Lugar donde se representaran los
   iuegos)
   (Cosa pertenesciente a aquel)
Iuez de la apellacion
Iuezes corrompidos por dineros
Iuyzio de astrologia (Aquella arte de
   diuinar por iuyzios)
   (Rayz de aq[ue]lla ju[n]cia)
Iuntar o echar en vno
Iuntura de los artejos
Iurar sin engaño
Iuzgar o pensar estimando
Yedra por si derecha
   (Estar la yegua caliente)
   (Cayda del yelo)
Igual cosa con otra cosa (Aquella ygual-
   dad con otra cosa)
Igualar vna cosa con otra
Igualar la tierra con çarzo
   (Hueco de los ijares)
   (Enfermo della)
Illuminador de libros
Inclinar hazia otra cosa
Inclinar la cabeça
Inconsiderancia
Indignidad de qualquier cosa
Infamia vergonçosa
Infincionada cosa o corrumpida
Ingenio assentado y reposado

Ingle
Intestino ciego
Intitular libro o edificio
Intitular poniendo titulo
Intractable cosa y desamorada
Ir al encuentro a saludar
Ir delante, o anticiparse
Ida de algun lugar
Ira que no permanesce
Labrar de çaquiçami
Labrar de martillo
    (Poner a vn lado, y a otro)
    (Ladrido de cachorros)
Lamina de plomo para escriuir
Lancero, que pelea con lança
Lançar tiro (Lançador de tiro)
Lapidario, que ve[n]de piedras preciosas
Lardo de puerco salado
    (Vaya de laurel)
Lauar juntamente
Lauar mucho
Lauar otra vez
Leche que saca de grano mojado
Leche de arroz
Leche de almendras
    (Medicina que cura en el lecho)
Lechuga parrada por el suelo
Lechuga montes
    (Mondaduras de legumbre)
    (Cosa que esta fuera del ley)
Ley consentida por muchos
    (Cosa de dos lenguas)
Lengua de balança
Lenteja de laguna
Leon domestico y manso
Leuantar de lugar
Leuantar hazia arriba
Leuantamiento assi
Lexos hazia delante
Librada cosa de peligro
    (Cosa perteneciente a la libreria)
Libro abreuiado
Libro manual, y que siempre se deue
    traer en la mano
Licensia que da el capitan al escudero
Licenciado, o dotor en derechos

(Parecer en el juyzio para contestar
    la lid, Aquella obra de parecer en
    iuyzio)
Lienta cosa que se puede doblegar
Limar enderredor
Limpiar la vassura o pozo
Limpiar el rio de arboles
Liños caberos de la viña
    (Cosa que habla lisonjas, Habla de
    lisonjas)
    (Cosa que se texe con dos lizos)
Logrero que lleua vno por ciento
Lombriguera yerua (Azeyte de
    lombriguera)
Lombrizes redondas y largas
Luchar vno con otro
Luchador en esta manera
Lucha assi
Luchar, y vencer luchando
Lugar para se assentar
Lugar priuilegiado para los malhechores
Lumbral sobre la puerta
Lumbral baxo en la puerta
Luto traer mucho tiempo
    (Cosa ante de la luz del dia)
Luzir mucho
Llaga que cresce
Llagada cosa como de mataduras
Llamar a otro apartandolo
Llamar mucho de lexos
Llamador que assi llama
Llamar otra vez
Llamar juntamente
Llaue contrahecha
Lleuar de alguno
Lleuar presto
Lleuar a cuestas
Lleuar antecogido
Llorar con otro (Lloro en esta manera)
Llouer juntamente
Lluuia de piedras o granero
Maderada cosa con madera
    (Hazer obras de madrastra)
    (Cosa del alua o madrugada)
Mayoral del ganado
Mayueta yerua

Mal de bubas
Mal de higado
Malauenturada cosa
  (Vsar de malicias)
Malla trasdoblanda
Mampesada [alphabetized under *Mam*-]
Manada de mill
Manar o rebossar lo liquido
Mancebo que comiença a baruar
  (Aquela quien se haze tal manda)
  (Vestidura de mangas luengas)
Mano de papel
Manto o vestidura de encima
  (Cosa que participa de dos mares)
  (Estrechura de mar entre dos tierras)
Marauedi moneda (Cosa desta moneda)
  (Cosa de marfil, Cosa cubierta con
    marfil)
Marido de la hermana
Marmol de porfido
Maromas
Maroma o cuerda para alçar
Mas que affaz
Mascar lo mascado
Mastratos yerua
Matador de ratones
Matador de hermano
Matar a hierro
Medicina de los brunos siluestres
Medicinas repercussiuas
Medidor de las tierras
Medio de los cabos (Media cosa entre
  dos cabos)
Medir rayendo (Medida raida)
  (Instrumento para medir la tierra)
Medir juntamente
Melancolia
Melocoton
Membrana que cubre el meollo
  (Carne de membrillos, Vino adobado
    con membrillos)
Mensagero de antes
Mentir con otro
Mercar juntamente
Mercaderias, echar en la mar (Perdida de
  mercaderias assi)

Merecer con otro
  (Cosa de espacio de dos meses)
  (Lo que se barre alçada la mesma,
    Frutas sobre mesa)
  (De tres ordenes)
Mesa redonda
Metal señalado para coronas
Metal que se labra a martillo
  (Chapa o hoja de metal, Arte de batir
    metal)
Meter en sacas o costales
Meter en el coraçon
Meter a dentro
Mezana, especie de velas
Mezclar otra vez
Miedo auerque te venga mal
Miedo auer de ti
Miel que no sabe a humo
Miesses en derredor
Minuta de la obra
Mirar y ver con los ojos (Cosa que mira
  la cabeça baxa)
Mirar a la vislumbre
Mitra de sacerdote o perlado
Mocos limpiar
Moler con otro
Mondaduras de legumbre
Mondaduras de vñas
Mondadura de mançana
Moneda que se coge para pagar sueldo
  (De monton en monton)
Morar en el campo
Morbo caduco
Morder lo de delante
Morir con otro
Morir muerte pestilencial
Mortaja, en que embueluen los muertos
Mosca que llega a las bestias
Mosquito de lagunas
Mosquito de higos
Mosquito de cabrahigos
Mostrar de antes
Mouida cosa o llamada muchas vezes
Mouer de baxo arriba, o Mouer a lexos
Muceta de obispo, o capirote de maestro
Mucho menos

Mudar el real
Muelle para hazer puerto
Muestra de lo que es el juego
Muerte de niño
Muger soltera
Muger que nunca se caso
Muger contrahazedora de personas
Muger casada muchas vezes
Muger que acompaña a otra
Muger casadera
Muladar de estiercol
Muñeca, parte de la mano
Murmurador
Murmurar vn poco
Muslos de calças
Nacer en derredor
Nacer saliendo a fuera
Nacido de mañana o amaneciendo
    (Nacida de pies)
Nariz muy remachado
Nariz donde se pone la mecha
    (Ornamentos de la naue)
Naue de dos, tres, quatro ordenes de
    remos
Naue para atalayar
Naue ligera de cossario
Naue real
Naue fornecida para encontrar
Necedades hazer o dezir
Negreta, genero de anade
Neuada cosa llena de nieue
Noche sin luna
Nombar antes
    (El que es del mismo nombre)
    (Cosa de dos nombres)
    (Linea del norte al mediodia)
Nueuas acarrear
Nuera de los abuelos
Nueza negra yerua
Nnudo de los artejos
Obejaruco, aue
Obispado dignidad de obispo
Obligar a otro con beneficios
Obra que se escriue en dialogo
Obra de hombre en quanto hombre
    (De obra en obrada)
Ochauada cosa

Ofrecerse con maldiciones
    (Ofrecimiento assi, Ofrecedor assi,
    Ofrecida cosa assi)
Ofrenda de muertos
Oyr escuchando (Aquella obra de oyr
    escucha[n]do, Cosa para assi oyr o
    escuchar)
    (Dolencia de los ojos, Cosa que tiene
    aquella dolencia)
    (Cosa llena de oliuas, Cosa que trae
    oliuas)
Olla generalmente
Ombre afrentado
Ombrezillos yerua
Omiziano de hermano
Ora igual de noche y dia
Ora que no es igual
Oracion suelta de ley de versos
Ordenar en partes
    (Cosa fuera de orden)
    (De comienço mal ordir)
Oreja de raton yerua
Oreja de abad yerua
(Mina de donde se saca el oro, Cosa de
    oro todo maçica, Lo que tiene hojas de
    oro, Cosa que trae oro, Tienda donde
    labra el platero, Hechura o lauor de oro,
    El que coge pedaçuelos de oro)
Oro para coronas
Oro sobre cobre
Ospital de huerfanos
Ospitalero, de tal hospital
Ostia de corteza aspera
Ostia de corteza a llana y lisa
Otra y otra vez
Oueja de dos años, o de dos dientes __
Pagar la deuda al creedor
Paga del meson
Paga de la buena obra
Page que lleua el estoque delante del rey
Pajar donde se guarda la paja
Pala de horno
    (Cosa de dos palmos en luengo)
    (Casillas del palomar)
Pan hecho de harina cernida con cedaço
    de cerdas
Pan de espelta

Pan de centeno
Pan de escandia
Pan de harina sin cernir los saluados
Pan cozido en padilla o al hogar
Pan amassado con mosto
Pan vizcocho
Pan o massa de cobre
Pan cozido de presto
Papel escrito de ambas partes (Como el
que de vna parte es escrito)
Papel que se passa
Papel de straça
Papuda cosa que tiene gran garguero
Pared de mampuesto (Maestro de hazer
paredes)
Pares en numero
Parir la muger mal y sin tiempo
(En dos, tres partes)
Partiendo en dos partes (Cosa abierta en
dos partes)
Partiendo en tajadas
Partidor de los cabellos
Passar juntamente por algun lugar
(Aquel passaje)
Passar cerca
Pauimiento o suelo de azulejos
Pecado por comision
Pechero estimado por la hazienda
(Cogedor de pechos)
Pedaço a pedaço
Pedaçuelo a pedaçuelo
Pedrezita
Peynar haziendo vello
Pelea a cauallo
Pelear vna cosa con otra
Pelo en piedras preciosas
Penacho del yelmo (Cosa con penacho)
Pensar con otro
Peones de armas liuiadas
Pepita
Percha de la parra (Parra de tal percha)
(Cantar la perdiz)
Peregrinar con otro
Peregrino con otro
Perla de la concha
Perla desbastada y limpia
(Hombre de cabeça de perro)

Perfiles en pintura
Pesar mucho
Pescar con anzuelo (Pescador de
anzuelo)
Peticion que se da al principe
(Cosa de does, tres, quatro pies)
(El que cria piedra)
Piedra de rayo
Piedra de que se haze la cal
Pilares que tienen medios cuerpos de
hombres y de mugeres
Pimienta blanca
Pimienta luenga
Pintada cosa en bueltas
Pixita de niños
Plaça de la fruta
Planta enderredor
Plantar por debaxo
(El que lleua el plato)
(Cargo quien tiene de los plazeres
del rey)
Plegada cosa muchas vezes (Plegadura
assi)
Pleyto ya contestado
Plomo quitar de la soldadura
(Maciço de la pluma del aue)
Poblador nueuo de algun lugar
Poder mucho
Poderosamente
Poeta escriptor de comedias (Cosa perte-
neciente a la comedia)
(Cosa perteneciente a polilla, Que
tiene o trae polilla)
Poluorear desmenuzando
Poluos para fregar dientes
Poma o buxeta de olor
(Medicina contra la ponçoña)
Poner en deposito o en terceria
Poniendo en terceria
Poner a serena, o al sereno
Ponerse a la ventura o peligro
Poner vno por otro
Postiza cosa assi
Poner vides en majuelo
Poner color delante
Poner a la puteria (Puesta estar a la
puteria)

Poner terminos
Poquedad de palabras
Por do[nde] quiera que
    (El que trae porra)
Portanario intestino
Pozo
Pozero que haze pozos
Pregonero que vende esclauo
Presentar la persona
Presentacion assi
Presentadora cosa para presentar
Presidencia tener
Presidente en las cuentas
    (El que tiene el registro de los
      presos)
Primera cosa engendrada
Primeramenti
Primicias de cada cosa
Principales del pueblo
Prometer por otro
Prometer otra vez
Protonotario apostolico
Proueer a alguna cosa
Puchas en los sacrificios
    (Contar el pueblo)
Puerco montes de mil libras
Puerco manso
Puerca que pario vna sola vez
Puertas cerradas con aldaua
    (El que tiene el pulgar del pie torcido
      a de[n]tro)
Punta hazer (De punta o con punta)
Punto que sierra la sentencia
Quebrantar mucho
Quebrar otra vez
Quebrar antes
    (Quebrantador de terrones)
Quebrar por debaxo
Quebrar el banco, o hazer bancarota
Quedar sin sentido
Quemadura assi
Querellarse de alguno acusandolo
Querer parir la muger
Queso de yeguas
Queso con mucho ojos
Quitar de la bestia silla o albarda
Quitar el cuero o hollejo

Quitar el pegujal
Quitar la pompa y soberuia
Quitar de lugar
Quitar la espuma
Rabo a viento en el aue
Raedura de la letra
Raer como con escofina
Raer la delantera
Rayas de las manos por donde adeuinan
    los chiromanticos
    (Lugar donde cayo rayo)
Rayz, qualquiera como de cebollas (Cosa
    de tal rayz, Cosa que tiene mucho de
    tal rayz)
Rayz de caña olorosa
Ramo de palma con datiles
Rana de mar
Ranciosa cosa como de azeite
    (Vestidura de raso)
Rastro sacar por olor
Rauia del can
Razonar o hablar en vno
Razonamiento que se haze en el concejo
    (El que razona en concejo)
Razonamiento tener en publico
    (Cosa de real, Assiento del real)
Recalcar vno con otro
Recalcadamente assi
Recalcar vna cosa sobre otra
Recobar lo perdido
Recoger lo perdido
Reconualecer
    (El que recuerda al rey lo que a de
      hazer)
Recebir de otro caucion y fianças
Recuajo de las lagunas
Recuesto cuesta arriba
Redarguir
Redarguir juntamente
Redarguir lo falso
Redondear por todas partes
Reflorecer
Regar el rio las tierras de donde corre
Regatonear por tauernas
    (Cosa fuera de regla)
Regir con templaça
Regidor assi

Regir la prouincia
Regozijada cosa con fiestas
Relinchando
Remiendo assi (Vestidura o obra de
 remiendos)
  (El que tiene doz remolinos en la
  cabeça)
Rentar la heredad
Renta que assi viene
Reñir con pariente o amigo
Repetir algo la segunda vez
Reprehender al que reprehende
Reprehender a pariente o amigo
 (Reprehension assi)
Resina no cuajada
  (Quien tiene difficultosa respiracion)
Resplandecer como perlas
Resplandecer mucho, o antes
Resplandecer de lexos
Responder a la pregunta
Responder al mandado de otro
Reteñir en cerco
Retuerta cosa, o de boueda
Retorno de recebido
  (Serrar lugar con rexas, Ventana con
  rexas)
Rezio, no flaco
Reziura, no flaqueza
Rio caudal y grande (Lugar donde se
 juntan dos rios)
  (Lugar donde el rio haze salto)
Robar el campo (Aquella obra de robar el
 ca[m]po, Robado del ca[m]po)
Roer enderredor
Rogar halagando
Rogar como llorando
Roido de gente armada
Rollo piedra lisa del rio
Roma cosa de narizes
Rompida cosa assi
Rompida gente y desbaratada
Rompimiento assi
Romper mucho
Roznido del asno
Rueda calçar que no vaya atras ni
 adelante
Ruego de muchos

Ruego como llorando
Ruida o sonido hazer lo que se quiebra
 (Ruido assi)
Ruido del regozijo que haze la gente
Sabidora cosa assi
Saber antes de tiempo
Sabiduria en esta manera
Sabidora cosa antes
Saber lo que se hizo
Sabuesos, especie de perros
Sacar las tripas
Sazar las hezes de lo liquido
Sacar a fuera guiando
Sacar el meollo o pepita de la fruta
Sacar fuera de numero
Sacar a fuera (Sacada cosa assi)
Sacar algo por el olor
Sacar de la despensa
Sacrificar cosa que se mata
Sacudir la cabeça
Sacudir vno con otro
Sacudimiento assi
Sacudir de arriba abaxo
Sacudimiento assi
Sacudir con varal
Sacudir otra vez
Salada cosa de antes
Sala baxa para cenar
Sala fresca por frio
Salario del corredor
Salir fuera del camino
Salida en esta manera
Salir a recebir alguno
  (Salida assi)
Salida fuera del ojo
Salida fuera del ombligo
Salida fuera de la madre
Saltadora cosa de vna parte a otra
Saltar o dançar delante
Saltar de lugar
Saltear o tomar de salto (Aquella obra de
 saltear)
Saluados de trigo
Sanar antes de tiempo
Sanar otra vez
Santos del cielo
Sarmiento para plantar

Sarmiento sopeton
Sarmiento fructifero
Sarmiento que no lleua fructo
Sarmiento para otro año
Sarnoso, lleno de sarna
Sarta de higos
Saucegatillo, arbol deste especie
Sauana de lienço
   (Cosa de seda, o de sirgo)
Segar hasta el cabo
Segazon de heno
Seguir juntamente
Segunda vez
Sellar con sello
   (Estar la tierra sazonada para
      sembrar, Aquella sazon de
      sementera)
Sembrada el restrojo
Sementera hecha en barruecho
Seno o golfo de mar
   (No tener sentido)
Sentir antes
Señalar alguna nouedad
   (Señalada cosa de heridas)
Señas hazer con los ojos
Sepultura sumptuosa y real
Sepulturas de familias
Serpa, sarmiento de la vid
   (El que es de aquella misma secta)
Sieruo vagabundo o que huye
Sieruo muchas vezes açotado
Sieruo bueno y modesto
Sieruo en la ciudad
Sieruo que siempre a de seruir
Silencio de la media noche
Silla de los assientos
Sin verdad
Sin duda
   (Platero que labra de sinzel)
Sobornar votos para dignidad
Socorrer despues de otro
Soldado a quien quitaron el sueldo
   (Soldadura assi)
Sombrero de pequeña falda
Sonar otra vez
   (Cosa que suena bien)
   (Aquello que assi suena)

Sonar la trompeta o bozina (Cosa que
   assi suena)
Soplar de lexos
Soplar hazia atras
Sopladora cosa que puede soplar
Subir debaxo arriba
Sudar ante de tiempo
Sudor que corre de las plantas
Suelo de argamassa
Suelta cosa para dezir o hazer
Suelta cosa de regla
Sueño subet
   (Cosa fuera de suerte)
Sulco mayor a que acuden los menores
Sulco para sangrar el agua lluuia
Sustentar antes
Sustentar debaxo
Suziedad cogida
Taça de oro tendida
Tajada de pan
Tajo para partir o picar carne
Tamarauiento yerua
Tañer para acometer batalla
Tañer para se retraer
Tañedor de cañutos
Tañedor de campanas
Tañedor de harpa
Tardarse juntamente
Tardança assi
Tardarse el que se fue (Tardança assi,
   Tardador en esta manera)
Tatara nieto, o chozno
Tender en derredor
Tener proposito de caminar
Tener respecto a alguna cosa
Tener mal prouecho
Tener acatamiento a otro
Teniendo en veneracion
Tentar de primero
Terciopelo alcarchofado
Terciopelo azeytuni o damasco
Termentina [as *pix* . . .]
   (Cosa vezina y cercana en terminos,
      Aquella vezindad en terminos)
   (Sin testamento)
Testimonio de loor o vituperacion
Texer antes

Texer por debaxo
Texillo ceñidura
Tienda de officiales
Tierra quasi toda cercada de mar
Tierra que se suele ahornagar
Tierra que echan sobre los muertos
Tierra para sembrar farro
Tierra que queda entre dos sulcos
Tierra virgen y no labrada
    (Lugar del assiento desta tina)
Tiña de la cabeça
Tinta de pintores
Tinta de purpura o carmesi
Tinta de grana para teñir
Tintorero de grana
Tirar tiro en contrario
Tirar coces atras
Tomar de lugar
Tomar por fuerça
Tomar para administrador
Tomar aguero por alguna cosa
Tomar a logro (Aquella obra de tomar a logro)
Tomar otro el juramento
Tomar algo emprestado de otro
Tomar algo para dar cuenta
Tomar a destajo
Tomar de primero
Tomamiento
    (Torcer sobre otra cosa)
Torcida cosa de lo derecho
Tornar algo a la memoria
Tornar a componer
Tornar otra vez a la amistad
Tornar lo traido
Tornar atras (Tornada assi)
Tornarse mancebo
Tornar a alcançar lo desseado
Tornar en su seso el loco
Torrezno de carne
Tortedad o trauiessa
    (Echar alguna cosa tossiendo)
Trabajo en balde
Trabajar con otro
Traer presto
Traer de algun lugar (Cosa traediza de algun lugar, Aquella obra de traer de lugar)

Traer llamas de fuego
Traer nueuas de antes
Traer hazia si
Traidor o aleuoso al principe
Traslapadura de tablas
Traspalar con pala instrumento
Traspassar te la possession
Trassegar el azeyte de alpechin (Aquella obra de trassegar)
Trassegador de azeite
Trastornar antes o primero
Tratar souajando la cosa (Aquel souajamiento)
Trauar por debaxo
Trauilla de la gorra
Trenca de la vid
    (Mucho tresquilar)
    (Cosa que se puede trocar con otra)
Trochisco
    (El que haze trompetas)
Veco de teatro
    (Cosa sin huessos)
Vuesso de qualquiera fruta
Veuo de gallina (Clara del hueuo, yema del hueuo)
Veno ya empellado
Vntar enderredor
Vntar juntamente
Vntar debaxo
Vua pisada para exprimir
    (Guardar las vacas, o bueyes)
Vayna de los testiculos
Vayo color
Vana cosa y de poco precio
Vanderizamente
Varon soltero
    (De vasito en vasito)
Vaso de la ceniza de los muertos
Vaso o nauezilla de encensio
Vassura de la casa do[nde] murio alguno
Vassura de lo que se barre
Vaziar el burujo de las vuas
Vaziar la sentina
Velloso aspereza assi
Vena que pertenesce a la cabeça
Vencer otra vez
Vencedor en juegos olimpiacos

Venir de lexos
Venir antes
Venida de antes
    (Cosa con ventanas o finiestras)
Ver antes
Ver otra vez
    (Poner a la verguença)
Vestidura en manera de bernia
Vestidura de carmesi
Vestidura de Damasco
Vestidura de color de llama
Vestidura redonda como manto
    (Vestido desta vestidura)
Vestir enderredor
    (Despoblacion de vides)
Vid armada sobre palos
Vides nueuas del majuelo
Viejo cercano a la muerte
Vieldo, instrumento para auentar
    (Cosa de aquel viento)
Vientos que corren de los golfos
Vientre de los animales que rumian (Lo
    vazio del vientre)
Vientre lugar donde concibe la muger
Vilecer otra vez
Villana cosa o descortes (Villania assi)
Vinagre hecho de aloxa
Vinagre hecho de cebolla albarrana
    (Bodega para tal vino)
Vino adobado con ensensios
Vino adobdo con espadañas
Vino que se puede detener
Vino del tintin
Viña apeada con rodrigones
Violar lo consagrado
Visitar otra vez
Visoño
Vista de antes
Voto que se atiene a otro
Xaharrar para encalar
Xaharrar la pared
Xaquima de cabestro
Xiringa
Zamarilla yerua
Zanganos con aguijon
    (Cosa que suena como zumbido)

7. CHANGES TO THE 1578 ANTEQUERA PRINTING

Entries added (25)

Acostarse de lado
Aguja de marear
Alharaz de huron
Almez arbol conoscido
Andar sobre las manos
Añudar hazer ñudo
Añudamiento
Arremeter el cauallo
Asaltos
Astil de alguna herramienta
Barajar palabras
Boca de calle, o puente
Bolcar sillar, o otra cosa
Borrador, libro en que se escriue para
    trasladar en otra parte
Bostezo [as *oscitatio . . .*]
Bostezar
Bostezo [as *consonido . . .*]
Carrillo para sacar agua
Charlatan, o chocarrero
Clarificar, exclarecer y aclarar, a otra cosa
Conspirar, o conjurar en vno
Conspiracion, o conjuracion
Correo, que va en troton o posta
Hallulo
Hintero o tablero do[nde] se amassa, o
    hiñe
Pan azedo

8. CHANGES TO THE 1581 ANTEQUERA PRINTING

Entries added (3)

Abaxar a alguno su estado
Abajar los mantenimientos caros
Asaltos [note that this entry did appear
    in the 1578 Antequera printing, but
    since the 1581 printing was based on
    the 1574 printing, this entry should be
    considered as one of the independently
    added entries to the 1581 printing]

9. CHANGES TO THE 1585 GRANADA PRINTING

Entries removed (3)

Cassador, y aniquilador de la ley
Corregida de afeytes
Vino que se puede detener

Entries added (53)

Abadejo pescado que llaman Bacallao
Abatida cosa, ques humillada
Abatidamente y baxamente
Ajada de ajo
Ajada cosa con ajo
Alameda
Al tiempo o plazo señalado
Ataude, para enterrar muertos
Azeytuna morada
Balas, con que se da tinta a las letras
Buey cuerni abierto
Busano
Cauallo o rocin castrado [the "o rocin castrado" specification is new]
Cauallo coceador
Caxa donde estan los Abecedarios de las letras para imprimir
Caxones do[n]de esta cada letra del Abecedario de molde
Chirlon o papirote
Cochinillas, que se crian junto a las tinajas de agua
Cortesia de la carta
Desbalijar
De tarde en tarde
Dexar o renunciar el cargo
Emprenta, o botica del impressor
Enagenada cosa
Encañado de cañas para Iardines
Grupera
Gusano ciento pies
Hartazga y tragazon
Hazer pie a los arbores
Maestro de capilla
Maestro de campo
Mantequilla
Matriz de la prensa de libros
Natas hechas de leche
Oydor, Iuez del Rey
Oydores de la Rota
Papel de marca mayor
Pescada cical
Pieça de artilleria
Pliego, o emboltorio de cartas
Poner en aprieto
Prepararse
Pretal
Pretender
Pretension y negociacion
Redomilla de tinta
Ropa de martas
Secreta cosa, que es econdida
Secretamente
Tragazon y hartazga
Verdugado, que vsan las Damas
Xarcia de nauio
Xaral lugar de xaras

Appendix B

A Royal Cedula from 1540, included in the opening pages of the 1574 Granada *Dictionarium.*

El Principe

POR QVANTO EL EMPERADOR Y REY MI SEñor por cedulas suyas dio licencia, y mando, que vos el Doctor Sancho de Lebrixa Alcalde del Crimen, que al presente soys de la Audiencia y Chancilleria que reside en la ciudad de Granada, y Sebastian de Lebrixa vuestro hermano, o quien vuestro poder ouiere y no otra persona alguna, pudiessen imprimir y vender en estos Reynos las obras que el Maestro Antonio de Lebrixa vuestro padre hizo, gloso y emendo, por ciertos años, segun mas largo en las dichas cedulas, a que nos referimos, se contiene. Y aora por parte de vos el dicho Doctor nos ha sido suplicado, que porque el termino contenido en las dichas cedulas se cumplira presto, y vos estays viejo, y no teneys que dexar a vuestros hijos, fuessemos seruidos prorrogar la dicha licencia por los dias de vuestra vida, y por los de Antonio de Lebrixa vuestro hijo, mandando que ninguna otra persona pudiesse imprimir ni vender los dichos tractados en estos reynos, ni traerlos a vender de otra parte, porque de algunos dias aca, de Francia, y otras partes los traen a vender contra lo contenido en las dichas cedulas de su Magestad, en que recebis daño, o como la nuestra merced fuesse. Y nos auiendo consideracion a lo que el dicho Antonio de Lebrixa vuestro padre trabajo en hazer las dichas obras, y vos nos aueys seruido continuamente, y por hazer bien y merced a vos, y al dicho vuestro hijo. Por la presente prorrogamos y alargamos el termino de la dicha merced y licencia, y siendo necessario os la damos de nueuo para en toda vuestra vida, y despues de ella al dicho Antonio de Lebrixa vuestro hijo tambien por toda su vida, contandose desde el dia que se cumpliere el termino de la dicha vltima prorrogacion que se os concedio en adelante. Y mandamos que durante los dias de vuestra vida, y despues della, de la del dicho vuestro hijo, vosotros, o quien el dicho vuestro poder ouiere, cada vno en su tiempo, y no otra persona alguna puedan imprimir y impriman, y vender, y vendan en estos Reynos y Señorios de Castilla las dichas obras que el dicho vuestro padre hizo, gloso y emendo, ni las traygan a vender de otra parte so pena que la persona, o personas que sin tener vuestro poder para ello las imprimieren, o vendieren, o hizieren imprimir, o vender en estos Reynos, o las traxeren a vender de otra parte, pierdan la impression que hizieren y vendieren, y los moldes y aparejos con que lo hizieren, y los libros que de otra parte traxeren a vender. E incurran mas cada vno dellos en pena de treynta mil marauedis por cada vez que lo contrario hizieren, la qual dicha pena mandamos que se reparta en esta manera. La tercia parte para la persona que lo acusare y la otra tercia parte para nuestra Camara y Fisco, y la otra tercia parte para el Iuez que lo sentenciare.

Y mandamos a los del nuestro Consejo Presidentes, y Oydores de las nuestras Audiencias, Alcaldes, Alguaziles, de nuestra Casas y Corte y Chancillerias, y a todos los Corregidores, Assistentes, Alguaziles, Merinos, Prehostes, y otras Iusticias y Iuezes qualesquier destos nuestros Reynos y Señorios, assi a los que aora son como a los que seran de aqui adelante, a quien esta nuestra cedula fuere mostrada, que os la guarden y hagan guardar en todo y por todo, como en ella se contiene, y guardando la, y cumpliendo la, no consientan que las dichas obras se impriman ni vendan enestos Reynos, ni las traygan a ve[n]der de fuera parte dellos, saluo por vosotros, o por quien vuestro poder ouiere, y no otra persona alguna, so las penas susodichas. Y no hagan ende al. Fecha en Valladolid, a cinco dias del mes de Diziembre, de mil y quinientos y quarenta años. Va entre renglones donde dize hizo. Vala.

YO EL PRINCIPE.

POR MANDADO DE SU ALTEZA

PEDRO DE LOS COBOS.

Esta concedida de nueuo esta merced a Aelio Antonio de Librixa, por su vida, y de su hijo, y nieto.

English translation

The Prince

WHEREAS THE EMPEROR AND KING MY LORD by his decrees gave license, and commanded, that you Doctor Sancho de Lebrixa [i.e., de Nebrija], Criminal Magistrate, which you are at present in the Court and Chancellery located in the city of Granada, and Sebastian de Lebrixa your brother, or whoever your will should allow and no other person, should print and sell in these kingdoms the works which Master Antonio de Lebrixa, your father, created, glossed, and corrected, for a certain number of years, as is outlined at greater length in the said decrees to which we refer. And now you, the said Doctor, have petitioned us that—because the term contained in these decrees will soon end, and you being old, and not having much to leave to your children—we should be served to extend the license for all the days of your life, and for those of Antonio de Lebrixa your son, commanding that no other person should be able to print nor sell the said tracts in these kingdoms, nor bring them to sell elsewhere (because recently here, from France and elsewhere, they are brought to sell in violation of that contained in the said decrees of his Majesty, by which you are harmed), or whatever our favor should be. And we, having respect for that which the said Antonio de Lebrixa did in creating the said works, and you having served us continually, and in order to grant benefit and favor to you, and to your son, for the present we extend and lengthen the limit of the said favor and license, and being necessary we grant it anew it for all your life, and afterwards for the life of the said Antonio de Lebrixa your son, starting from the day on which ends the last extension which we granted, in continuation. And we command that during the days of your life, and after it, during that of your son, you, or whoever your will should allow, each one in his time, and no other person, can print or will print, can sell or will sell, in these kingdoms and dominions of Castile the said works which your said father created, glossed, and corrected, nor bring them to sell from elsewhere, under penalty that the person or persons who without having your permission for it should print them, or should sell them, or should have them printed, or sold in these kingdoms, or should bring them to sell from another part, will lose the copies which they created and sold, and the type and equipment with which it was done, and the books which from elsewhere they should bring to sell. And they will also incur, each one of them, a fine of 30,000 maravedis for each of their violations, the said fine we command be divided in this way: a third to the person who makes the accusation, and the other third for our Chamber and Exchequer, and the other third to the sentencing judge.

And we command to those of our Council, Presidents and Judges of our Courts, Magistrates, Sheriffs of our Houses and Court and Chancelleries, and all the Corregidors, Assistants, Sheriffs, Judges, Provosts, and other Justices and Judges whosoever of our kingdoms and dominions, both those at present as well as those who will be henceforth, to whom this our decree should be shown, that they should observe and have it observed in full, just as it says, and observing it, and carrying it out, not allow that the said works be printed nor sold in these kingdoms, nor that they be brought to sell from outside of them, except by you, or by whoever your will allows, and no other person at all, under the said penalties. And they shall not act contrary to this. Done in Valladolid, on the fifth day of the month of December, 1540. (The part added between the lines, where it says "was done," is valid).

I THE PRINCE

BY COMMAND OF HIS HIGHNESS

PEDRO DE LOS COBOS.

This decree is once again granted to Aelio Antonio de Librixa, for his lifetime, and that of his son, and grandson.

Notes

Introduction

Epigraphs:

"TRADVZIR, del verbo Latino traduco.is. por lleuar de vn lugar a otro alguna cosa, o encaminarla. Gra[m]matici traduco, ad locum aliquem duco, vel de loco in locum duco: transfero, a tra[n]s & duco. En lengua Latina tiene otras algunas sinificaciones Analogicas, pero en la Española sinifica el boluer la sentencia de vna lengua en otra, como traduzir de Italiano, o de Frances algun libro en Castellano." Folio 50v. The Latin part of Covarrubias's definition was taken from Ambrogio Calepino's best-selling Latin dictionary, first published in 1502; thanks to Mary Bellino for bringing this to my attention.

"TRASLADAR, passar de vn lugar a otro alguna cosa de consideracion como trasladar el cuerpo, o reliquias de algun santo." Folio 52r.

"TRASLADAR, vale algunas vezes interpretar alguna escritura de vna lengua en otra, y tambien vale copiar: y este se llama traslado. Algunos son simples, y otros estan autenticados." Folio 52r.

1. Throughout, I use "Castilian" as a more precise name—both historically and geographically—for the central Iberian language usually called Spanish today.

2. On the rescue of saintly relics from Protestant lands in the early modern period, and their translation to safer havens (including churches in the Americas), see Morales, *La vida;* Campos, *Relacion;* Hernández, *Vida;* Johnson, *An Edition;* Christian, *Local Religion,* 133–40; Carneiro da Cunha, "Da guerra"; Morales, *Carta;* Freitas Carvalho, "Os recebimentos"; Smith, "Repatriating Sanctity"; Smith, "Salvaging Saints"; and Archivo General de la Nación (Mexico City), Inquisición, vol. 81, exp. 1 (1576). Note that both Morales and Hernández refer explicitly to the "translacion" of relics in their titles (from 1568 and 1591, respectively). On the medieval theory and practice of *translatio,* see Geary, *Furta Sacra;* and Bartlett, *Why,* 10–13, 282–311; thanks to Aaron Hyman for these two references.

3. It is striking that Covarrubias begins his definition of **Tradvzir** with the Latin

meaning; normally he cites Latin (and Greek, and Hebrew) roots and etymologies only after providing a Castilian definition.

4. For catalogs of the various editions of Nebrija's works, see Odriozola, "La caracola"; Esparza Torres and Niederhe, *Bibliografía Nebrisense;* Wilkinson, *Iberian Books,* 30–38; and (for publications up to 1520) Abad, *Post-incunabules ibéricos,* 97–112. Invaluable online databases for Nebrijan research include Pedro Martín Baños's Corpus Nebrissense (http://corpusnebirssense.com), the Universal Short Title Catalog (www.ustc.ac.uk) for works prior to 1601, as well as the ongoing Iberian Books Project (http://iberian.ucd.ie), which currently extends through the first half of the seventeenth century.

5. In previous studies of Nebrija's dictionaries and their influence on dictionary production in the New World, there has been some confusion as to when the "first" and "second" editions of Nebrija's *Dictionarium* were printed (Clayton and Campbell, "Alonso de Molina," 338–39; Clayton, "Evidence," 99; Smith-Stark, "Lexicography," 16). In this book I will refer to separate *printings:* the 1503 Seville printing, the 1514 Zaragoza printing, the two different Alcalá printings of 1520, and so on.

6. To my knowledge, the only previous studies of entry-variation in Nebrija's Castilian–Latin vocabulary as it developed over time are by María Lourdes García Macho ("Novedades léxicas"; "Sobre los vocablos suprimidos"; "Variantes léxicas"; "Actitud de Nebrija"; "Procesos internos"), who compares the 1495 and 1516 printings; and Carmen Codoñer ("Evolución"), who examines the transformations in the Latin–Castilian 1492 and 1512 printings. Gloria Guerrero Ramos (*El léxico*) traces the relationship between Nebrija's 1492 Latin–Castilian and 1495 Castilian–Latin dictionaries.

7. On language, genealogy, and parentage, see also Masten, *Queer Philologies.*

8. More subtly, Smith-Stark ("El 'primer Nebrija indiano,'" 535) points out that Nebrija's Castilian categories of **no poder, no querer,** and **no saber,** faithfully copied into Alonso de Molina's 1555 Castilian–Nahuatl vocabulary, are derived from the Latin *nequeo, nolo,* and *nescio,* negative verbs (formed with the combining particle *ne-*) that have no real equivalent in Castilian (or Nahuatl, for that matter).

9. For discussions of this transformation in the entries of Alonso de Molina's Nebrija-inspired Nahuatl vocabularies of 1555 and 1571, see Hernández de León-Portilla, "Nebrija," 216; and Galeote, "Estudio preliminar," xxiv, xxx–xlvii. The idea that Nebrija's publications were used to blindly straitjacket indigenous languages and categories into Latin models has been critiqued by Nansen Díaz ("Nebrija," 82), Manrique Castañeda ("La estructura," 97), and Galeote ("Originalidad," 1726).

10. Molina, *Aqui comiença,* v recto; the full quotation is included in chapter 4.

11. Note that from 1503 onward this was usually accompanied by a Latin–Castilian half as well, modeled on Nebrija's 1492 Latin-to-Castilian *Lexicon.* See chapter 1.

12. Danto, "Translation and Betrayal"; Allen, "The Happy Traitor."

13. There is of course a large body of theoretical writings on translation, such as Walter Benjamin's famous "The Task of the Translator," first published in 1923 (see also Tedlock, *The Spoken Word;* Tawada, "The Translator's Gate"). These writings, how-

ever, are above all engaged with complex, grammatically structured "semiotic organizations": dialogues, oral narratives, literary works. As Michael Silverstein argues, the transformation of these complex semiotic organizations from one language to another is better understood as a process of *transduction;* the concept of *translation,* technically speaking, should be reserved for the focused transformations of one sense category to another, transformations that are central to the structure of translating dictionaries: "We can translate English (my) father with a term in another language, say Worora (northwestern Australia) (ngayu) iraaya" (Silverstein, "Translation," 78). In other words, the theoretical issues involved in the translations from one word to another that we find in dictionaries are related to, but distinct from, the theoretical issues involved in more extended transductions. Throughout this book, then, my references focus on the (much smaller) corpus of writings engaged with Silverstein's *translation* in the narrow sense.

14. Smith-Stark ("Lexicography," 25–26) estimates the number of entries as 19,179; my own counts generated a total of 19,393 entries.

15. Galeote, "El acervo," 2209–10; Guerrero Ramos, *El léxico,* 157–70; Hernández, "Influencias," 64; Hernández, "La lexicografía," 191–92.

16. On allochronism and the denial of coevalness, see Fabian, *Time and the Other,* and the concluding chapter in this volume.

17. This book participates in a larger tradition of writing "connected histories" of the early modern world; see Wolf, *Europe;* Mintz, *Sweetness and Power;* Sahlins, "Cosmologies"; Subrahmanyam, "Connected Histories"; Subrahmanyam, "Holding the World"; Brook, *Vermeer's Hat;* Hamann, "Chronological Pollution"; Hamann, "The Mirrors"; Hamann, "Bad Christians"; and the section "Printing Conquers the World" in chap. 6 of Febvre and Martin, *Coming of the Book,* 198–215. At the same time, this study also connects to an emerging field of global lexicography, alongside Greene, *Five Words;* Levy and Mills, *Lexikon;* and Ogilvie, *Words of the World*—all published in 2013.

1. Nebrija and the Ancients

1. Because early modern spelling was not consistent, Antonio de Nebrija's last name had a number of variant forms: Lebrija, Lebrixa, Librixa, and Nebrissa (in Castilian) as well as Nebrissensis (in Latin). For a brief biography of Nebrija and his interest in recovering Latin as it existed in the classical past, see Guzmán Betancourt, "La lengua"; on his stay in Italy (the exact dates of which are debated), see Caro Bellido and Tomassetti Guerra, *Antonio de Nebrija,* 78–87; Esparza Torres and Niederehe, *Bibliografía,* 12–13.

2. Esparza Torres and Niederehe, *Bibliografía,* 13; surviving evidence, however, suggests Nebrija was more interested in his own studies than in teaching; see Elliot van Liere, "After Nebrija." On early modern Latin more generally, see Burke, *Languages,* 43–60.

3. See the table of printings from 1481 to 1565 in Odriozola, "La caracola," between

pages 12 and 13. Sarmiento ("Antonio de Nebrija") considers the impact of the *Introductiones* on the creation of grammars for three indigenous New World languages: Quechua (in 1560), Nahuatl (in 1571), and Guarani (in 1640).

4. Antonio began substituting his family name for that of his town of origin (Antonio Lebrixa or de Lebrixa) a few years earlier, when he was a student in Salamanca and later in Bologna; on this and Elio/Aelius, see Caro Bellido and Tomassetti Guerra, *Antonio de Nebrija,* 39; Guzmán Betancourt, "La lengua," 26; and Esparza Torres and Niederehe, *Bibliografía,* 11–12. On ancient Roman remains in the region of Lebrija, see Caro Bellido and Tomassetti Guerra, *Antonio de Nebrija,* 62–74. On Nebrija's own writings about archaeological remains, see Morán, *La memoria,* 60–61, 121–22.

5. This version dates to around 1488; see Esparza and Niederehe, *Bibliografía,* 16; Niederehe, "La *Gramática,*" 42.

6. Guzmán Betancourt, "La lengua," 29.

7. Although this *Gramatica castellana* went through only one printing in the early modern period (Esparza Torres and Niederehe, *Bibliografía,* 17), Esparza Torres ("Los prólogos") argues that its influence—such as on the creation of grammars for indigenous New World languages—was greater than has been appreciated. On the "authorization" of vernaculars through the writing of grammars, see Burke, *Languages,* 89–90, 95.

8. Technically speaking—as Thomas Smith-Stark ("Lexicography," 11) points out—Fernández de Palencia's text was "not really a bilingual dictionary, but rather a monolingual Latin dictionary with a translation of the Latin texts into Spanish"; see also García Macho, "Macroestructura." The earliest bilingual dictionary to be printed in Europe was the Latin–German *Vocabularius ex quo,* published as early as 1467. Considine, *Dictionaries,* 113.

9. On Nebrija's various innovations in the creation and structuring of dictionaries, see Lope Blanch, "Nebrija"; on the relationship between Nebrija's 1492 and 1495 dictionaries, see Guerrero Ramos, *El léxico.*

10. See the excellent comparative analysis in Guerrero Ramos, *El léxico,* 23–50. The creation of the *Oxford English Dictionary,* too, was based on a start-from-scratch method (Ogilvie, *Words,* 29, 31).

11. "Nunca dexe de pensar alguna manera por donde pudiesse desbaratar la barbaria por todas las partes de España tan ancha y luenga mente derramada. . . . Assi, io, para desarraigar la barbaria de los ombres de nuestra nacion, no comence por otra parte sino por el estudio de Salamanca, el qual, como una fortaleza, tomado por combate, no dudava io que todos los otros pueblos de España vernian luego a se me rendir." [I never stopped thinking about how I might be able to banish the barbarity which is spilled so far and wide across all parts of Spain. . . . And so I, to rip up the barbarity of the men of our nation, began nowhere else but in the studies at Salamanca, which, taken in combat like a fortress, I did not doubt that all the other towns of Spain would then come surrender before me.] Nebrija, *Lexicon,* a.ii verso–a.iii recto, quoted in Caro Bellido and Tomassetti Guerra, *Antonio de Nebrija,*

81–82. Nebrija's earlier *Gramatica* complained about the linguistic and epigraphic mischief committed by the medieval Goths: "Los cuales, no solamente acabaron de corromper el latin i la lengua romana, que ia con muchas guerras avia començado a desfallecer, mas aun torcieron las figuras i traços de las letras antiguas, introdu-ziendo i mezclando las suias, cuales las vemos escriptas en los libros que se escri-vieron." [They not only ended up corrupting Latin and the Roman language, which already with many wars had begun to decline, but they even twisted the figures and outlines of the ancient letters, introducing and mixing their own, which we see written in the books which they wrote.] Quoted in Bellido and Tomassetti Guerra, *Antonio de Nebrija*, 87. See also Lope Blanch, "Nebrija," 45.

12. Sextus Pompeius Festus was a Roman grammarian of the second century and the author of a lexicon based on Verrius Flaccus' *De verborum significatu*. When a sin-gle manuscript was rediscovered in the Renaissance, only about half of the work had survived, covering entries from M to V. According to the Universal Short Title Catalog (www.ustc.ac.uk), at least eight printings of Festus' text were published before 1500.

13. Folio LXXX verso. Another list of examples is provided by García Macho, "Pro-cesos internos," 1322. In part because some of Nebrija's dictionaries are not foliated and others are paginated by section, in most of what follows I do not include page references for word entries.

14. The list of authors takes up all of folio a ii recto. A thorough discussion of classi-cal authors cited in Nebrija's works is provided by Caro Bellido and Tomassetti Guerra, *Antonio de Nebrija*, 129–47.

15. Guerrero Ramos, *El léxico*, 35–37. See also the brief discussion of possible fif-teenth-century neo-Latin authors used by Nebrija in García Macho, "Sobre los vocablos suprimidos," 143–45; her best evidence is for Nebrija's references to the work of the humanist poet Juan de Mena (1411–1456).

16. On Nebrija's hypothetical "fichero," or card file, see García Macho, "Procesos inter-nos," 1320. On the use of slips elsewhere in Europe, see Considine, *Dictionaries*, 270; Blair, "Note Taking," 104–6; Blair, "Rise of Note-Taking"; many thanks to Ann Blair for drawing my attention to these sources. The use of slips would have a long history in lexicography, including the making of the *Oxford English Dictionary* (Ogilvie, *Words*, 2–3, 9–10, 14).

17. Erasmus also made wry observations about early modern "Ciceronians" who used medieval Latin vocabulary; see Burke, *Languages*, 58.

18. On Nebrija's various innovations in the creation and structuring of dictionaries, see Lope Blanch, "Nebrija."

19. On documented cases of Cromberger piracy, see Norton, *Printing in Spain*, 79; and Griffin, *The Crombergers*, 68. On the early modern cultures of book piracy more generally, see Johns, *The Nature of the Book*; Johns, *Piracy*.

20. Other contrastive examples include **Xabonera ierva** (1495) versus **Xabonera yerua** (1503, 1506); **Zorzal ave conocida** (1495) versus **Zorzal aue conocida** (1503, 1506). On these possibly Andalusian variants (discussed in connection with the

1516 Seville printing), see Gerald J. MacDonald's introduction to his 1973 edition of Nebrija's *Vocabulario de romance en latín*. Critiques of Nebrija's work in the sixteenth century complained that his writings represented a too-Andalusian version of Castilian (Burke, *Languages*, 97), but these claims have been evaluated and rejected by more recent scholarship; see Guilarte, "Alcance y sentido"; Guerrero Ramos, *El léxico*, 189–98.

21. The teacher who held Nebrija's university post during his long absence had also just died; Esparza Torres and Niederehe, *Bibliografía*, 26.

22. On the collaboration of Guillén de Brocar and Nebrija in general, see Sáez Guillén and García de la Concha Delgado, "Obras de Nebrija"; Abad, "Nebrija"; and Cátedra García, "Arnao Guillén de Brocar" (the printing of the 1512–1513 dictionary is discussed on 63–64). On the relationship between the 1512 and 1513 printings, see Abad, *Post-incunabules ibéricos*, 100–102; on concurrent printing in early modern England, see Johns, *The Nature of the Book*, 99–100.

23. Fernández Valladares, *La imprenta*, 133–34; on the locations of Nebrija's house and Guillén de Brocar's workshop in Alcalá, see Torre, "La casa de Nebrija"; on the important role authors had in overseeing the printing of their books, see Johns, *The Nature of the Book*, 101–4.

24. Cátedra García ("Arnao Guillén de Brocar," 63) suggests the second half of the revised *Dictionarium* was printed in Salamanca so that Nebrija could oversee its production.

25. On Guillén de Brocar and Alcalá, see Abad, "Nebrija," 26–27; Abad also notes that Arnao's Logroño workshop continued to function after his move to Alcalá.

26. Fadrique de Basilea had published Nebrija's work before: his pamphlet on Iberian antiquities from the 1490s. On Fadrique de Basilea more generally, see Fernández Valladares, *La imprenta*, 127–46.

27. On Nebrija's revisions, see García Macho, "Novedades léxicas"; García Macho, "Sobre los vocablos suprimidos"; García Macho, "Variantes léxicas"; García Macho, "Actitud de Nebrija"; García Macho, "Procesos internos." A complete list of terms excluded from the 1513 Castilian–Latin dictionary (compared with the 1495 printing) is published in García Macho, "Variantes léxicas," 188–92. Note that Nebrija did add 125 Castilian–Latin entries to the 1513 printing, a complex mix of revisions, corrections, and actual additions; see Garcia Macho, "Novedades léxicas." The same desires for classical purification and medieval excision were present in other early modern dictionary projects as well, such as Robert Estienne's 1531 Latin–French dictionary (Considine, *Dictionaries*, 32). On language and purification more generally in the early modern period, see Burke, *Languages*, 141–59.

28. Cátedra García, "Arnao Guillén de Brocar," 64.

29. On these versions and their dating, see Abad, *Post-incunabules ibéricos*, 101–2. Abad also points out that the Latin–Castilian and gazetteer sections of the (first) 1516 printing were actually printed in 1517—probably the result of a concurrent printing arrangement like that used for the 1512 Burgos / 1513 Salamanca printing of the *Dictionarium*.

30. Thus **Azeituna** (1495, 1513) versus **Azeytuna** (1503, 1506); **Cabezcaido** (1495, 1513)

versus **Cabezcaydo** (1503, 1506); **Carniceria este mesma** (1495, 1513) versus **Carniceria esta mesma** (1503, 1506); **Cassador de escriptura** (1495, 1513) versus **Cassador de la escriptura** (1503, 1506); **Cassar la scriptura** (1495, 1513) versus **Cassar la escriptura** (1503, 1506); **Xenabe o mostaça** (1495, 1513) versus **Xenabe o mostaza** (1503, 1506).

31. Thus **Cantar el grillo** (1513, 1516) versus **Cantar el gryllo** (1514), **Cabestero que faze cabestros** (1513, 1516) versus **Cabestrero que haze cabestros** (1514), **Ueuo de aue o reptilia o pece** (1513, 1516) versus **Ueuo de aue o reptilia o peçe** (1514).

32. Thus **Cabezcaido** (1495, 1513) versus **Cabezcaydo** (1503, 1506, 1516), **Xabonera ierva** (1495) versus **Xabonera yerua** (1503, 1506, 1516), **Xativa ciudad de aragon** (1495) versus **Xatiua cibdad de aragon** (1503, 1506), **Xatives cosa desta ciudad** (1495) versus **Xatiues cosa desta cibdad** (1503, 1506).

33. The titles of the two versions, with their variant spacing, are given in Esparza Torres and Niederhe, *Bibliografía Nebrisense*, 87–88.

34. The foliated version is represented by copies in Madrid at the library of the Universidad Complutense (Res.270(1); a PDF scan is available on Google Books) and the Biblioteca Nacional de España (*R2700); and in London at the British Library (C.63.c.14). The unfoliated version is represented by copies at the library of the Universidad Complutense (FOA 158; a PDF scan is available on Google Books) and the Biblioteca Nacional de España (*R2219), both in Madrid; and in the British Library (C.63.c.15).

35. Rental documents suggest that Nebrija began living in Alcalá in October 1513; Torres, "La casa de Nebrija," 184.

36. Academic politics at Salamanca may also have played a role in Nebrija's move; see Esparza Torres and Niederhe, *Bibliografía Nebrisense*, 30. For Nebrija's on-again off-again involvement with the Complutensian Bible project, see Revilla Rico, *La Políglota*, 34–36, 111; Esparza Torres and Niederhe, *Bibliografía Nebrisense*, 24; for Guillén de Brocar's role, see Revilla Rico, *La Políglota*, 37–40; Sáez Guillén and Concha Delgado, "Obras," 432–33; Torre, "La casa de Nebrija." Actual circulation of the bible's printed volumes had to wait several years for papal approval; see Revilla Rico, *La Políglota*, 39–48.

37. Wilkinson, *Iberian Books*, 33–34.

38. For general biographies and for the collaborations of these two printers with Nebrija (and their continued posthumous printing of his works), see Cátedra García, "Arnao Guillén de Brocar"; and Abad, "Nebrija."

39. The presumably first 1520 printing is represented by a copy in the British Library (*C.63.i.7); the presumably second 1520 printing is represented by a copy in the Biblioteca Nacional de España (*R7701).

40. Spelling variations are found throughout the 1513 and 1514 versions, as well as the two pairs of volumes dated 1516 and 1520. Spellings in the 1513, 1520, and 1528 printings, however, are consistently parallel, diverging from the 1514 and 1516 printings. Further spelling variations in the 1532 printing are documented in notes 41 and 43 in this chapter. Thus **Cantar el grillo** (1513, 1516, 1520, 1528, 1532) versus **Cantar el gryllo** (1514); **Cabestero que faze cabestros** (1513, 1516, 1520, 1528) versus

Cabestrero que haze cabestros (1514); Cada ruin (1513, 1514, 1520, 1528) versus Cada ruyn (1516); Callecer hazer callos (1513, 1514, 1520, 1528) versus Callecer fazer callos (1516); Cantar el buitre (1513, 1514, 1520, 1528, 1532,) versus Cantar el buytre (1516); Caridad amor onesto (1513, 1514, 1520, 1528, 1532) versus Caridad amor honesto (1516); Casa en la eredad (1513, 1514, 1520, 1528, 1532,) versus Casa en la heredad (1516); Casamiento la dote que se da (1513, 1514, 1520, 1528, 1532) versus Casamiento el dote que se da (1516); Cassador de escriptura (1513, 1514, 1520, 1528) versus Cassador de scriptura (1516); Xenabe o mostaça (1513, 1514, 1520, 1528, 1532) versus Xenabe o mostaza (1516).

41. Thus Borron de escritura (1528, 1532, 1533, 1536) versus Borron de escriptura (1513, 1520); Vihuela (1528, 1532, 1533, 1536) versus Viyuela (1520, spelling from the revised 1520 version as represented by the Biblioteca Nacional de España copy).

42. The title page declares that it was printed "Cum priuilegio," though what that privilege was is unclear—was it permission to print the *Dictionarium,* or do these words indicate only that Díaz Romano was a licensed printer?

43. Thus Borrico hijo de asna (1532, 1533, 1536) versus Borrico de fijo asna (1513) and Borrico fijo de asna (1520, 1528); Cabestrero que haze cabestros (1532, 1533, 1536) versus Cabestero que faze cabestros (1513, 1520, 1528); Camara lo que assi se haze (1532, 1533, 1536) versus Camara lo que assi se faze (1513, 1520, 1528); Cassador de escritura (1532, 1536) versus Cassador de escriptura (1513, 1520, 1528); Visitar yr a ver (1532, 1533, 1536) versus Visitar ir auer (1513, 1520, 1528).

44. Abad, "Nebrija," 32–33; Wilkinson, *Iberian Books,* 35–36.

45. References in the text of a 1554 royal cedula, or decree, granting Sancho and Sebastián (as well as Sancho's son Antonio) the right to print and sell Nebrija's works in the Americas suggest that the sons of Nebrija had already been granted the power to print and authorize publications of "las obras que el maestro antonio de lebrixa vuestro padre hizo gloso y emendo por ciertos años" [the works which the Master Antonio de Nebrija your father created glossed and corrected for some years]; the document goes on to say this power had been extended to two lifetimes: "y despues por otra cedula firmada del serenisimo rey principe don felipe nuestro muy caro e muy amado hijo se os prorrogo la dicha licencia por los dias de la vida de vos el dicho doctor [Sancho] y despues della por los de antonio de lebrixa vuestro hijo" [and after by another decree signed by the most serene King-Prince don Felipe our very dear and much loved son were extended to you the said license for the days of the life of you the said Doctor [Sancho] and after them for those of Antonio de Nebrija your son]. Quoted in Bermúdez Plata, "Las obras," 1031, from a cedula in the Archivo General de Simancas; the same document is printed on the verso of the title page of the 1567 Granada printing of the *Dictionarium.* The "otra cedula" may be one from Prince Philip (later King Philip II) dated December 5, 1540, and reprinted in the opening pages of the 1574 Antequera version of the *Dictionarium* (see appendix B in this volume). This 1540 cedula, in turn, refers to cedulas granted by Philip's father, Charles V, to Sancho and Sebastián (although the date of these grants is not stated). Such royal grants parallel the copyright-like

privileges or "letters patent" issued by the king to authors and printers in seventeenth-century England. Johns, *The Nature of the Book*, 248–55; for Iberia, see García Oro, *Los reyes*.

46. Cátedra García, "Arnao Guillén de Brocar," 50–51.

47. Carrera de la Red, "El *Dictionarium medicum*," 401; see also Torre, "La casa de Nebrija," 186–87; on the surviving inventory of these manuscripts, see Odriozola, "La caracola," 55.

48. For details on these Granada editions, see Esparza Torres and Niederehe, *Bibliografía*, 126–7; Gallego Morell, *Cinco impresores*, 46–7; for individual summaries, see Odriozola, "La caracola," 53, 68, 73, 78–79.

49. On the publications of Sancho, Sebastián, and Antonio in Granada, see Gallego Morell, *Cinco impresores*, 33–68.

50. See note 43 in this chapter, which shows how lexical variations separating the 1532 printing from the 1520 and 1528 printings are shared by the 1536 printing. Most are also shared by the 1533 Valencia printing, but that version, in turn, has spelling variations that do not appear in 1536. Thus **Callosa cosa con callos** (1532, 1536) versus **Calloso cosa con callos** (1533); **Cassar la escritura** (1532, 1536) versus **Cassar la escriptura** (1533); **Cassador de escritura** (1532, 1536) versus **Cassador de scriptura** (1533). In other categories, the 1533 version departs from spelling variations otherwise shared from 1513 to 1536 (perhaps a reflection of Levantine traditions and spelling and speaking). Thus **Faisan aue** (1513, 1520, 1528, 1532, 1536) versus **Faysan aue** (1533); **Faisa por la faxa** (1513, 1520, 1528, 1532, 1536) versus **Faysa por la faxa** (1533); **Faisa pequeña** (1513, 1520, 1528, 1532, 1536) versus **Faysa pequeña** (1533); **Faisar por faxar** (1513, 1520, 1528, 1532, 1536) versus **Faysar por faxar** (1533); **Musaica obra antiuga** (1513, 1520, 1528, 1532, 1536) versus **Musayca obra antigua** (1533).

51. As discussed later in this chapter, this ordering was corrected twice (and independently) in two different Nebrijan lineages: the Antwerp edition of 1545 (and its descendants), and the Granada edition of 1552 (and its descendants). The Granada series also removed the redundant second **Vihuela** entry. But because this corrected Granada series (unlike its Antwerp cousin) had no extended progeny, the purging of the second **Vihuela** lasted only for the Granada printings of 1552, 1554, and 1555.

52. Thus **Cabruno cosa deste cabron - Cabrituno cosa de cabrito - *Carcarear el gallo - Caça de aues** (1536) versus **Cabrituno cosa de cabrito - Cabron para casta - Cabron castrado - Cabruno cosa desta linaje - Caburno assi - Cabruno cosa deste cabron - *Carcarear el gallo - Caça de aues** (1540); **Marfil dientes de elefante - Margomar antiguo verbo - Margen de libro - *Marhojo o moho d los arboles - Marido de muger** (1536) versus **Marfil dientes del elephante - Margen de libro - Margomar antiguo verbo - *Marhojo o moho d los arboles - Marido de muger casada** (1540); **Ruego al ygual o menor - Ruego como quiera - *Rufian o alcaguete - *Rufianeria o alcagueteria - *Rufianear o alcaguetear - Ruga de cosa arrugada - *Rugimiento de las tripas - Rugoso cosa arrugada** (1536) versus ***Rufian o alcaguete - *Rufianeria o alcagueteria - *Rufianear o alcaguetear - Ruego al**

ygual o menor - Ruego como quiera - Ruga de cosa arrugada - *Rugimiento de
las tripas - Rugoso cosa arrugada (1540).

53. That the 1545 Granada printing was used as a source for the 1552 printing is made
    clear by the spellings of **Xaraue de medicina** and **Xenabe o mostaza** (1545, 1552)
    versus **Xarafe de medicina** and **Xenabe o mostaça** (1536, 1540, 1543, 1548, 1550), as
    well as an alphabetization glitch introduced in 1543: **Guedeja de cabellos - Guede-
    judo - Guedeja enhetrada** (1543, 1545, 1552) versus **Guedeja de cabellos - Guedeja
    enhetrada - Guedejudo** (1536, 1540, 1548, 1550).

54. Cuesta Gutiérrez, "El enigma," 112–13; Gallego Morell, *Cinco impresores,* 40–45.

55. These include a 1545 printing of Nebrija's *Segmenta ex epistolis* (a selection of
    extracts from the apostolic letters), represented by a copy in the Universidad de
    Salamanca, Biblioteca General 12192(3); and an abridged 1559 printing of the *Dic-
    tionarium* with only Latin–Spanish and gazetteer sections, represented by a copy
    in the Universidad de Granada, Biblioteca H. Real / A-026-207 (note that the
    online catalog misdates this volume to 1550).

56. Esparza Torres and Niederhe claim that a 1561 Granada volume was printed, with
    surviving copies in the British Library and the Biblioteca Nazionale Centrale in
    Rome (*Bibliografía Nebrisense,* 153–54). But the British Library copy includes only
    the Latin–Castilian and gazetteer sections, not the Castilian–Latin section (and
    thus is like the 1559 printing mentioned in the previous note), and the Rome copy
    seems not to exist: it is not listed in the current online catalog, nor does it appear in
    any of the bibliographic sources Esparza Torres and Niederhe cite as references for
    this edition, which list only the British Library copy. Only the British Library copy
    is listed in Wilkinson, *Iberian Books,* 36.

57. Gallego Morell, *Cinco impresores,* 43. Antonio followed this with additional vol-
    umes in 1564, 1565, and 1566.

58. This woodcut, which includes curving lines in front of Nebrija's face, was used for
    the 1555, 1567, and 1572 printings of the dictionary—another publishing heirloom
    handed from father to son.

59. See notes to the section "Antonio's Grandson from Granada to Antequera" later in
    this chapter.

60. Basic biographical information on Jan Steels, and his second wife, Anna van Ert-
    born(e), who continued publishing books after Jan's death, can be found in Rouzet,
    Dictionnaire, 94–96; and Bietenholz and Deutscher, *Contemporaries of Erasmus,*
    191–92. Nuyts (*Jean Steelsius*) published a full list of known publications. Depend-
    ing on the language he was printing in, Jan's last name may appear as Steelsius,
    Esteelçeo, Steelij, Steelsio, Steelsman, Steelsmanus, Stelsio, Stelsius, or Steltius.

61. Carrasco Montero and Carrera de la Red, "Lexicografía," 115.

62. The Castilian–Latin entries added to the 1545 Antwerp printing are, in general, not
    medical terms, and the Castilian definitions for the Latin–Castilian entries men-
    tioned by Montero Cartelle and Carrera de la Red ("El *Dictionarium medicum,*"
    408–9) are not among them. See appendix A, section 5.

63. Braudel, *The Perspective of the World,* 143.

64. Wilkinson, *Iberian Books*, xvii.

65. Pérez's translation went through two printings, in 1550 and 1556. Nuyts, *Jean Steelsius*, 33, 44; González Palencia, *Gonzalo Pérez*, 201–2.

66. Montero Cartelle and Carrera de la Red, "El *Dictionarium medicum*," 399–400; Carrasco Montero and Carrera de la Red, "Lexicografía," 116. A reconstruction of the contents of this manuscript has been edited by Avelina Carrera de la Red (see Nebrija, *Dictionarium medicum*).

67. Luis Nuñez's letter of dedication to the 1545 printing complains "sic omnia lacera, immutata, corrupta, et deprauata erant" ("all were ragged, changed, corrupted, and distorted"). See Montero Cartelle and Carrera de la Red, "El *Dictionarium medicum*," 402.

68. Pines, "Les médecins marranes," 549–50.

69. See quotations in Nuyts, *Jean Steelsius*, 24–25.

70. Montero Cartelle and Carrera de la Red, "El *Dictionarium medicum*," 403.

71. "Secondary entries" are Castilian categories included as subheadings after the definition of a primary entry; they do not begin on a new line of text. Thus the primary category of **Autor que primero inuenta alguna cosa** is followed by a Latin equivalent, which is then followed on the same line by **Cosa que tiene autoridad**, that category's Latin equivalent, then **Autores ruynes**, that category's Latin equivalent, and finally **Autores principales** and its Latin equivalent. In many cases, categories already included in earlier editions of the *Dictionarium* are, in the 1553 printing, followed by new secondary terms (such as the new categories of **Ordeñador de las cabras** and **Cosa que tiene pies de cabras** added to the existing primary category of **Cabruno, cosa deste linaje.**

72. Note that the 1553 and 1560 printings also share the same page-entry layouts (the 1570 Antwerp printing, in contrast, uses a different layout, a layout then copied in the 1574 Antequera printing, discussed later in this chapter).

73. For spelling variations that link the 1560 and 1570 printings in contrast to their predecessors, see the examples given in notes 74, 75, and 79 in this chapter. Finally, at least one alphabetization glitch was corrected in the 1570 printing: the entry for **Guarda, en lugar de otro** was placed before **Guarda, la persona que guarda**, correcting a minor misalphabetization present ever since **Guarda, en lugar de otro** was added as a category in 1553.

74. Thus **Cassadora cosa para cassar la ley** (1553, 1567, 1572) versus **Cassadora cosa para cassa la ley** (1560, 1570); **Echar de si rayos de luz** (1553, 1567, 1572) versus **Echar de si rayz de luz** (1560, 1570); **Mirar ala vislumbre** (1553, 1567, 1572) versus **Mirar ala vislombre** (1560, 1570); **Mouer debaxo arriba, o Mouer a lexos** (1553, 1567, 1572) versus **Mouer debaxa arriba, o Mouer a lexos** (1560, 1570); **Ochauada cosa** (1553, 1567, 1572) versus **Ochaua cosa** (1560, 1570); **Puerco montes de mil libras** (1553, 1567, 1572) versus **Puerco montes de mill libras** (1560, 1570); **Resina no cuajada** (1553, 1567, 1572) versus **Resina no cujada** (1560, 1570); **Seno o golfo de mar** (1553, 1567, 1572) versus **Sino o golfo de mar** (1560, 1570).

75. Spelling variations shared by the 1567 and 1572 printings, in contrast to the 1553

and 1560 printings (and usually the 1570 printing as well), include **Afeytada cosa assi** (1567, 1572) versus **Afeitada cosa assi** (1553, 1560, 1570); **Bañador, y Bañadora** (1567, 1572) versus **Bañedor, y Bañedora** (1553, 1560) and **Bañador, y Bañedora** (1570); **Empulgueras de arco o ballesta** (1567, 1572) versus **Empulgueras del arco o ballesta** (1553, 1560) and **Empulguera del arco o ballesta** (1570); and **Lamina de plomo para escreuir** (1567, 1570, 1572) versus **Lamina de plomo para escriuir** (1553, 1560). The 1553 Antwerp and 1567 and 1572 Granada printings also place the initial entries in the *Z* section in correct order: **Zamarilla yerua** followed by **Zangano de colmena**. In contrast, the 1560 Antwerp printing places **Zagano** (with only one *n*) **de Colmena** first, followed by **Zamarilla**; the **Zagano** spelling is maintained in 1570.

76. On Antonio's publishing career in Antequera, see Leiva Soto, "La imprenta de Antequera," 30–34.

77. Spelling variations showing that the 1570 Antwerp printing was the source for the 1574 Antequera printing (in contrast to the Antwerp printings of 1553 and 1560 and the Granada printings of 1567 and 1572) include **Desañuda** (1570, 1574) versus **Desañudar** (1545-Antwerp, 1553, 1560, 1567, 1572); **Habla abbreuiada** (1570, 1574) versus **Habla abreuiada** (1553, 1560, 1567, 1572); **Hazer, o señalar alguno nouedad** (1570, 1574) versus **Hazer, o señalar alguna nouedad** (1553, 1560, 1567, 1572); **Hilazas de lienço** (1570, 1574, 1578, 1581, 1585) versus **Hilazas del lienço** (1553, 1560, 1567, 1572); **Traspalar con palo instrumento** (1570, 1574, 1581) versus **Traspalar con pala instrumento** (1553, 1560, 1567, 1572); **Vesso de qualquiera fruta** (1570, 1574, 1578, 1581, 1585) versus **Vuesso de qualquiera fruta** (1553, 1560, 1567, 1572). In addition, the 1570 and 1574 printings place **Guarda, en lugar de otro** before **Guarda, la persona que guarda**, in correct alphabetical order and in contrast to their reversed placement in the printings of 1553, 1560, 1567, and 1572.

78. The "Heirs of Juan de Canova" was specifically his widow, Juana de Vergara, who is known to have been printing books until 1578. See Mano González, *Mercaderes e impresores,* 56; Díez Ménguez, "Tesoros"; Reyes and Nadales, "The Book in Segovia," 355.

79. As mentioned earlier, **Zangano de colmena** had been placed before **Zamarilla yerua** in the Antwerp printing of 1560 (an order carried on to the printings of 1570, 1574, 1578, in contrast to the correct alphabetical order in the printings of 1553, 1567, 1572). Spelling variations that connect the 1578 printing to the 1570 and 1574 printings (and separate it from earlier Antwerp printings as well as the 1567–1572 Granada series) include **Cauallo de alquilar** (1570, 1574, 1578, 1581, 1585) versus **Cauallo de alquiler** (1553, 1560, 1572); **Despoluerizar quebrando** (1570, 1574, 1578, 1581, 1585) versus **Despoluorizar quebrando** (1553, 1560, 1572); **Hilazas de lienço** (1570, 1574, 1578, 1581, 1585) versus **Hilazas del lienço** (1553, 1560, 1567, 1572); **Vesso de qualquiera fruta** (1570, 1574, 1578, 1581, 1585) versus **Vuesso de qualquiera fruta** (1553, 1560, 1567, 1572).

80. Spelling variations that link the 1578 printing to the 1545-Antwerp–1553–1560–1572 series in contrast to the 1570–1574–1581 series include **Azedura desta manera**

(1545-Antwerp, 1553, 1560, 1572, 1578) versus **Azedera desta manera** (1570, 1574, 1581); **Desañudar** (1545-Antwerp, 1553, 1560, 1572, 1578, 1581) versus **Desañuda** (1570, 1574); **Destriur ermando** (1545-Antwerp, 1553, 1560, 1572, 1578) versus **Destruir armando** (1570, 1574, 1581); **Hazer, o señalar alguna nouedad** (1553, 1560, 1572, 1578, 1581) versus **Hazer, o señalar alguno nouedad** (1570, 1574); **Intractable cosa y desamorada** (1553, 1560, 1572, 1578, 1581) versus **Intrastable cosa y desamorada** (1570, 1574); **Traspalar con pala instrumento** (1553, 1560, 1572, 1578) versus **Traspalar con palo instrumento** (1570, 1574, 1581). Spelling variations that further separate the 1553, 1572, and 1578 printings from the Antwerp printings of 1560 and 1570 include **Manpesada** (1553, 1572, 1578, 1581) versus **Mampesada** (1545-Antwerp, 1560, 1570, 1574); **Resina no cuajada** (1553, 1572, 1578) versus **Resina no cujada** (1560, 1570) and **Resina no quajada** (1574, 1581). Narrowing the field of source candidates one step further are two details connecting the 1578 printing to the 1553 printing in particular, and not to the 1572 printing (or the 1574 printing for that matter): **Aldea o hiez, de colmena** (1545-Antwerp, 1553, 1560, 1570, 1578) versus **Aldea o hez de colmena** (1572, 1574, 1581); **Curar al enfermo** (1545-Antwerp, 1553, 1560, 1578) versus **Curar el enfermo** (1570, 1574, 1581) and **Curar enfermo** (1572).

81. Spelling variations indicating that the 1574 printing was used as a source for the 1581 printing, in contrast to the 1578 (and 1585) printings, include **Azedera desta manera** (1574, 1581) versus **Azedura desta manera** (1578, 1585); **Chiriar la golondrina** (1574, 1581) versus **Chiar la golondrina** (1578, 1585); **Destruyr armando** (1574, 1581) versus **Destriur ermando** (1578, 1585); **Resina no quajada** (1574, 1581) versus **Resina no cuajada** (1578, 1585); **Primera cosa engendrada** (1574, 1581) versus **Primero cosa engendrada** (1578, 1585). See also note 80 in this chapter.

82. On Antonio's publishing career in Granada, see Leiva Soto, "La imprenta de Antequera," 33–34.

83. On the relationship between the 1578 and 1585 printings, in contrast to the 1574 and 1581 printings, see note 81 in this chapter.

84. "Van añadidos en nuestra vltima impression pocos vocablos, porque en el primero del Latin se añidieron muchos." For the entries added to the 1585 Granada printing, see appendix A, section 9. Oddly—probably because of simple typesetting errors—three Castilian entries which had been part of the Antwerp–Granada dictionary lineage for decades were left out of the 1585 version: **Cassador, y aniquilador de la ley; Corregida de afeytes;** and **Vino que se puede detener.**

85. In the 1585 printing, this new section is titled "Compendio de algvnos vocablos arabigos introdvzidos en la le[n]gua Castellana en alguna manera corruptos, de que co[m]munmente vsamos, puestos por orden alphabetico: recopilados por el Illustre señor Francisco Lopez Tamarid Racionero de la sancta yglesia de Granada, familiar, y Interprete de la lengua Arabiga en el sancto Officio. Visto por el Licenciado Alonso de Castillo Interpretes de su Magestad." [Compendium of some Arabic words introduced into the Castilian language in a somewhat corrupt manner, which we commonly use, placed in alphabetic order: compiled by the Illustrious Señor Francisco López Tamarid, Lesser Prebend of the holy church of

Granada, familiar [of the Inquisition] and interpreter of the Arabic language in the Holy Office [of the Inquisition.] Reviewed by the Licentiate Alonso de Castillo, interpreter for his Majesty.] López Tamarid was a Christian of Muslim ancestry (Morisco), and in the late 1580s and 1590s would be deeply involved in controversies over the (forged) "Lead Books" and other Arabic-Christian relics "discovered" in and around Granada (García-Arenal, "The Religious Identity").

86. On Agustín, see Leiva Soto, "La imprenta de Antequera," 33–35. By the time the last of Antonio de Nebrija's editions was published, in 1589, his grandfather's Castilian–Latin dictionary had at least one competitor: Alfonso Sánchez de la Ballesta's *Dictionario de vocablos castellanos aplicados a la propiedad latina*, published in Salamanca in 1587. Another, long-lived competitor arrived a decade later: Bartolomé Bravo's *Thesaurus verborum* (first edition Zaragoza, 1597).

87. The slow morphing of the 1589 version into the 1595 version, and of the 1595 version into the 1600 version, can be seen in the shifting *-ue* to *-be* endings for **Xaraue:** **Xaraue de medicina - Xaraue para vomitar** (1589); **Xarabe de medicina - Xaraue para vomitar** (1595); **Xarabe de medicina - Xarabe para vomitar** (1600, 1610). Spelling changes introduced in 1595 and maintained in subsequent printings include **Cadaño** (1589) versus **Cada año** (1595, 1600, 1610); **Cada ruin** (1589) versus **Cada ruyn** (1595, 1600, 1610); **Caer en tierra moriendo** (1589) versus **Caer en tierra muriendo** (1595, 1600, 1610); **Calador de cirurgiano** (1589) versus **Calador de cirujano** (1595, 1600, 1610); **Calauerna de cabeça** (1589) versus **Calauerna, o calauera de cabeça** (1595, 1600, 1610); **Maciça, hazer maciço** (1589) versus **Maciza, hazer maciço** (1595, 1600, 1610).

88. On the 1602 contract, and for information on Alonso Rodríguez Gamarra in general, see Leiva Soto, "La imprenta de Antequera," 35–36.

89. "consentimiento de don Augustin antonio de Nebrissa para esta impression."

90. Smith-Stark, "Lexicography," 11–18; see also Considine, *Dictionaries*, 27–30.

2. Arabic, Nahuatl, Tuscan, Tagalog . . .

1. Esparza Torres and Niederhe, *Bibliografía Nebrisense*, 63, 94. Pedro de Arenas's 1611 *Vocabulario manual de las lenguas castellana y mexicana* is not included because its entries (organized by topic: ways of counting, religious phrases, kinship terms) are not based on Nebrija (Arenas, *Vocabulario*; Brain, "Aprendizaje," 293–95); also excluded is Luys de Valdivia's non-Nebrijan 1607 *Vocabvlario breve en lengva millcayac*. Considine (*Dictionaries*, 91) mentions the commissioning of a Spanish–Latin–Czech dictionary by Juan Borja y Castro, the Spanish ambassador in late sixteenth-century Prague—but his source for this (Chuboda, *Spain*, 160) actually describes a Latin–Spanish–Czech dictionary. Chuboda's en-masse blocs of references at the end of the book don't clarify where he read about this project, and I haven't been able to track down a copy (for example, in Wilkinson, *Iberian Books*), if indeed such a three-way dictionary ever existed.

2. Bolles, "The Mayan," 61; Smith-Stark, "Lexicography," 20–21.

3. Previous scholarship on the influence of Nebrija on subsequent dictionaries in both the Old World (Steiner, *Two Centuries*, 17–35; Guerrero Ramos, "La lexicografía"; Nieto Jiménez, "Coincidencias") and the New (Moreno Fernández, "Antonio de Nebrija," 92–102; Galeote, "Guardianes," 140, 142; Galeote, "El primer vocabulario," 544; Hernández, "El vocabulario náhuatl"; Hernández, "En torno al diccionario," 1791; Hernández, "Influencias," 68; Hernández, "La lexicografía," 198; Karttunen, "The Roots"; Laughlin, *The Great Tzotzil Dictionary*, 11–17; Lope Blanch, "La lexicografía," 555–58; Romero Rangel, "La originalidad," 141–42; Smith-Stark, "El 'primer Nebrija indiano,'" 534; Smith-Stark, "Lexicography"; Torero, "Entre Roma y Lima," 280–84) has focused comparisons on the entry lists of the 1495 and (one of the) 1516 printings of Nebrija—both of which were reissued in the twentieth century. These two versions, however, were seldom the models for spinoff dictionary production in either the Americas or in Europe (but see Clayton, "A Trilingual"; Clayton, "Evidence"; and Tellez Nieto, *Vocabulario*, 161). Karttunen ("The Roots") does make reference to the 1560 Antwerp printing of Nebrija, but her statistical analyses focus on the 1516 printing (hence confusion about the shared appearance of entries for **Queso** in Molina 1555 and Nebrija 1560). Prior statistical comparisons of the entry lists in New World dictionaries with the entry lists in Nebrija (1495 and 1516) are therefore flawed, being based on the wrong source editions.

4. Studies of Alcalá's *Arte* include Drost, "El Arte"; Pezzi Martínez, *El vocabulario*; Peñalver Castillo and González Aranda, "Pedro de Alcalá"; Framiñán de Miguel, "Manuales"; Smith-Stark, "Lexicography," 7.

5. "vna de las copilaciones que ay de vocablos para la trasladar en arauigo . . . que hizo el honrrado y prudente varon maestro antonio de lebrixa. ala qual yo añadi algunos nonbres y verbo[s] y otras partes de la oracion que me ocurrieron. y dexe algunas de las que alli estaua[n] que carecian de traslacio[n] arauiga."

6. "esta obra y vocabulista de romance en arauigo." Drost ("El Arte") argues that the delay between composition and publication can be explained by the fact that the city of Granada did not have a printer in residence until late 1504. Note that the spellings of terms in Alcalá do not always match the spellings of Nebrija 1495, instead paralleling orthographies used in the 1503 or 1506 Seville printings. These latter parallels, however, must be due to broader Andalusian spelling traditions, as opposed to direct copying from the Seville publications (which appeared after Alcalá says he finished his book project in 1501). Spellings shared by Alcalá with the 1495 printing of Nebrija include **Azeituna** (1495, 1505) versus **Azeytuna** (1503); **Azeite** (1495, 1505) versus **Azeyte** (1503); **Cada ruin** (1495, 1505) versus **Cada ruyn** (1503). Spellings in Alacalá that parallel those of the 1503 Seville printing of Nebrija include **Ueuo guero** (1503, 1505) versus **Uevo guero** (1495); **Xalon rio de calatayud** (1503, 1505) versus **Xalon rio de calataiud** (1495); **Xatiua cibdad de aragon** (1503, 1505) versus **Xativa ciudad de aragon** (1495); **Xabonera yerua** (1503, 1505) versus **Xabonera ierva** (1495); **Xenabe o mostaza** (1503, 1505) versus **Xenabe o mostaça** (1495).

7. Percyvall's 1591 Castilian–English–Latin dictionary translates *zarzahan* as "a kinde of cloth which the mores make."

8. Studies of the Newberry manuscript include Clayton, "A Trilingual"; Clayton, "Evidence"; Karttunen, "The Roots," 78–80; Hernández, "La lexicografía," 196–97; Tellez Nieto, *Vocabulario.*

9. Clayton ("A Trilingual," 396–99) argues that the current manuscript is a clean copy of a text compiled earlier. It is quite possible—given the glossed printed dictionaries discussed in chapter 4—that this source was a printed copy of Nebrija with Nahuatl translations added in the margins. In any case, an examination of the spacing in the Newberry manuscript strongly suggests that all the black entries were made first; in many cases the red Nahuatl entries have been squeezed into a narrower-than-ideal space (see fig. 4.5).

10. Tellez Nieto provides an overview of prior suggestions for the dating of this text; her own analysis argues that work on it began in the 1540s and was completed by 1555 (*Vocabulario*, 20–21, 195).

11. Clayton, "Evidence," 109–10, 101, 104.

12. Clayton, "A Trilingual," 393; Clayton, "Evidence," 117n2. The usefulness of MacDonald's edition is limited for a number of reasons. He does not indicate what book from which library was used as a model for his "critical edition"—a major problem given that there are two distinct versions of the "1516" *Dictionarium.* He also chose to regularize spelling variations in the text, which makes his edition basically unusable (as well as actually misleading—see comments on the entry for **Barreña** in note 50 in this chapter) for close textual analysis. For other evaluations of MacDonald's much-cited edition, see Ricciardelli, "Review," 410; see also Smith-Stark, "Lexicography," 16. Historiographically speaking, MacDonald was editing according to a "critical edition" model of textual scholarship, in which early modern uses of spelling and typography, as well as variations between one textual edition and another, were homogenized and regularized according to twentieth-century standards and assumptions. This problematic model of edition was overturned in the early 1980s; see manifestos in McGann, *A Critique;* McKenzie, *Bibliography.*

13. Tellez Nieto, *Vocabulario*, 161.

14. I have double-checked these spellings against copies of the original 1516 printing at the Universidad Complutense (Res.270(1)), the Hispanic Society of America, and the British Library (C.63.c.14), as well as against a copy of the pirated "1516" (that is, circa 1520) printing at the Universidad Complutense (FOA 158).

15. Remember that my study refers to different "printings" of dictionaries, in order to avoid the confusing and not very accurate references to "editions" of Nebrija by previous scholars (as discussed in the introduction, note 5). I bring this up again because unclear references to "first" and "second" editions of the *Dictionarium* are extremely common in discussions of MacDonald's 1973 publication and its use as a model for studies of the entries in the Newberry manuscript.

16. Tellez Nieto (*Vocabulario*, 175–77) also points out that the spacing, and spelling, of the Newberry manuscript's title, ("Dictionarium ex hisniensi in lati= | num sermonem. interprete Aelio | Antonio Neprissensi. Lege foeliciter") is different from the

three-line title that heads begins the list of *A* entries of the published versions (as it happens, both legitimate and pirated copies share the same title spacing: "Dictionariu[m] ex hispanie[n]si in latinu[m] ser= | monem. interprete Aelio Antonio Ne= | brissensi. Lege foeliciter." Note also that, as mentioned in chapter 1, both "1516" volumes also have separate title-only opening pages, which differ slightly from each other in their layout and spelling. But after reviewing a half-dozen surviving copies of the two "1516" printings of the *Dictionarium* (and not finding any variations in their short-format printed title at the start of the *A* entries), my interpretation of this difference is that the Nahua scribe (who was also expanding the abbreviations of Nebrija's original title) chose to insert his own spacing divisions, thinking ahead to his manuscript's two-column format. The spelling variation of *Neprissensi* as opposed to *Nebrissensi* probably relates to the unconscious influence of Nahuatl phonology (see Tellez Nieto, *Vocabulario*, 155).

17. A facsimile version with supporting material prepared by Thelma Sullivan was finally published in 1985, with René Acuña as editor (Olmos, *Arte*); more recent studies include Hernández, "Influencias"; Hernández, "La lexicografía," 197; Dakin, "The Organization"; and Dakin, "El *Vocabulario*."

18. Dakin, "The Organization"; Dakin notes that her ideas were developed in conversation with Mercedes Montes de Oca.

19. Hernández, "Influencias," 1792.

20. All of this means that Hernández's claim that the "parte castellano-náhuatl no tiene en absoluto deuda con el *Vocabulario* de Nebrija" [the Castilian–Nahuatl part has absolutely no debt to the *Vocabulary* of Nebrija] ("Influencias," 1791) needs to be revised.

21. For studies of the 1555 printing of Molina, see Clayton and Campbell, "Alonso de Molina"; Galeote, "El *Vocabulario*"; Galeote, "Estudio preliminar"; Galeote, "Originalidad"; Galeote, "Guardianes"; Galeote, "El primer vocabulario"; Hernández de León-Portilla, "Hernando de Ribas"; Hernández de León-Portilla, *Obras*; Lockhart, "Sightings," 224–26; Karttunen, "The Roots," 81–82; and López Bernasocchi and Galeote, *Tesoro castellano*. Bibliography on the 1571 printing of Molina is cited in notes 36–38 in this chapter.

22. Laughlin, *The Great Tzotzil Dictionary*, 9–19; Karttunen, "The Roots," 81–82; Hernández, "El vocabulario náhuatl"; Clayton and Campbell, "Alonso de Molina," 338–41, 360–63; Hernández, "Influencias."

23. The 1555 version of Molina does contain two of the 114 terms added to the Antwerp printing of 1545—**Agua rosada**, 'rosewater,' and **Agua miel**, 'honeywater.' But since none of the other 1545 terms appear in the 1555 *Vocabulario*, and given that the 1555 text also adds dozens of other **Agua** categories to the base list of water terms from Nebrija, it is most likely that the entries **Agua rosada** and **Agua miel** were independently added by Molina and his colleagues, rather than being copied from an Antwerp-series printing. Furthermore, the structure of Molina's entries, as discussed in the next paragraph, shows key divergences from the Granada printing of 1540—the version that was used as the model for the Antwerp series.

24. See the brief reference in Smith-Stark, "Lexicography," 71–72; eight pages from this copy have been reproduced in René Acuña's edition of Alonso Urbano's *Arte breve de la lengua otomí y vocabulario trilingüe* (xxxiii–xl).

25. See Schuller, "An Unknown"; as well as the brief reference in Smith-Stark, "Lexicography," 73, which mentions the manuscript's previous home, the Museum of the American Indian Library in New York City. Two pages from the volume can be seen as part of Cornell's *Vanished Worlds, Enduring People* online exhibit at http://nac.library.cornell.edu/exhibition/language/language_3.html; others are reproduced in Schuller, "An Unknown." My thanks to Doris Bartholomew, Yolanda Lastra, and Etna T. Pascacio for helping me track down this volume's present location, which is the subject of Pasacio's forthcoming doctoral dissertation at the Instituto de Estudios Mesoamericanos, Universidad Nacional Autónoma de México, Mexico City. See also the forthcoming study edited by Lastra, Pasacio, and Leopoldo Valiñas (*Vocabulario castellano-matlatzinca de Fray Andrés de Castro*).

26. See Karttunen, "The Roots," 82–83; Acero Durántez, "En los comienzos"; Acero Durántez, "Una aportación"; Monzon, "The Tarascan"; Hernández, "La lexicografía," 199–200.

27. These dropped entries include **Alcançar a alguno de cuenta entendiendo sus propositos o yntincion, Auisar a alguno con piedad para que biua como a de biuir porque no le suceda algun mal**, and **Çahareño. busca esquiuo.**

28. On Juan Pablos, see López Bernasocchi and Galeote, *Tesoro castellano*, 15–18.

29. See brief references in Schuller, "An Unknown," 191–94; and Smith-Stark, "Lexicography," 72.

30. See Porras Barrenechea, prologue to *Léxicon vocabulario*; MacCormack, "Ubi Ecclesia?," 90–92; Moreno Fernández, "Antonio de Nebrija"; Torero, "Entre Roma y Lima"; Hernández, "La lexicografía," 200; and Dedenbach-Salazar Sáenz, "Dictionaries," 236–37.

31. "este vocabulario va por el mismo orden que el del Antonio de Nebrissa por el alphabeto" (Santo Tomás, *Lexicon*, v verso).

32. On these untranslated Castilian categories, see Torero, "Entre Roma y Lima," 284.

33. For a discussion of Andean-specific entries, see ibid., 283–84. The use of *oueja* ('sheep') in the entry on bloodletting indicates that the word's meaning was extended to cover the native camelid species of the Andes; earlier in the dictionary **Oueja, animal conoscido** is translated as "llama, o paco [alpaca], o guaca, o guanaco, o vicuña."

34. Thus the Sevillan 1570 and 1583 printings run **Traghiotire - Traguggiare - Traghiottire - Tranguggiare**; whereas the Venetian 1576, 1582, and 1587 printings use the double-*t* spelling of **Traghiottire** twice: **Traghiottire - Traguggiare - Traghiottire - Tranguggiare**. Spelling irregularities in the 1583 Seville printing make it clear this version was not used as a model for later Venetian publications: thus **Xarcias** (1570, 1576, 1582, 1587, 1591) versus **Xarcia** (1583) and **Virtud** (1570, 1576, 1582, 1587, 1591) versus **Virtu** (1583).

35. The expanded *Z* entries in 1582 and their reuse in the 1587 and 1591 printings,

discussed earlier in this chapter, make clear the connection of those three editions. The expanded X entries of 1591 were, in turn, carried over to 1597. Spelling variations between the 1591 and 1597 printings make clear that the 1597 printing was used for all subsequent printings. Thus Torçal (1591) versus Torcial (1597, 1600, 1604, 1608); Traylla (1591) versus Trayla (1597, 1600, 1604, 1608); and Trauezon (1591) versus Trauuezon (1597, 1600, 1604; 1608). Spelling variations shared between the 1597 and 1608 printings, but which contrast with spellings in the 1600 and 1604 printings, make clear that the 1608 printing was based on the 1597 printing, at the same time as they reveal the 1600 printing to be the model for the 1604 printing. Thus Tomba (1597, 1608) versus Tumba (1600, 1604); Axara (1591, 1597, 1608) versus Xara (1600, 1604) and Zurrator (1591, 1597, 1608) versus Zarrator (1600, 1604). Finally, the 1604 printing contains spelling variations not shared with the 1597, 1600, or 1608 printings. Thus Taluiua (1597, 1600, 1608) versus Taluina (1604), Tromba (1597, 1600, 1608) versus Trompa (1604), and Zebretana (1597, 1600, 1608) versus Zebreana (1604).

36. Karttunen, "The Roots," 83–85; Galeote, "El *Vocabulario*"; Galeote, "Guardianes," 147–50; Clayton and Campbell, "Alonso de Molina."

37. Clayton and Campbell, "Alonso de Molina," 338; see also entry estimates by Smith-Stark, "El 'primer Nebrija indiano,'" 534–35 (citing prior statistical work by Hernández de León-Portilla and Joseph Campbell).

38. Karttunen, "The Roots," 85; for a general discussion of differences between the two printings see Clayton and Campbell, "Alonso de Molina," 379–80, 386–89.

39. See Smith-Stark, "Lexicography," 71; Hernández, "La lexicografía," 202; Hernández, "Vocabularios," 141–42.

40. Thus Alonso's manuscript includes an entry for Maiz desgranado, an entry absent from Molina's 1555 *Vocabulario* but added to the 1571 printing. A similar expansion and transformation involves entries for *coa* ('digging stick'). Molina's 1555 listing of Coa para cauar la tierra, followed by Cobarde persona, became in 1571 Coa o pala para cauar o deseruar - Coa de hierro - Cobarde persona. In turn, the 1571 transformation was copied by Alonso: Coa o pala p[ar]a cauar o deseruar - Coa de hierro - Cobarde persona.

41. Hernández, "Vocabularios," 141–42.

42. Jackson, "Continuity and Change," 688–90. The Tzeltal vocabulary contains a number of entries and spelling variations found in Molina's 1571 *Vocabulario* but not in the 1555 version, such as Llama de fuego (Molina 1571 and Ara) versus Llama de huego (Molina 1555); the entry series of Mensajero - Mensajero hazer - Mensaje (Molina 1571) and Mensagero - Mensajero haçer - Mensaje (Ara) versus Mensajero - Mensaje (Molina 1555), the entry Zangotear el cuero o basija q[uan]-do no esta lleno (present in Ara and Molina 1571 but absent from Molina 1555); and the integration of the entry for Luçiernaga (which, in Molina 1555, appeared in the appendix of additional terms) into the main list of entries, after Luchador and before Ludir o fregar—the same location as its integration in Molina 1571.

43. "Fray Alonso de Guzman traslado este bocabulario el sobre dicho P. el año de 1620

años en la provincia de Tzeldales en el pueblo de Taquin Vitz." [The said Father Friar Alonso de Guzman copied this vocabulary the year 1620 in the Province of the Tzeltales in the town of Taquin Vitz.]

44. See the 1918 letter by Adela C. Breton quoted in a typed note at the beginning of the University of Pennsylvania manuscript; digital scan available at www.famsi.org/research/mltdp/item185 (page 4). The letter is also briefly quoted in Ara, *Vocabulario de la lengua tzeldal*, 25.

45. For what is known of Ara's biography, see Ara, *Vocabulario de la lengua tzeldal*, 36–44.

46. See Ara, *Vocabulario de la lengua tzeldal*, 264, 265, 273 (transcription with modernized spelling), as well as the facsimile pages reproduced in the same volume. The category of **Piedra sobre que sacrificaban**, borrowed from Molina into the Tzeltal–Castilian manuscript, appears in the Castilian–Tzeltal manuscript as "**Piedra de sacrif[ici]o. chimbaltó sobre q[ue]**."

47. See Karttunen, "The Roots," 85–86; Smith-Stark, "Mujeres"; Smith-Stark, "Dioses"; Smith-Stark, "Lexicography," 39, 53, 59, 68; Thiemer-Sachse, "El 'Vocabulario'"; Rojas Torres, "La categoría 'adjetivo.'" Thanks to Adam Sellen for sharing with me a copy of Thomas Smith-Stark's text file version of Córdova's vocabulary.

48. Hernández, "La lexicografía," 201; cf. Karttunen, "The Roots," 85.

49. Thus where Molina 1555 has the entry string of **Coa para cauar la tierra - Cobarde persona**, Molina 1571 has **Coa o pala para cauar o deseruar - Coa de hierro - Cobarde persona**, matched by Córdova's **Coa de palo para cauar los Indios - Coa de hierro para lo mismo - Cobarde y cobardia**. Where Molina 1555 has **Echar cacao a una xical a otra para hazer espuma**, Molina 1571 has **Echar cacao de una xical en otra para hazer espuma**, matched by Córdova's **Echar cacao de vna xicara en otra**.

50. Hernández ("Influencias," 68–69) argues that Córdova used both the 1495 and 1516 printings of Nebrija as a source, citing Córdova's inclusion of **Barreña** (which she argues was present in the 1495 printing but absent from the 1516 printing). The "absence" of this term in 1516 is illusory, however; it is present in both "1516" versions printed in the sixteenth century, but left out of Gerald J. MacDonald's "transcripción crítica" of 1973, which is what Hernández uses as a source. Terms added in the 1553 Antwerp expansion, absent in Molina, and present in Córdova include **Fresno arbol** and **Papel de straça** (which appears in Córdova as **Papel de straça o desta tierra**); Córdova also includes **Verenjena**, which was added to the 1545 Antwerp printing.

51. In general see Bolles, "The Mayan"; Hernández, "La lexicografía"; Hernández, "Vocabularios"; Hanks, *Converting Words*; Jackson, "Continuity and Change," 688–90. Another Castilian–Yucatec manuscript dictionary once existed, found by Juan Pío Pérez in the church of Ticul. Dated January 26, 1690, this manuscript was copied and published by Pérez in 1898, but he reordered the entries, a modernization strategy that makes it problematic for the kinds of textual analyses pursued here. See Bolles, "The Mayan," 69–70.

52. Note that the published transcriptions of both the "Bocabulario de maya than" (René Acuña's 1993 edition) and the "Diccionario de San Francisco" (Oscar Michelon's 1976 edition) have revised and transformed the Castilian–Yucatec sections for present-day users, so that in both cases these editions depart significantly from their manuscript sources. The transcription of the "Bocabulario" reorders entries to conform with contemporary assumptions about alphabetization (fortunately, however, photographs of the original manuscript are also included in Acuña's edition, as well as in Ernst Mengin's 1972 edition, which includes only photographed pages). The Castilian–Yucatec section of Michelon's "Diccionario" transcription has been expanded by inserting terms culled from the Yucatec–Castilian section. As discussed in note 12 of this chapter, these editorial transformations were informed by an older, "critical edition" approach to publishing manuscripts and early modern texts.

53. All four dictionaries include entries that were added to Nebrija's dictionary in the 1585 Granada printing (see appendix A, section 9). Most significant is the pair of **Secreta cosa, Secretamente** (in the "Bocabulario," "Diccionario," Solana, and Motul II). Other 1585 additions occur in three of the four manuscripts, variations that are the result of copying omissions in the complex descent chains that connect these manuscripts (as explained in the next few paragraphs of the main text). These include **Papel de marca mayor** (which appears as **Papel de marca** in the "Diccionario," Solana, and Motul II, but is absent from the "Bocabulario") and **Pretender** (which appears as **Pretender ignorancia** in the "Bocabulario," **Pretender algo** in the Solana and Motul II, and is absent from the "Diccionario"). Tellingly, all four manuscripts also contain entries added to the 1578 Antequera printing of Nebrija, which was the immediate source for the 1585 printing: **Boca de calle** (in the "Bocabulario," "Diccionario," Solana, and Motul II); and see also **Asaltos** (in the "Diccionario," Solana, and Motul II, but not the "Bocabulario"). For critiques of the 1580 date for the Solana, see Bolles, "The Mayan," 70–71, 73.

54. On the Solana attribution, see Bolles, "The Mayan," 70–71.

55. The *breton* category in Nebrija is **Breton de berça**; Molina's **Breton de col** appears in all four Castilian–Yucatec dictionaries. Molina's **Adular, busca lisongear** appears as **Adular o linsojear** in the "Bocabulario," as **Adular, o lisongear** in the Solana, as **Adular, vide lisogear** in the Motul II, and simply **Adular** in the "Diccionario." (No **Adular** lead entry appears in the Nebrijan Castilian–Latin dictionaries). Molina's **Bruñir lo encalado** appears as **Bruñir lo encalado y otras cosas** in the "Bocabulario," is repeated in the Solana and Motul II, and is shortened to **Bruñir** in the "Diccionario." (The equivalent entry in the Nebrijan Castilian–Latin dictionaries is **Bruñir para que reluza**). On these non-Nebrijan categories shared by Molina and the Solana, see Hernández, "La lexicografía," 116–17.

56. Note the spelling shift from **Maçorca** to **Mazorca** in most "Bocabulario" entries which are not shared by the "Diccionario," Solana, and Motul II, further underscoring how these are added categories not present in YucatecMsA.

57. Most significantly, the "Bocabulario" includes an entry at the very beginning for

Abadejo o bacalao, **pexe del mar**, which is probably adapted from one of the new categories added to the 1585 Granada printing of Nebrija: **Abadejo pescado que llaman Bacallao**. The "Bocabulario" also uniquely incorporates a number of other Nebrijan entries that first appeared in earlier Nebrijan editions, entries then carried forward in all subsequent generations. These include **Armaçon o cama de madera** and **Corona de oro** (added in the 1553 Antwerp printing), **Cama o lecho donde dormimos** (added in the 1513 Salamanca printing), **Cauerna o cueba de piedra** (compare with the Nebrijan **Cauerna de tierra o piedra**, added in the 1513 Salamanca printing), and **Collado de Monte** (compare with the Nebrijan **Collado del Monte**, added in the 1536 Granada printing).

58. These conclusions are different from those of David Bolles ("The Mayan," 61, 73), who proposes that the "Bocabulario de maya than" was created first (1590), then the Solana and the Motul II (1600) and last the "Diccionario de San Francisco" (1680); and of Hernández ("Los vocabularios hispano-mayas," 139–40, "En torno al vocabulario," 115), who suggests that the Solana was the direct source for the Motul II.

59. This transmission pattern explains other shared entries that unite the "Bocabulario," Solana, and Motul II but which skip the "Diccionario," such as **Pretender** (which appears as **Pretender algo** in the Solana and Motul II, as **Pretender ignorancia** in the "Bocabulario," but is absent from the "Diccionario") or the **Adular** and **Bruñir** entries that YucatecMsA copied from Molina's Nahuatl vocabulary (see note 55). Of course, entries that were present in YucatecMsA may have sometimes been left out of the "Bocabulario" copy, which may explain why **Asaltos** (one of several entries the Yucatec vocabularies borrow from the 1578 Antequera printing of Nebrija) is absent from the "Bocabulario," even though it is included in the other three manuscripts (see note 53).

60. Mannheim, "Lexicography," 2682; Dedenbach-Salazar Sáenz, "Dictionaries," 237–38. A copy of the 1586 printing is available at the Biblioteca Digital Hispánica website, http://bdh.bne.es; copies of the 1604 and 1614 printings are available at the Biblioteca Virtual of the Biblioteca Nacional del Perú, http://bvirtual.bnp.gob.pe.

61. The Castilian–Quechua entries also include two terms added to the 1585 printing of Nebrija—**Secretamente** and **Portal**—but these are apparently accidental parallels, since according to its front matter, the 1586 dictionary had been approved for publication on August 12, 1585. The added-in-1578 entries of **Añudar hazer ñudo**, **Bostezar**, and **Charlatan, o cocharrero** are paralleled by **Añudar, dar ñudo**, **Bostezar** and **Charlatan** in the 1586 publication. Of the terms added to the 1553 Antwerp expansion, fifteen have possible parallels in the Lima volume: compare the Nebrijan entries of **Dolorse con otro**, **Hermoso hazer**, **Muladar de estiercol**, **Sacudir con varal**, and **Vayo color** with **Dolerse de otro**, **Hermoso hazerse**, **Muladar**, **Sacudir con vara**, and **Vayo de color**.

62. Spelling corrections include **Yr a riba** and **Xerlinga** in 1586 emended to **Yr arriba** and **Xeringa** in 1603.

63. The layout on the verso of the penultimate folio of the 1614 printing runs from **Xeringa** to **Yerro** in column 1 and **Yerto** to **Yo solo** in column 2, whereas in the 1586

and 1603 printings page layout runs from **Xeringa** to **Yerto** in column 1 and **Yerua** to **Yo solo** in column 2. Diagnostic spelling variations include **trompa de caracol** (1586, 1614) versus **trompeta de caracol** (1604) and **Xabon de los yndios** (1586, 1614) versus **xabó de los indios** (1604). See also Aguilar Páez, *Gramática*, 222–27.

64. Höpfner, "De la vida," 71–74.
65. Smith-Stark, "Lexicography," 71.
66. Steiner, *Two Centuries*, 17–35.
67. Suggestive are terms included in Percyvall but not in Casas, and that have variant spellings in different printings of Nebrija. These include **Manpesada** (Nebrija 1553, 1572, 1578, 1581, and Percyvall 1591) versus **Mampesada** (Nebrija 1545-Antwerp, 1560, 1570, 1574, 1585, 1589); **Arroyarse el rio** (Nebrija 1553, 1574, 1581, and Percyvall 1591) versus **Arrojarse el rio** (Nebrija 1560, 1570, 1572, 1578, 1585, 1589; note that this category is absent altogether from the 1545 Antwerp printing), and **Mastratos** (Nebrija 1553, 1560, 1574, and Percyvall 1591) versus **Mastrates** (Nebrija 1570, 1578, 1581, 1585, 1589) and **Mastrantos** (Nebrija 1572; this is another category absent from the 1545 Antwerp printing). Percyvall also spells *syringe* as **Xiringa** (a category added to the 1553 Antwerp printing). This matches the spelling in the 1553, 1560, 1570, 1572, 1574, and 1581 printings of the *Dictionarium,* and contrasts with the **Xeringa** spelling used both in Casas and in the 1578, 1585, and 1589 printings of the *Dictionarium.* Finally, Percyvall includes none of the Castilian terms added to the 1578 or 1585 printings of Nebrija (repeated in subsequent publications) or in the 1581 printing (which had no progeny).
68. See Smith-Stark, "Lexicography," 31; as well as Karttunen, "The Roots," 86; Hernández, "Influencias," 69; Hernández, "La lexicografía," 203–4.
69. Alvarado and the 1571 printing of Molina both share entries for **Batata** and **Batea**—entries absent from Córdova (and Nebrija as well). Molina (1571) has **Coa o pala para cauar o deseruar** and Alvarado copies the first section (**Coa o pala para cauar**); in contrast Córdova has **Coa de palo para cauar los Indios.** Molina follows **Mandragula** with **Manera de vestidura o faldriquera,** mirrored by Alvarado's **Mandragora** and **Manera de vestidura faldiquera** (terms absent in Córdova and present in Nebrija as **Mandragula yerua** and **Manera de vestidura**).
70. Karttunen ("The Roots," 86) first pointed out Alvarado's probable debt to Córdova (although citing a different example). Both Córdova and Alvarado share parallel entries for the traditional ball game known as *batey* (**Batey juego de pelota d[e]los yndios el lugar** and **bate o juego de pelota, el lugar que solian tener los yndios**), a category absent from Molina (and Nebrija). Córdova and Alvarado also share categories for types of maize not present in either the 1555 or 1571 printings of Molina: **Maiz cadañero, Maiz tostado.**
71. The following complex entries are shared by Alvarado and the 1553 Antwerp printing of Nebrija (and thus all later printings as well), but are not found in Córdova (or in Molina either, for that matter): **Alexarse de algun lugar, Azul escuro, Balança para pesar, Bonança en la mar, Hallar lo perdido, Meter en el coraçon, Mocos limpiar, Muger soltera.**

72. Or at least no 1578/1585 *Dictionarium* terms not also already included (as category additions independent from a Nebrijan source) in either Córdova (**Bostezar, Secretamente**) or Molina (**De tarde en tarde**).

73. **Manta que suelen traer los principales que parece cuero de tigre**; on Alvarado's fascinating categories for slavery, see Hamann, "Inquisitions," 166–67.

74. For a general description see Steiner, *Two Centuries*, 38–51.

75. Entries not included in Percyvall but added to Minsheu from the 1591 printing of Casas include **Argulloso** (contrast with the 1597 **Arguilloso**), **Baraza** (contrast with the 1597 **Baraz**), **Cursar** (contrast with the 1597 **Cusar**), and **Sortija** (contrast with the 1597 **Sorrija**).

76. Steiner, *Two Centuries*, 39–40.

77. For the English–Castilian section, Minsheu also borrowed entries from John Rider's English–Latin *Bibliotheca Scholastica: A Double Dictionarie* (probably the original 1589 printing; see Steiner, *Two Centuries*, 49).

78. A published version is available: Warren, *Diccionario grande*.

79. On these irregularities, see Laughlin, *The Great Tzotzil Dictionary*, 30; see also his general discussion of manuscript interrelationships on 28–33.

80. Cooper, "El Recueil," 300; Guerrero Ramos, "La lexicografía," 468–70.

81. Consider three Castilian categories shared by Nebrija, Minsheu, and Pallet: **Abadexo**, **Xaral**, and **Xarcia**. **Abadexo** is translated by Pallet into French as "merlus," "poisson," and "mouche cantaride." *Mouche cantaride* does not appear as a leading French entry in either Hornkens or Pallet. Hornkens does have a French leading entry for **Merlus ou stocfiz**, which is translated into Spanish as "merluza seca especie de cecial." Pallet's corresponding entry is **Merlus, poisson**, translated into Spanish first as "merluza" (after Hornkens) and then as "abadexo" (a term probably culled from Minsheu). That is, although the Spanish category of *merluza* is present in Hornkens, the category *abadexo* is not. The presence of "abadexo" as the second translation for **Merlus, poisson** in the French–Castilian section of Pallet suggests the category of *abadexo* was copied first into the Castilian–French section, and then added (cross-reference fashion) to an existing French–Castilian category (*merluza*) borrowed from Hornkens. Pallet's Castilian–French entry for **Xaral** is translated as "lieu plein de tel bois"—a long French phrase not found in either Hornkens or in the French–Castilian section of Pallet. **Xaral**, then, seems to have been imported directly from Minsheu, but never added as a cross-reference in the French–Castilian section of the *Diccionario*. As a third example, **Xarcia** is translated by Pallet into French as "corde de nauire" and "amarre." Hornkens—but not Pallet—does have a leading French entry for **Cordaille de nauire**, translated into Castilian as "Mura, osta, scota, triça" (but not *xaral*). Hornkens also has a category for **Amarres**, translated into Castilian as "maromas, cables." Curiously, one line earlier Hornkens translates the French word **Amarrage** into Castilian as "xarcia de naue." Nevertheless, **Amarrage** is not copied as a leading French entry by Pallet. Instead, Pallet uses the leading entry **Amarre de nauire**, which he translates into Castilian (following Hornkens, although with some orthographic errors) as

"maroma" and "cabre." In sum, although the term *xarcia* does appear in Hornkens, it (and the accompanying French entry) are themselves not copied by Pallet. The presence of *xarcia* in the Castilian–French section of Pallet, but not in the French–Castilian section, suggests that this entry was copied into the Castilian–French section directly from Minsheu, but—like *xaral*—never cross-reference-copied into Pallet's French–Castilian section. Analyzing the categories of **Viuienda** and **Xara**—which I argue Pallet copied from Minsheu, who in turn copied them from a 1591 printing of Casas—produces similar results. Pallet translates **Viuienda** into French as "nourriture." In Pallet's French–Castilian section, **Nourriture** is translated as "Cria, criança, mantenimiento, viuienda." Turning to Pallet, we find **Nourriture** translated only as "mantenimiento." All this suggests that Hornkens was not Pallet's source for the entry term **Viuineda**. Instead, I argue, Pallet copied **Viuienda** from Minsheu into the Castilian–French section of his dictionary, decided on "nourriture" as a translation, and then added "viuienda" to the list of translations given for **Nourriture** in the French–Castilian section of his *Diccionario*. A much less complicated story is told by the term *xara*. Pallet translates **Xara** into French as "bois, d'oic l'on fait les dards"; however, this long French phrase has no parallel either in Pallet or in Hornkens. This strongly suggests that the entry **Xara** was copied by Pallet directly from Minsheu, but never reversed for cross-referenced integration into the French–Castilian section. This is quite a lengthy note, but it shows just how complicated—but not impossible—it is to trace the sources for Pallet's Castilian categories.

82. As we saw earlier, pre-1585 printings of Nebrija's *Dictionarium* spelled this entry **Xarafe** or **Xarabe**. The spelling was briefly changed to **Xaraue** in the 1585 and 1589 Granada printings, and slowly changed into **Xarabe** in the Antequera printings of 1595 and 1600. Pallet translates **Xaraue** as the French "syrop." **Syrop**, in turn, was one of the lead categories in Hornkens, but translated as "arrope." The appearance of **Xaraue** in Pallet is not due to Hornkens—and I also argue in the main text that Pallet's translation spellings of "jaraue, xarope" are indebted first and foremost to Minsheu.

83. Bibliothèque Nationale de France, Département des manuscrits, Manuscrit Américain 8. Evidence for the use of Molina 1555 as a source is presented in Karttunen, "The Roots," 86–87; see also Lastra, "El vocabulario."

84. For his French–Castilian section, Oudin also drew on the French-to-Castilian-and-Latin *Recveil de dictionnaires francoys, espagnolz et latins* of Heinrich Hornkens (1599); on this, and on Oudin more generally, see Cooper, "El Recueil"; Guerrero Ramos, "La lexicografía," 470–71; Zuili, *César et Antoine Oudin*; Zuili, "César Oudin."

85. Spelling variations in terms taken by Oudin from Pallet (terms not present in Minsheu) make it clear that the 1604 printing was Oudin's source. Thus **Abouedado** (Pallet 1604, Oudin) versus **Abobedado** (Pallet 1606); **Acarilar** (Pallet 1604, Oudin) versus **Acarillar** (Pallet 1606); **Acuerdar** (Pallet 1604, Oudin) versus **Acordar** (Pallet 1606). See also the more general discussion of differences between the 1604 and 1606 printings of Pallet in Cooper, "El Recueil," 300–301. Zuili ("César

Oudin," 280) suggests that Casas may be one of the direct sources for Oudin, but (for example) many of the *Z* entries included in Oudin are not found in any of the Casas printings. The parallels between entries in Casas and Oudin are due, as we have seen, to the use of Casas as a direct source by Minsheu as well as the use of Casas (in an earlier printing) by Minsheu's model Percyvall.

86. Oudin also published a reorganized version of the *Tesoro* in Paris in 1621, and a reissue of the 1616 version in Brussels in 1625 (Zulli, "César Oudin").

87. Mannheim, "Lexicography," 2682–83; Dedenbach-Salazar Sáenz, "Dictionaries," 238–39; Hernández, "La lexicografía," 202–3.

88. Thus **trompeta de caracol** (1604, 1608) versus **trompa de caracol** (1586, 1614); **xabō de los indios** (1604) and **xabon de los indios** (1608) versus **Xabon de los yndios** (1586, 1614).

89. Compare the 1586 series of **Maçorca de maiz verde** - **Maçorca de maiz seco** - **Maçorca de mayz verde cozido y seco** with the 1608 series of **Maçorca de maiz verde** - **Maçorca podrida en la caña** - **Maçorca en leche tierna que comiença** - **Maçorca nacer hazerse** - **Maçorca coger** - **Maçorca de maiz seca** - **Maçorca podrida requemada como hollina** - **Maçorcas pegadas** - **Maçorca de mayz verde cozido y secado en el sol** - **Maçorca verde tostada o assada**.

90. Thus the 1586 series of **Mayz bla[n]co** - **Mayz dulce** - **Mayz cozido** - **Mayz tostado** - **Mayz naudo, para hacer chica** - **Mayz blando** - **Mayz duro** - **Mayz tostado para hazer chicha** becomes the 1608 series of **Mayz en grano** - **Mayz blanco** - **Mayz dulze** - **Mayz cozido** - **Mayz tostado** - **Mayz renacido para chicha** - **Mayz duro para chicha de yuncas vuina** - **Mayz morado** - **Mayz hazer que renazca** - **Mayz retoñecer** - **Mayz blando de comer** - **Mayz duro** - **Mayz vn poco tostado para hazer chicha** - **Mayz tostar assi**.

91. **Papas** - **Papas crudas** - **Papas secas** - **Papas al yelo despues de cozidas** - **Papas en remojo, y luego eladas**.

92. Cooper, "Girolamo Vittori."

93. Ibid., 5.

94. Ibid., 10–12.

95. At least two Nebrijan categories from the 1578 Antequera expansion, **Añudamiénto** and **Asaltos**, are included in Vittori but not found in either Minsheu or Oudin; another Nebrijan entry (since the 1495 printing on) specific to Vittori is **Ablandar lo duro**. Entries from Minsheu included in Vittori but not found in Nebrija (even in late printings) include **Acomplimento, Acrescentador, Abatido, Abandonar, Aba el lobo, Acrevillar, Fonsadera**. The Nebrijan category **Aguja de mareár** (added in the 1578 Antequera printing) was also borrowed by Vittori directly from Minsheu (the category does not appear in Oudin).

96. Albó and Layme, introducton to *Vocabulario de la lengua aymara;* Dedenbach-Salazar Sáenz, "Dictionaries," 244–46.

97. Compare the **Maçorca** categories from 1586 and 1608 in note 89 with this list from Bertonio: **Maçorca de mayz si es verde** - **Maçorca, o espiga de la quinua** - **Maçorca quando esta en leche** - **Maçorca podrida** - **Maçorca de mayz cozido, y seco**.

98. Thomas Pinpin is discussed in detail by Vicente Rafael, although the *Vocabvlario* is mentioned only in passing (Rafael, *Contracting Colonialism,* 124, 142–43); for more extensive discussions see Scott, "Sixteenth-Century Tagalog Technology"; Sánchez-Fuertes, "El *Vocabulario*"; García-Medall, "Notas," and "La traducción"; for general historical and lexicographic background, see Phelan, "Philippine Linguistics," and Postma, "Tagalog *Vocabularios.*"

99. The three "marias" were either three women present at the Crucifixion (the Virgin Mary, Mary Magdalene, and Mary wife of Cleopas) or three women who discovered Christ's empty tomb (Mary Magdalene, Mary the mother of James, and Mary Salome). These two lists overlap with another group of three Marys: the daughters, by different husbands, of Saint Anne (the Virgin Mary, Mary wife of Cleopas, and Mary Salome). For the debate in Mesoamerican studies on the identification of the Aztec Mamalhuaztli constellation as either Gemini or Orion, see Coe, "Native Astronomy"; on the three Marys and ritual crossdressing in medieval and early modern Resurrection dramas, see Webster, *Art and Ritual,* 145–46.

100. We can confirm this equivalence by activating another node in the global network of Nebrijan dictionaries: the corresponding entry in the Newberry library's Castilian–Latin–Nahuatl manuscript reads "**Astilejos costelacion del cielo.** Orion. mamaluãztli."

101. "No lleua esta letra . x este Vocabulario como xabon.xeme.xerga &c pero va puesta en la .I."

102. Specifically, Joaquín García-Medall compares San Buenaventura with the Castilian entries found in Alonso de Molina's 1555 Castilian–Nahuatl *Vocabulario* but *not* found in Nebrija's 1495 *Vocabulario,* and finds that some 50 percent of Molina's "added" terms are shared by San Buenaventura. He thus argues Alonso de Molina was a source for San Buenaventura. As we have seen, however, Molina was actually based on a 1545 Granada printing of Nebrija's text, a printing with far more Castilian entries than the 1495 first edition. García-Medall does not provide the details of his lexical analysis of San Buenaventura, but it seems likely that the proposed parallels with Molina are actually parallels shared with versions of Nebrija's *Dictionarium* from the 1536 Granada printing on. García-Medall's more detailed discussion of his analysis of the entries in a Philippine dictionary of circa 1637 reveals that most of Molina's New World–specific entries were *not* included. García-Medall, "Notas," 209; 206–7.

103. Shared Z-entries between Minsheu and San Buenaventura are **Zabullir, Zanca, Zancadilla, Zanja, Zaraguelles, Zaranda, Zarça, Zarçillos, Zarço, Zebolla, Zeçear, Zedaço, Zedro, Zedula, Zegajoso, Zeguera, Zeja, Zeloso, Zenteno, Zeñidor, Zumbar, Zumbido, Zumo, Zurdo.**

104. On the role of Spain in early English travels to the East Indies, see Hackel and Mancall, "Richard Hakluyt," 429–30, 432–33; Barbour, "The East India Company," 256–57; on the early history of the English East India Company generally, see Ogborn, "Writing Travels"; Fang Ng, "Global Renaissance," 304–6.

105. An online transcription is available at http://sb.tagalogstudies.org/.

3. From the Shores of Tripoli to the Halls of Montezuma

1. Pagden, *The Fall*; MacCormack, *On the Wings*; John Pohl and Claire Lyons are editing a volume on these themes from their 2010 conference at the Getty Villa in Malibu: "*Altera Roma: Art and Empire from the Aztecs to New Spain*." Such antique comparisons did not simply try to explain indigenous cultures by reference to a more familiar (to Europeans) Greco-Roman tradition; they could also provide models to justify European empires, as Michael Dietler has made clear ("'Our Ancestors the Gauls,'" "The Archaeology").

2. Laird, "Aztec and Roman Gods"; Olivier Durand, "The Mexica Pantheon."

3. Marcus, "Archaeology and Religion," 173–74; for critiques of her dismissal of Meso-american "anthropomorphized 'gods' from some kind of 'pantheon,'" see Houston and Stuart, "Of Gods"; Sellen, "Storm-God Impersonators," 3; Sellen, *El cielo compartido*; Houston and Inomata, *The Classic Maya*, 193–217; Lind, *Ancient Zapotec Religion*, 6–11.

4. Marcus, *Women's Ritual*, 12; see also similar lists on 11.

5. Ibid., 14–15.

6. These categories do not appear in Molina's 1571 Castilian–Nahuatl dictionary, the other source of entries for Córdova's *Vocabulario*. On the fate of Nebrijan divinatory categories in the Quechua dictionary of Santo Tomás, see Torero, "Entre Roma y Lima," 282.

7. Smith-Stark, "Dioses," 144.

8. Ibid., 166.

9. Ibid., 147.

10. The initial *ti-* is a habitual mood/aspect marker (roughly a "present tense" prefix); the final *-ya* indicates the first person. On first-person vocabulary entries in general, see Thiemer-Sachse, "El 'Vocabulario,'" 160–61.

11. Lockhart, "Some Nahua Concepts," 477.

12. Marcus, *Women's Ritual*, 11–12. For divination and reflective surfaces, see also Mason, "Mirrors"; Carlson, "Olmec"; Carlson, "The Jade Mirror"; Pendergast, "Ancient Maya Mercury"; Taube, "The Iconography"; Austin, "Mercury"; Nelson et al., "Composite Mirrors"; Healy and Blainey, "Ancient Maya." For prehispanic archaeological sortilege divination, see also Morris, "Description," 187–88; Colby and Colby, *The Daykeeper*, 46; Brady and Prufer, "Caves"; Brown and Sheets, "Distinguishing," 14, Earley, "Ritual Deposits"; and Love, "Early States"; as well as folio 21 of the sixteenth-century Codex Borbonicus; thanks to Julia Guernsey and David Freidel for their help tracking down several of these references to prehispanic sortilege. On water-scrying in early modern Europe, see Cirac Estopañán, *Los procesos*, 55, 56, 138; Thomas, *Religion*, 215; Ciruelo, *Pedro Ciruelo's*, 148, 116; and Duffy, *The Stripping*, 73.

13. Marcus, *Women's Ritual*, 12; see also 4, 13, 15. On the reality effect, see Barthes, "The Reality Effect." Silverstein ("Translation," 88–89) provides a useful critique of indigenous-term fetishism in the writings of anthropologists.

14. Joyce, "Gender."

15. González, *Zapotec Science*, 52; Zeitlin, *Cultural Politics*, 71.

16. The Codex Muro, also known as the Codex Ñunaha, is a screenfold book currently housed in the National Library of Anthropology and History in Mexico City. Photographs of all of its pages, with commentary, were first published in Smith, "The Relationship"; a more recent reproduction and commentary is Hermann Lejarazu, *El Códice Muro*.

17. Smith, "The Relationship," 91, 93, 95; Jansen and Pérez Jiménez, *Codex Bodley*, 45.

18. Alvarado, *Vocabvlario*, 17v, 22r, 63v, 113v, 189v; the various meanings of *chiyo* were first gathered in Smith, *Picture Writing*, 45, 47.

19. Jansen, *Huisi Tacu*, 199; Jansen and Pérez Jiménez, *Codex Bodley*, 25, 45.

20. For the Classic Maya, see Houston and Inomata, *The Classic Maya*, 200; for Postclassic and twentieth-century examples, see Montes de Oca Vega, "Semantic Couplets," 246–47; Jansen, *Huisi Tacu*, 195–97; Monaghan, "Performance," 134–36.

21. Theimer-Sachse, in a discussion of Córdova's Zapotec vocabulary ("El 'Vocabulario,'" 158–59), draws attention to other entries that separate European and Zapotec forms of very similar practices, including religious ones.

22. Torero, in a study of Santo Tomás's 1560 Quechua dictionary, also reveals how a single Nebrijan category (**Templo**) was expanded to accommodate European views of New World religious practices ("Entre Roma y Lima," 282).

23. On Molina's use of *lo mismo*, see Clayton and Campbell, "Alonso de Molina," 357–59; on his use of the Latin *vel*, see Clayton and Campbell, "Alonso de Molina," 350.

24. On the Nahuatl *momoztli* as 'raised altar, platform, land boundary, or mojonera,' see Osowski, *Indigenous Miracles*, 52.

25. *Pezeeláo* was used in Córdova to define the word *demonio* (116v), but as Smith-Stark has shown ("Dioses," 111–12) the term's more literal reference was to an indigenous god of the underworld.

26. It is important to point out, however, that ruined sites and buildings were and are revered locations throughout Mesoamerica, places for offerings and sacrifices; Hamann, "Heirlooms," 136–38.

27. The prehispanic Codex Nuttall, also known as the Codex Zouche-Nuttall, is housed in the British Museum. The first facsimile edition was published by the Peabody Museum in Cambridge, Massachusetts, in 1902; more recent facsimiles were published by Akademische Druck- und Verlagsanstalt in Graz, Austria (1974) and Fondo de Cultura Económica in Mexico City (1992).

28. The prehispanic Codex Vienna, also known as the Codex Vindobonensis Mexicanus I, is housed in the Austrian National Library in Vienna. A facsimile edition was published by Akademische Druck- und Verlagsanstalt in Graz, Austria, in 1974; another facsimile was published by Fondo de Cultura Económica in Mexico City in 1992.

29. Hamann, "The Social Life"; Hamann, "Heirlooms"; see also Hermann Lejarazu, "El sitio."

30. Monaghan and Hamann, "Reading"; Hamann, "'In the Eyes'"; Hamann, "How Maya Hieroglyphs," 58–68.

31. Clayton and Campbell ("Alonso de Molina," 366) provide a similar example with Molina's various Castilian entries for **Arder**, 'to burn,' which were created to capture the nuances of Nahuatl terminology.

32. For classic overviews of alphabetic writing in Nahuatl, see Lockhart, *The Nahuas*; Lockhart, *Nahuatl as Written*.

33. Wood, "The Origin"; Sahlins, "Colors and Cultures"; Eco, "How Culture"; also relevant here is Bille and Sørenson's 2007 proposal for an anthropology of luminosity ("An Anthropology").

34. Gellius, *Noctes Atticae* 2.26; Eco ("How Culture," 158–59) expands Gellius' examples with others from Latin literature.

35. Eco, "How Culture," 171.

36. Alexis Wimmer's excellent online Nahuatl dictionary (with translations into English, French, Spanish, and German) provided a key resource for tracking down examples of Molina's categories in context: http://sites.estvideo.net/malinal/index.html. *Tlanextia* in context (in this and subsequent notes, FC refers to the twelve-volume edition of Sahagún, *Florentine Codex*): the moon (*itlanestiliz; FC* 7:3); Venus (*tlanestia; FC* 7:11); *icpitl* ['glowworm'] (*tlanextli; FC* 11:101).

37. *Pepetzca* in context: *xalquani* [*Mareca americana*, 'widgeon'] (*pepetzca; FC* 11:36); red quetzal feathers (*pepetzca; FC* 11:19); *tzinitzcan tototl* feathers [*Trogon mexicanus*, 'green Mexican trogon'] (*pepepetzca; FC* 11:20); quetzal feathers (*ontzimitzcapepetzcatinenemi*; Bierhorst, *Cantares Mexicanos*, 1:418, line 15); *tlecocozpapalotl* ['smoky yellow butterfly'] (*pepetzca; FC* 11:95); the sun (*pepetzcaticah; FC* 2:98); gold (*pepetzcatihuitz*; Bierhorst, *Cantares Mexicanos*, 1:392, line 13); *mayatl* insect [*Hallorina duguesi*, 'scarab'] (*pepetzca; FC* 11:101).

38. *Pepetlaca* in context: *mayatl* insect [*Hallorina duguesi*, 'scarab'] (*pepetlaca; FC* 11:101); gold earrings (*pepetlaca; FC* 2:91); *itzquauhtli* feathers ['golden eagle'] (*pepetlaca; FC* 11:41); quetzal crest feathers (*pepetlaca; FC* 11:19); *eptli* ['pearl'] (*pepetlaca; FC* 11:60); *tezatetlilli* ['mirror stone earth'] (*pêpepetlaca; FC* 11:238); indigo-dyed hair (*pepetlaca; FC* 8:47); iron lances and halbreds (*tlapepetlaca; FC* 12:30); shields (*petlâtiuitz*; Bierhorst, *Cantares Mexicanos*, 2:265).

39. *Cuecueyoca* in context: turquoise mask (*cuecueyoca; FC* 2:159); *chalchivitl* ['greenstone'] (*cuecueioca; FC* 11:222); *quetzalchalchivitl* ['greenstone'] (*cuecueioca; FC* 11:223); *coztic çintli* ['yellow ears of maize'] (*cuecueioca; FC* 11:280); *tlacuilolquauitl* wood [used for making drums and guitars] (*cuecueioca; FC* 11:111); *capuli* fruit [*Prunus capuli*, 'black cherries'] (*cuecueiochauhquj; FC* 11:121); black eggs of the *tecalatl* frog (*cuecueiochauhticate; FC* 11:63); *amanalli* ['pool of water'] (*cuecueioatimanj; FC* 11:250); *ixtlaoatl* ['trackless desert'] (*cuecueiocatimanj; FC* 11:262); see also Clayton and Campbell, "Alonso de Molina," 371–72.

40. *Pepeyoca* in context: eyes (*pepeioca; FC* 10:102).

41. I was only able to find this word attested in dictionary entries.

42. *Tzotzotlaca* in context: *cacalotl* [*Corvus corax sinuatus*, 'raven'] (*tzotzlotlanj; FC* 11:43); *yiamolli* leaves [*Phytolacca octandra* Linn., 'red inkplant'] (*tzotzolaca; FC* 11:133); *Iollosuchiquavitl* leaves [*Talauma mexicana* Don, 'magnolia'] (*ixtzotzotlaca;*

FC 11:201); *amaquahitl* leaves [*Ficus benjamina*, 'ficus tree'] (*tzotzotlaca; FC* 11:111); *tetzmolin* [*Quercus fusiformis* Smal., 'evergreen live oak'] (*tzotzotlactic; FC* 11:196); *ilin* ['ash tree'] (*tzotzotlaca; FC* 11:108).

43. Peterson, "The Florentine Codex."

44. On the Codex Magliabechiano textiles, see Boone, *The Codex Magliabechiano,* 168–74; the manuscript also contains a year count and images of Central Mexican deities and ceremonies. The Lienzo de Tlaxcala was a massive painted cloth (five meters tall and two meters wide) comissioned by the indigenous town council of Tlaxcala in 1552. Its images told how the Tlaxcalans helped the Spaniards to overthrow the Aztec empire. The original cloth disappeared during the French occupation of Mexico in the nineteenth century; fortunately, color tracings survived, and were used to publish a lithograph facsimile in 1892. See Hamann, "Object"; a digital re-creation is available online at www.mesolore.org. The "General History" (also known as the Florentine Codex) is a massive encyclopedia of prehispanic Nahua life completed by the Franciscan friar Bernardino de Sahagún and indigenous collaborators in 1570s Central Mexico; it is currently housed in the Biblioteca Medicea Laurenziana in Florence (see Peterson, "The Florentine Codex").

45. This conceptual association is found in other Mesoamerican languages as well; see Hamann, "How Maya Hieroglyphs," 60–61.

46. Peterson, "The Florentine Codex"; Leibsohn, "Seeing In-Situ."

47. Partially compiled from indigenous records and captured by pirates en route to Spain, the Codex Mendoza has three sections: a list of the Aztec kings and their conquests, a record of tribute provinces in the Aztec empire, and an account of daily life and the life cycle. It is currently housed in the Bodleian Library at Oxford University; for a facsimile, see Berdan and Anawalt, eds., *The Codex Mendoza.*

48. These comments are based on observations by a number of my art-historical interlocutors; see also Pillsbury, "Reading Art." For a recent summary of Panofskian iconology in a Mesoamericanist context, see Jansen and Pérez Jiménez, *The Mixtec,* 186–99; see also Didi-Huberman, "Before the Image," 34–35, for a sharp critique of textually constrained art history. It should be said, however, that Panofsky himself did not see alphabetic texts as an exclusive end-all solution for visual analysis. One of his opening examples from *Studies in Iconology* (on how to distinguish Salome from Judith) stresses that textual descriptions may take us only so far: "Thus we have two literary sources applicable to our picture with equal right and equal inconsistency. We should be entirely at a loss did we depend on literary sources alone. Fortunately we do not" (12–13). He then continues by bringing in additional visual sources. Panofsky's principles today, then, are often oversimplified, and he would probably have been surprised at the current alphabetic bias in visual analysis.

49. As Magaloni Kerpel reveals ("Painters"), Nahua artists were able to draw on allusion and hieroglyphic puns to specify the color qualities of particular substances when— after the devastating epidemics in mid-1570s Mexico—they could not longer acquire colored pigments and had to fall back on black ink alone. In these cases, however,

artists depicted the particularized qualities of particular substances—the red *xilo-suchitl* flower versus the green *quetzaliztli* stone—and not broader reflective qualities shared by different substances (*pepetlaca* versus *pepeyoca*). In other words, Nahua artists indicated surface qualities in general (*ixtli*) as well as specific manifestations (the *quetzaliztli* stone), but appear not to have registered the "middle range" of shared reflective properties indicated by Molina and attested in other Nahuatl texts. In contrast, Classic Maya artists used "differing eye forms [to] denote two qualities of reflective light, one a bright gleam from hard, shiny surfaces, and the other more muted and opaque." Houston and Taube, "An Archaeology," 284.

50. Derrida, *Margins*, 3–27.

4. Margins of Vocabularies

1. Clanchy, *From Memory*; Chartier, "Texts"; Illich, *In the Vineyard*; Stallybrass et al., "Hamlet's Tables"; Hamann, "Object."

2. Sherman (*Used Books*, 59) describes how early modern printed books might have "a whole notebook's worth of blank paper" in their margins and flyleaves; Considine (*Dictionaries*, 61) points out that blank pages for writing down new examples were included after each chapter of the 1565 *Traicte de la conformite du langage françois auec la grec* ('Treatise on the conformity of the French language with Greek'). On the challenge and cost of producing early modern paper, see Febvre and Martin, *Coming of the Book*, 29–44; Griffin, *The Crombergers*, 54–56; Lucas, "Industrial"; Montellano Arteaga, "Culhuacán"; see also Piedra, "The Value."

3. For examples from northern Europe, see Considine, *Dictionaries*, 68, 71, 237, 252–54.

4. See Garibay Kintana, "'Códice Carolino'" for references to a (now lost) copy of Molina glossed with additional Castilian–Nahuatl entries. Also of relevance here is the 1555 copy of the *Dictionarium* held by the Jagiellonian Library in Kraków, which has 28 additional Castilian–Latin entries (spanning the letters A to V) added to the margins of the Castilian–Latin section.

5. See Caie, "The Significance"; Slights, "The Edifying Margins"; Jardine and Grafton, "'Studied for Action'"; Camille, *Image*; Tribble, *Margins*; Boehrer, "Renaissance Classicism"; Blanshard and Sowerby, "Thomas Wilson's *Demosthenes*"; Richards, "Gabriel Harvey"; Sherman, *Used Books*; and for a discussion of early modern marginal graffiti that has little or no direct connection with its book's content, see Scott-Warren, "Reading Graffiti."

6. Jackson, *Marginalia*, 85; Slights, "Review of *Marginalia*," 127–28.

7. Grafton, "Is the History," 147–48.

8. On the traces of these conversations in the very grammar of vocabulary entries, see Thiemer-Sachse, "El 'Vocabulario,'" 160–61.

9. Chartier, "Texts," 158; see also Fish, *Is There a Text*, 167–73; Houston and Stuart, "The Ancient Maya Self," 92; on the related topic of recitation literacy, see Houston, "Literacy"; Monaghan, "The Text in the Body."

10. Interpretive conversations played a central role in Dennis Tedlock's translations of indigenous narratives from the Americas (Tedlock, *The Spoken Word*), most famously the sixteenth-century *Popol Vuh* (1996) and *Rabinal Achi* (2003). Conversation is also a central theme in Laura Murray's discussion of indigenous vocabularies from seventeenth- through nineteenth-century North America ("Vocabularies"; see also Bishop, "Qu'y a-t-il de si drôle").

11. Derrida, *Margins*, xi–xii.

12. Ibid., xii, xiii.

13. Ibid., xvii.

14. The obvious exception in this study is the Newberry's "Vocabulario trilingüe" manuscript, which (as we saw in chapter 2) seems to have been created by Nahuatl speakers, for Nahuatl speakers. But this exception only underscores my arguments about translation and dialogue. The nature of many of the Nahuatl translations in that manuscript (which misunderstand the basic semantic contours of the Castilian–Latin category pair being translated) make clear just how important two-way conversations about language were in producing translating dictionaries. The Nahuatl-speaking creators of this document were not working in tandem with a native speaker of Castilian, who could have explained (for example) that a *botilleria* was a place, not a person.

15. For North American examples, see Murray, "Vocabularies," 603, 608. For other examples, we could also consider the indigenously authored "Vocabulario trilingüe," in which the hand-copied entries of the Nebrijan model were maintained (no doubt reflecting their perceived alien authority) even when they were not understood (see chapter 2).

16. On Maya concepts of *ik*, see Houston, Stuart, and Taube, *The Memory*, 143–46.

17. Molina, *Aquí comiença*, 171r; see also 45v, 184r, 185r.

18. See also Lockhart, "Sightings," 225, on "ad hoc" neologisms.

19. Lockhart, "Sightings," 227—both terms are included in Molina's 1555 vocabulary; see also Clayton and Campbell, "Alonso de Molina," 351–59, 364–67 for a nuanced treatment of how entries and translations in Molina's vocabularies were generated.

20. "En este vocabulario se ponen algunos romances, que en nuestro Castellano no quadran, ni se vsan mucho: y esto se haze por dar a entender mejor la propriedad de la lengua de los indios, y assi dezimos. Abaxador aunque no se vsa en nuestro romance: por declarar lo que quiere dezir esta palabra. tlatemouiani, la qual en buen romance quiere dezir, el que abaxa algo." Molina, *Aquí comiença*, v recto.

21. Derrida, *Margins*, xxiii. Of course, if a book had blank pages at the end (see note 2), these too could be the site for adding new terms and translations—as is the case with the Newberry's "Vocabulario trilingüe," as well as the Jagiellonian Library's 1555 copy of the *Dictionarium* (some additions there are from Castilian to Italian, not Latin). But as is shown in figures 4.4 and 4.5, the Newberry manuscript includes page-edge marginal additions as well (as does the Jagiellonian *Dictionarium*; see note 4 in this chapter). Remember that early modern paper was expensive, and so any blank space was fair game for annotation.

Conclusions

1. These foundations extend far beyond Nebrijan vocabulary lists; our current understandings of the structures of the Mesoamerican calendar, the contours of divine forces, and the basics of the Maya writing system (to give just three examples) all take their points of departure from the writings of early modern Europeans.

2. Latour, "Drawing," 20–21.

3. Chakrabarty, *Provincializing Europe*, 7.

4. The "denial of coevalness" is a phenomenon first described by Johannes Fabian in *Time and the Other*: he used it to analyze the then-common tendency (in 1983) for ethnographers to write about the people they lived with and studied as if those people were from the distant past, an era separate from the ethnographer's own present (see Fabian, *Time*, 31). Note also that the adjective *colonial* is anachronistic before the turn of the nineteenth century. According to Mark Davies's *Corpus del Español* database (www.corpusdelespanol.org), the word *colonial* doesn't appear in Spanish usage until 1796, in Servando Teresa de Mier's *Segunda carta de un americano al español* ('Second letter of an American to a Spaniard'); the apparent hit in Sepúlveda is actually to a twentieth-century translation. The first recorded use of *colonización* isn't until 1843, in Antonio Ferrer del Río's *Historia del reinado de Carlos III en España* ('History of the reign of Charles III in Spain'). *Colonialismo* doesn't occur until the twentieth century. None of these words appears in the Nebrijan corpus studied here. In English (according to the *Oxford English Dictionary*), *colonial* is first attested (tellingly) in 1776, and although *colonialism* appears in 1853, its initial meaning was akin to 'provincial' ("a practice or idiom peculiar to or characteristic of a colony"). The use of *colonialism* to refer to "the colonial system" doesn't appear until 1886. The OED dates *colonization* to 1770. See also Gosden, *Archaeology and Colonialism*, 1. The category of "early modern," of course, has its own issues (Goldstone, "The Problem"; Bentley, "Early Modern Europe"; and Fasolt, "Saving Renaissance and Reformation"); my concerns here are the effects of temporal-geographic separations of the "colonial" from the "early modern." For other critiques of the concept of "coloniality" in New World studies, and the ways assumptions about the "colonial" Americas cut them off from "early modern" Europe (in classic denial-of-coevalness form), see Armitage, "Greater Britain," and Warner, "What's Colonial" (on British North America); Klein, "Not Like Us" (on Latin America); and above all Levene, *Las Indias*; Klor de Alva, "Colonialism"; Klor de Alva, "The Postcolonization"; Bauer and Mazotti, "Creole Subjects"; and Hamann, "Bad Christians." For colonialist readings of the translation process, see Fabian, *Language*; Greenblatt, "Learning to Curse"; Mignolo, *The Darker Side*; Rafael, *Contracting Colonialism*; Cohn, *Colonialism*; Murray, "Vocabularies"; Durston, *Pastoral Quechua*; Hanks, *Converting Words*; and cf. McKenzie, "The Sociology of a Text" (a study of missionary printing in nineteenth-century New Zealand for which "the colonial" is not a key category of analysis); as well as Ogilvie's challenges to prior interpretations of the *Oxford English Dictionary* as transparently imperialist (*Words*, 74–90).

5. Latour, *The Pasteurization*, 219–21; Latour, *We Have Never Been Modern*, 117–20; Cooper, *Colonialism in Question*, 3–31, 91–112.

Works Cited

Abbreviations

BC   Biblioteca Colombina, Seville
BL   British Library, London
BNE   Biblioteca Nacional de España, Madrid
BNF   Bibliothèque Nationale de France, Paris
BNP   Biblioteca Nacional de Portugal, Lisbon
BPR   Biblioteca del Palacio Real, Madrid
BUC   Biblioteca de la Universidad Complutense, Madrid
JL   Jagiellonian Library, Early Printed Book Section, Kraków
HSA   Hispanic Society of America, New York
RAE   Real Academia Española, Madrid

Abad, Julián Martín. "Nebrija en los talleres de Arnao Guillén de Brocar y Miguel de Eguía." In *Nebrija V Centenario: Actas del Tercer Congreso Internacional de Historiografía Lingüística,* edited by Ricardo Escavy Zamora, José Miguel Hernández Terrés, and Antonio Roldán Pérez, vol. 1, 23–58. Murcia: Universidad de Murcia, 1994.

———. *Post-incunabules ibéricos.* Madrid: Ollero y Ramos, 2001.

Acero Durántez, Isabel. "En los comienzos de la lingüística mesoamericana: El influjo de Alonso de Molina en la obra de Maturino Gilberti." *Anuario de lingüística hispánica* 12, no. 1 (1999): 199–211.

———. "Una aportación a la historia de la lexicografía americana: Sobre el *Vocabulario en lengua de Michoacán* de fray Maturino Gilberti." In *Estudios de lexicografía diacrónica del español (V Centenario del Vocabularium Ecclesiasticum de Rodrigo de Santaella),* edited by Antonia M. Medina Guerra, 81–102. Málaga: Universidad de Málaga, 2001.

Acuña, René. Introduction to *Arte breve de la lengua otomí y vocabulario trilingüe* (1605), by Alonso Urbano, xix–lxx. Mexico City: Universidad Nacional Autónoma de México, 1990.

————, ed. *Bocabulario de maya than: Codex Vindobonensis N.S. 3833: Facsímil y transcripción crítica anotada.* Mexico City: Universidad Nacional Autónoma de México, 1993.

Aguilar Paéz, Rafael. *Gramática quechua y vocabularios.* Lima: Universidad Nacional Mayor de San Marcos, 1970.

Albó, Xavier, and Félix Layme. Introduction to *Vocabulario de la lengua aymara,* by Ludovico Bertonio, ix–lviii. Cochabamba, Bolivia: Ediciones Ceres, 1984.

Alcalá, Pedro de. *Arte para ligerame[n]te saber la le[n]gua arauiga.* Granada: Juan Varela de Salamanca, 1505.

Allen, Roger. "The Happy Traitor: Tales of Translation." *Comparative Literature Studies* 47, no. 4 (2010): 472–86.

Alvarado, Fray Francisco de. *Vocabvlario en lengva misteca.* Mexico: Pedro Balli, 1593.

Ara, Domingo de. "Vocabulario de la lengua española y tzeldal." Berendt-Brinton Linguistic Collection, Ms. Coll. 700, item 185. Rare Book and Manuscript Library, University of Pennsylvania.

————. *Vocabulario de la lengua tzeldal según el orden de Copanabastla.* Edited by Mario Ruz. Mexico City: Instituto de Investigaciones Filológicas, Universidad Nacional Autónoma de México, 1986.

Arenas, Pedro de. *Vocabulario manual de las lenguas castellana y mexicana.* Edited by Ascensión H. de León-Portilla. Mexico City: Universidad Nacional Autónoma de México, 1982.

Armitage, David. "Greater Britain: A Useful Category of Historical Analysis?" *American Historical Review* 104, no. 2 (1999): 427–45.

Arte, y vocabvlario en la lengva general del Perv llamado Quichua, y en la lengua Española. Lima: Antonio Ricardo, 1586.

Arte, y vocabvlario en la lengva general del Perv llamado Quichua, y en la lengua Española. Lima: Francisco del Canto, 1614.

Austin, Patricia A. "Mercury and the Ancient Maya." MA thesis, Trent University, 1994.

Barbour, Richmond. "The East India Company Journal of Anthony Marlowe, 1607–1608." *Huntington Library Quarterly* 71, no. 2 (2008): 255–301.

Barthes, Roland. "The Reality Effect." In *The Rustle of Language,* translated by Richard Howard, 141–48. Oxford: Blackwell, 1986.

Bartlett, Robert. *Why Can the Dead Do Such Great Things? Saints and Worshippers from the Martyrs to the Reformation.* Princeton, NJ: Princeton University Press, 2013.

Bauer, Ralph, and José Antonio Mazzotti. "Creole Subjects in the Colonial Americas." In *Creole Subjects in the Colonial Americas: Empires, Texts,*

Identities, edited by Ralph Bauer and José Antonio Mazzotti, 1–57. Chapel Hill: University of North Carolina Press for the Omohundro Institute of Early American History and Culture, 2009.

Benjamin, Walter. "The Task of the Translator." In *Illuminations,* translated by Harry Zohn, edited by Hannah Arendt, 69–82. New York: Harcourt Brace Jovanovich, 1968.

Bentley, Jerry H. "Early Modern Europe and the Early Modern World." In *Between the Middle Ages and Modernity: Individual and Community in the Early Modern World,* edited by Charles H. Parker and Jerry H. Bentley, 13–31. Lanham, MD: Rowman and Littlefield, 2007.

Berdan, Frances F., and Patricia Rieff Anawalt, eds. *The Codex Mendoza.* 4 vols. Berkeley: University of California Press, 1992.

Bermúdez Plata, Cristóbal. "Las obras de Antonio de Nebrija en América." *Anuario de estudios americanos* 3 (1946): 1029–32.

Bertonio, Ludovico. *Vocabvlario de la lengva aymara.* Juli: Francisco del Canto, 1612.

Bierhorst, John. *Cantares Mexicanos: Songs of the Aztecs.* 2 vols. Stanford, CA: Stanford University Press, 1985.

Bietenholz, Peter G., and Thomas Brian Deutscher. *Contemporaries of Erasmus: A Biographical Register of the Renaissance and Reformation.* 3 vols. Toronto: University of Toronto Press, 2003.

Bille, Mikkel, and Tim Flohr Sørensen. "An Anthropology of Luminosity: The Agency of Light." *Journal of Material Culture* 12, no. 3 (2007): 263–84.

Bishop, John E. "Qu'y a-t-il de si drôle dans la chasse au canard? Ce que les ouvrages linguistiques nous disent de la rencontre entre les Jésuites et les Nehiraw-Iriniw." *Tangence: À la recherche d'un signe oublié: Le patrimoine latin du Québec et sa culture classique* 92 (Winter 2010): 39–66.

Blair, Ann. "Note Taking as an Art of Transmission." *Critical Inquiry* 31, no. 1 (2004): 85–107.

———. "The Rise of Note-Taking in Early Modern Europe." *Intellectual History Review* 20, no. 3 (2010): 303–16.

Blanshard, Alastair J. L., and Tracey A. Sowerby. "Thomas Wilson's *Demosthenes* and the Politics of Tudor Translation." *International Journal of the Classical Tradition* 12, no. 1 (2005): 46–80.

Boehrer, Bruce Thomas. "Renaissance Classicism and Roman Sexuality: Ben Jonson's Marginalia and the Trope of 'Os Impurum.'" *International Journal of the Classical Tradition* 4, no. 3 (1998): 364–80.

Bolles, David. "The Mayan Franciscan Vocabularies: A Preliminary Survey." *Estudios de cultura maya* 24 (2003): 61–84.

Boone, Elizabeth Hill. *The Codex Magliabechiano and the Lost Prototype of the Magliabechiano Group.* Berkeley: University of California Press, 1983.

Brady, James E., and Keith M. Prufer. "Caves and Crystalmancy: Evidence for the Use of Crystals in Ancient Maya Religion." *Journal of Anthropological Research* 55, no. 1 (1999): 129–44.

Brain, Cecelia. "Aprendizaje de lenguas indígenas por parte de españoles en Nueva España en los primeros cien años después de la conquista." *Colonial Latin American Review* 19, no. 2 (2010): 279–300.

Braudel, Fernand. *The Perspective of the World.* Vol. 3 of *Civilization and Capitalism, 15th–18th Century.* New York: Harper and Row, 1985.

Brook, Timothy. *Vermeer's Hat: The Seventeenth Century and the Dawn of the Global World.* London: Bloomsbury Press, 2008.

Brown, Linda A., and Payson Sheets. "Distinguishing Domestic from Ceremonial Structures in Southern Mesoamerica: Suggestions from Cerén, El Salvador." *Mayab* 13 (2000): 11–21.

Burke, Peter. *Languages and Communities in Early Modern Europe.* Cambridge: Cambridge University Press, 2004.

Caie, Graham D. "The Significance of the Early Chaucer Manuscript Glosses (with Special Reference to 'The Wife of Bath's Prologue')." *Chaucer Review* 10, no. 4 (1976): 350–60.

Camille, Michael. *Image on the Edge: The Margins of Medieval Art.* Cambridge, MA: Harvard University Press, 1992.

Campos, Manuel de. *Relacion del solemne recibimiento que se hizo en Lisboa a las santas reliquias que se llevaron a la yglesia de San Roque de la Compañia de Jesus a veinte y cinco de Enero, 1588.* Alcalá de Henares: Juan Iñiguez de Lequerica, 1589.

Carlson, John B. "Olmec Concave Iron Ore Mirrors: The Aesthetic of a Lithic Technology and the Lord of the Mirror." In *The Olmec and Their Neighbors: Essays in Memory of Matthew W. Stirling,* edited by Elizabeth P. Benson, 117–47. Washington, DC: Dumbarton Oaks, 1981.

———. "The Jade Mirror: An Olmec Concave Jadeite Pendant." In *Precolumbian Jade: New Geological and Cultural Interpretations,* edited by Frederic W. Lange, 242–50. Salt Lake City: University of Utah Press, 1993.

Carneiro da Cunha, Manuela. "Da guerra das relíquias ao quinto império: Importação e exportação da história no Brasil." *Novos estudos CEBRAP* 44 (March 1996): 73–88.

Caro Bellido, A., and J. M. Tomassetti Guerra. *Antonio de Nebrija y la Betica (sobre arqueologia y paleografía del Bajo Guadalquivir).* Cádiz: Servicio de Publicaciones, Universidad de Cádiz, 1997.

Carrera de la Red, Avelina. "Dioscórides en la obra médica de E. A. Nebrija." In *Humanismo y pervivencia del mundo clásico: Homenaje al profesor Luis Gil,* edited by José María Maestre Maestre, Joaquín Pascual Barea, and

Luis Charlo Brea, vol. 1, 121–28. Cádiz: Universidad de Cádiz, 1997.

Carrera de la Red, Micaela. "Lexicografía contrastiva castellano–catalana en el *Dictionarium medicum* de E. A. de Nebrija: Campo léxico de los árboles." *Revista de filología románica* 14, no. 1 (1997): 113–34.

Casas, Cristóbal de las. *Vocabvlario de las dos lengvas toscana y castellana.* Seville: Casa de Francisco de Aguilar, 1570.

——. *Vocabvlario de las dos lengvas toscana y castellana.* Venice: Casa de Damiano Zenaro, 1576.

——. *Vocabvlario de las dos lengvas toscana y castellana.* Venice: Casa de Damiano Zenaro, 1582.

——. *Vocabvlario de las dos lengvas toscana y castellana.* Seville: Casa de Andrea Pescioni, 1583.

——. *Vocabvlario de las dos lengvas toscana y castellana.* Venice: Casa de Damiano Zenaro, 1587.

——. *Vocabvlario de las dos lengvas toscana y castellana.* Venice: Casa de Damiano Zenaro, 1591.

——. *Vocabvlario de las dos lengvas toscana y castellana.* Venice: Casa de Damiano Zenaro, 1597.

——. *Vocabvlario de las dos lengvas toscana y castellana.* Venice: Olivier Alberti, 1600.

——. *Vocabvlario de las dos lengvas toscana y castellana.* Venice: i Guerra fratelli, 1604.

——. *Vocabvlario de las dos lengvas toscana y castellana.* Venice: Matthio Valentino, 1608.

Cátedra Garcia, Pedro M. "Arnao Guillén de Brocar, impresor de las obras de Nebrija." In *El libro antiguo español III: El libro en Palacio y otros estudios bibliográficos,* edited by María Luisa López-Vidriero and Pedro M. Cátedra, 43–80. Salamanca: Universidad de Salamanca, 1996.

Chakrabarty, Dipesh. *Provincializing Europe: Postcolonial Thought and Historical Difference.* Princeton, NJ: Princeton University Press, 2000.

Chartier, Roger. "Texts, Printing, Readings." In *The New Cultural History,* edited by Lynn Hunt, 154–75. Berkeley: University of California Press, 1989.

Christian, William A., Jr. *Local Religion in Sixteenth-Century Spain.* Princeton, NJ: Princeton University Press, 1981.

Chuboda, Bohdan. *Spain and the Empire, 1519–1643.* New York: Octagon Books, 1977.

Cirac Estopañán, Sebastián. *Los procesos de hechicerías en la Inquisición de Castilla la Nueva, tribunales de Toledo y Cuenca.* Madrid: Diana Artes Gráficas, 1942.

Ciruelo, Pedro. *Pedro Ciruelo's A Treatise Reproving All Superstitions and Forms of*

Witchcraft: Very Necessary and Useful for All Good Christians Zealous for Their Salvation. Translated by Eugene A. Maio and D'Orsay W. Pearson; edited by D'Orsay W. Pearson. Rutherford, NJ: Fairleigh Dickinson University Press, 1977.

Clanchy, M. T. *From Memory to Written Record: England, 1066–1307,* Cambridge: Cambridge University Press, 1979.

Clayton, Mary L. "A Trilingual Spanish–Latin–Nahuatl Manuscript Dictionary Sometimes Attributed to Fray Bernardino de Sahagún." *International Journal of American Linguistics* 55, no. 4 (1989): 391–416.

———. "Evidence for a Native-Speaking Nahuatl Author in the Ayer *Vocabulario Trilingüe*." *International Journal of Lexicography* 16, no. 2 (2003): 99–119.

Clayton, Mary L., and R. Joe Campbell. "Alonso de Molina as Lexicographer." In *Making Dictionaries: Preserving Indigenous Languages of the Americas,* edited by William Frawley, Kenneth C. Hill, and Pamela Munro, 336–90. Berkeley: University of California Press, 2002.

Codex Magliabecchiano XIII: Manuscrit mexicain post-Colombien de la Bibliothèque nationale de Florence; reproduit en photochromographie aux frais du duc de Loubat. Rome: Danesi, 1904.

Codex Vindobonensis Mexicanus I. Graz: Akademische Druck- und Verlagsanstalt, 1974.

Codex Zouche-Nuttall. Graz: Akademische Druck- und Verlagsanstalt, 1974.

Codoñer, Carmen. "Evolución en los diccionarios de Antonio Nebrija (1492–1512)." *Historiographia linguistica* 23, no. 3 (1996): 267–86.

Coe, Michael D. "Native Astronomy in Mesoamerica." In *Archaeoastronomy in Pre-Columbian Mesoamerica,* edited by Anthony Aveni, 3–31. Austin: University of Texas Press, 1975.

Cohn, Bernard. *Colonialism and Its Forms of Knowledge: The British in India.* Princeton, NJ: Princeton University Press, 1996.

Colby, Benjamin N., and Lore M. Colby. *The Daykeeper: The Life and Discourse of an Ixil Diviner.* Cambridge, MA: Harvard University Press, 1981.

Considine, John. *Dictionaries in Early Modern Europe.* Cambridge: Cambridge University Press, 2008.

Cooper, Frederick. *Colonialism in Question: Theory, Knowledge, History.* Berkeley: University of California, 2005.

Cooper, Louis. "Girolamo Vittori y César Oudin: Un caso de plagio mutuo." *Nueva revista de filología hispánica* 14, no. 1–2 (1960): 3–20.

———. "El Recueil de Hornkens y los diccionarios de Palet y de Oudin." *Nueva revista de filología hispánica* 16, no. 3–4 (1962): 297–328.

Córdova, Juan de. *Vocabvlario en lengva çapoteca.* Mexico: Pedro Charte and Antonio Ricardo, 1578.

Covarrubias Orozco, Sebastián de. *Tesoro de la lengua castellana, o española.* Madrid: Luis Sánchez, 1611.

Cuesta Gutiérrez, Luisa. "El enigma de la imprenta del humanista Elio Antonio de Nebrija y sus sucesores." *Gutenberg-Jahrbuch* 36 (1961): 107–14.

Dakin, Karen. "The Organization of the Verbs in the Vocabulario of the Tulane Manuscript of Olmos' *Arte*." Paper presented at the V Congreso Internacional de Lingüística Misionera, Universidad Nacional Autónoma de México, Mérida, Yucatán, 2007.

———. "El *Vocabulario* del Ms. del *Arte* de Olmos de la Universidad de Tulane: ¿Es una herramienta válida para estudiar la derivación verbal en el náhuatl?" In *De morfología y temas asociados: Homenaje a Elisabeth Beniers Jacobs,* edited by Francisco Arellanes Arellanes, Sergio Ibáñez Cerda, and Cecilia Rojas Nieto, 47–56. Mexico City: Universidad Nacional Autónoma de México, 2011.

Danto, Arthur C. "Translation and Betrayal." *Res: Anthropology and Aesthetics* 32 (Autumn 1997): 61–63.

Dedenbach-Salazar Sáenz, Sabine. "Dictionaries, Vocabularies, and Grammars of Andean Indigenous Languages." In *Guide to Documentary Sources for Andean Studies, 1530–1900,* edited by Joanne Pillsbury, vol. 1, 235–64. Norman: University of Oklahoma Press, 2008.

Derrida, Jacques. *Margins of Philosophy.* Translated by Alan Bass. Chicago: University of Chicago Press, 1982.

"Diccionario de San Francisco." Latin American Library, Tulane University. [Consulted in photographic facsimile: MS 1617, vol. 2, Ayer Collection. Newberry Library, Chicago.]

Didi-Huberman, Georges. "Before the Image, before Time: The Sovereignty of Anachronism." In *Compelling Visuality: The Work of Art In and Out of History,* edited by Claire Farago and Robert Zwijnenberg, 31–44. Minneapolis: University of Minnesota Press, 2003.

Dietler, Michael. " 'Our Ancestors the Gauls': Archaeology, Ethnic Nationalism, and the Manipulation of Celtic Identity in Modern Europe." *American Anthropologist* 96, no. 3 (1994): 584–605.

———. "The Archaeology of Colonization and the Colonization of Archaeology: Theoretical Challenges from an Ancient Mediterranean Colonial Encounter." In *The Archaeology of Colonial Encounters: Comparative Perspectives,* edited by Gil Stein, 33–68. Santa Fe, NM: School of American Research, 2005.

Díez Ménguez, Isabel. "Tesoros de la Biblioteca Histórica Complutense: Manuscritos, impresos parisinos del siglo XVI y ediciones dieciochescas de los Libros de Horas." *Pecia Complutense* 8, no. 15 (2011): 1–28.

Drost, Gerrit. "El *Arte* de Pedro de Alcalá y su vocabulista: De tolerancia a represión." In *Las prácticas musulmanas de los moriscos andaluces (1492–1609): Actas del III Simposio Internacional de Estudios Moriscos,* edited by Abdejelil Temimi, 57–69. Zaghouan: Publications du Centre d'Etudes et de Recherches Ottomanes, Morisques, de Documentation et d'Information, 1989.

Duffy, Eamon. *The Stripping of the Altars: Traditional Religion in England, c. 1400–c. 1580.* 2nd ed. New Haven, CT: Yale University Press, 2005.

Durston, Alan. *Pastoral Quechua: The History of Christian Translation in Colonial Peru, 1550–1650.* South Bend, IN: University of Notre Dame Press, 2007.

Earley, Caitlin Cargile. "Ritual Deposits and Sculpted Stones: The Construction of Identity at Late Preclassic Chiapa de Corzo." MA thesis, University of Texas at Austin, 2008.

Eco, Umberto. "How Culture Conditions the Colours We See." In *On Signs,* edited by Marshall Blonsky, 157–75. Baltimore, MD: Johns Hopkins University Press, 1985.

Elliot van Liere, Katherine. "After Nebrija: Academic Reformers and the Teaching of Latin in Sixteenth-Century Salamanca." *Sixteenth Century Journal* 34, no. 4 (2003): 1065–1105.

Esparza Torres, Miguel Ángel. "Los prólogos de Alonso Molina (c. 1514–1585): Destrucción de una ideología." *Península: Revista de estudios ibéricos* 2 (2005): 69–91.

Esparza Torres, Miguel Ángel, and Hans-Josef Niederhe. *Bibliografía Nebrisense: Las obras completas del humanista Antonio de Nebrija desde 1481 hasta nuestros días.* Amsterdam and Philadelphia: John Benjamins, 2001.

Fabian, Johannes. *Time and the Other: How Anthropology Makes Its Object.* New York: Columbia University Press, 1983.

———. *Language and Colonial Power: The Appropriation of Swahili in the Former Belgian Congo, 1880–1938.* Cambridge: Cambridge University Press, 1986.

Fang Ng, Su. "Global Renaissance: Alexander the Great and Early Modern Classicism from the British Isles to the Malay Archipelago." *Comparative Literature* 58, no. 4 (2006): 293–312.

Fasolt, Constantin. "Saving Renaissance and Reformation: History, Grammar, and Disagreements with the Dead." *Religions* 3 (2012): 662–80.

Febvre, Lucien, and Henri-Jean Martin. *The Coming of the Book: The Impact of Printing, 1450–1800.* 1958. Reprint, London: Verso, 1984.

Fernández Valladares, Mercedes. *La imprenta en Burgos, 1501–1600.* Madrid: Arco Libros, 2005.

Fish, Stanley. *Is There a Text in This Class? The Authority of Interpretive Communities.* Cambridge, MA: Harvard University Press, 1980.

Framiñán de Miguel, María Jesús. "Manuales para el adoctrinamiento de neoconversos en el siglo XVI." *Criticón* 93 (2005): 25–37.

Freitas Carvalho, José Adriano de. "Os recebimentos de relíquias em S. Roque (Lisboa 1588) e em Santa Cruz (Coimbra 1595). Relíquias e espiritualidade. E alguma ideologia." *Via Spiritus: Revista de história da espiritualidade e do sentimento religioso* 8 (2001): 95–155.

Galeote, Manuel. "El *Vocabulario en lengua castellana y mexicana* de Fray Alonso de Molina (1555, 1571)." In *Antiqua et Nova Romania: Estudios lingüísticos y filológicos en honor de José Mondéjar en su sexagesimoquinto aniversario,* vol. 1, 272–99. Granada: Servicio de Publicaciones de la Universidad de Granada, 1993.

———. "Estudio preliminar." In *Aquí comiença vn vocabulario en la lengua castellana y mexicana,* by Alonso de Molina, edited by Manuel Galeote, xi–lxiii. Málaga: Universidad de Málaga, 2001.

———. "Originalidad y tradición gramatical en las artes de las lenguas indígenas americanas (siglo XVI)." In *Actas del V Congreso Internacional de Historia de la Lengua Española,* edited by María Teresa Echenique Elizondo and Juan Sánchez Méndez, vol. 2, 1719–27. Madrid: Editorial Gredos, 2002.

———. "Guardianes de las palabras: El vocabulario bilingüe de Fray Alonso de Molina." *Anales del Museo de América* 11 (2003): 137–54.

———. "El primer *Vocabulario* (1555) de Alonso de Molina, primer Nebrija de las Indias." In *Nuevas aportaciones a la historiografía lingüística: Actas del IV Congreso Internacional de la SEHL,* edited by Cristóbal Corrales Zumbado, 543–50. Madrid: Arco Libros, 2004.

———. "El acervo léxico romance e indígena en el primer vocabulario de las Indias Occidentales (Alonso de Molina, 1555): Vegetales." In *Actas del VI Congreso Internacional de Historia de la Lengua Española,* edited by Jose Luis Girón Alconchel and José Jesús de Bustos Tovar, vol. 3, 2205–15. Madrid: Arco Libros, 2006.

Gallego Morell, Antonio. *Cinco impresores granadinos de los siglos XVI y XVII.* Granada: Universidad de Granada, 1970.

García-Arenal, Mercedes. "The Religious Identity of the Arabic Language and the Affair of the Lead Books of the Sacromonte of Granada." *Arabica* 56, no. 6 (2009): 495–528.

García Macho, María Lourdes. "Novedades léxicas en el *Vocabulario español-latino* de 1516." *Insula* 47, no. 551 (1992): 13–14.

———. "Sobre los vocablos suprimidos en la edición de 1516 del *Vocabulario español-latino* de Nebrija." *Anuario de letras* 30 (1993): 135–59.

———. "Variantes léxicas y derivados en dos ediciones del *Vocabulario español-latino* de Elio Antonio de Nebrija." *Cahiers de linguistique hispanique médiévale* 20 (1995): 187–209.

———. "Actitud de Nebrija en las ediciones posteriores del *Vocabulario.*" In *Palabras, norma, discurso. En memoria de Fernando Lázaro Carreter,* edited by Luis Santos Río et al., 537–57. Salamanca: Ediciones Universidad de Salamanca.

———. "Macroestructura y microestructura en los diccionarios de Alonso de Palencia, Antonio de Nebrija, y Sebastián de Covarrubias." In *Actas del V Congreso Internacional de Historia de la Lengua Española*, edited by María Teresa Echenique Elizondo and Juan P. Sánchez Méndez, 2075–92. Madrid: Editorial Gredos, 2005.

———. "Procesos internos en los cambios de una obra, condicionados en alguna manera por el humanismo, en las ediciones posteriores a los príncipes del *Diccionario latino-español* y del *Vocabulario español-latino* de Antonio de Nebrija." In *Actas del VII Congreso Internacional de Historia de la Lengua Española*, edited by Concepción Company and José G. Moreno, vol. 2, 1319–28. Madrid: Arco Libros, 2008.

García-Medall, Joaquín. "Notas de lexicografica hispano-filipina: El *Bocabulario de lengua bisaya, hiligueyna y haraya de la isla de Panay y Sugbu y para las demas islas*, de Fray Alonso de Méntrida, OSA (ca. 1637)." In *Missionary Linguistics / Lingüística misionera: Selected Papers from the First International Conference on Missionary Linguistics*, edited by Otto Zwartjes and Even Hovdhaugen, 201–32. Amsterdam and Philadelphia: John Benjamins, 2004.

———. "La traducción codificada: Las artes y vocabularios hispano-filipinos." *Hermeneus: Revista de la Facultad de Traducción e Interpretación de Soria* 9 (2007): 117–44.

García Oro, José. *Los reyes y los libros: La política libraria de la Corona en el Siglo de Oro (1475–1598)*. Madrid: Cisneros, 1995.

Garibay Kintana, Ángel María. "'Códice Carolino': Manuscrito anónimo del siglo XVI en forma de adiciones a la primera edición del 'Vocabulario de Molina.'" *Estudios de cultura náhuatl* 7 (1967): 11–58.

Geary, Patrick J. *Furta Sacra: Thefts of Relics in the Central Middle Ages*. Princeton, NJ: Princeton University Press, 1978.

Gilberti, Maturino. *Vocabulario en lengua de Mechuacan*. Mexico: Juan Pablos Bressano, 1559.

Goldstone, Jack A. "The Problem of the 'Early Modern' World." *Journal of the Economic and Social History of the Orient* 41, no. 3 (1998): 249–84.

González, Roberto Jesús. *Zapotec Science: Farming and Food in the Northern Sierra of Oaxaca*. Austin: University of Texas Press, 2001.

González Holguín, Diego. *Vocabvlario de la lengva general de todo el Perv llamada lengua Qquichua, o del Inca*. Lima: Francisco del Canto, 1608.

González Palencia, Ángel. *Gonzalo Pérez, secretario de Felipe II*. Madrid: Instituto Jerónimo Zurita, 1946.

Gosden, Chris. *Archaeology and Colonialism: Cultural Contact from 5000 B.C. to the Present.* Cambridge: Cambridge University Press, 2004.

Grafton, Anthony. "Is the History of Reading a Marginal Enterprise? Guillaume Budé and His Books." *Papers of the Bibliographical Society of America* 91, no. 2 (1997): 139–57.

Grammatica y vocabolario en la lengva general del Perv llamada Quichua, y en la lengua Española. Seville: Clemente Hidalgo, 1603.

Greenblatt, Stephen. "Learning to Curse: Aspects of Linguistic Colonialism in the Sixteenth Century." In *Learning to Curse: Essays in Early Modern Culture,* 16–30. London: Routledge, 1990.

Greene, Roland. *Five Words: Critical Semantics in the Age of Shakespeare and Cervantes.* Chicago: University of Chicago Press, 2013.

Griffin, Clive. *The Crombergers of Seville: The History of a Printing and Merchant Dynasty.* Oxford: Clarendon Press, 1988.

Guerrero Ramos, Gloria. "La lexicografía bilingüe desde Nebrija a Oudin." In *Actas del IV Congreso Internacional de EURALEX (Benalmádena, 1990),* 463–71. Barcelona: Biblograf, 1992.

———. *El léxico en el* Diccionario *(1492) y en el* Vocabulario *(¿1495?) de Nebrija.* Seville: Universidad de Sevilla, 1995.

Guilarte, Guillermo L. "Alcance y sentido de las opiniones de Valdés sobre Nebrija." In *Homenaje a Ángel Rosenblat en sus 70 años: Estudios filológicos y lingüísticos,* 247–88. Caracas: Instituto Pedagógico, 1974.

Guzmán Betancourt, Ignacio. "La lengua, ¿compañera del imperio? Destino de un 'presagio' nebrisense en la Nueva España." In *Memoria del coloquio La Obra de Antonio de Nebrija y su Recepción en la Nueva España: Quince estudios nebrisenses (1492–1992),* edited by Ignacio Guzmán Betancourt and Eréndira Nansen Díaz, 23–38. Mexico: Instituto Nacional de Antropología e Historia, 1997.

Hackel, Heidi Brayman, and Peter C. Mancall. "Richard Hakluyt the Younger's Notes for the East India Company in 1601: A Transcription of Huntington Library Manuscript EL 2360." *Huntington Library Quarterly* 67, no. 3 (2004): 423–36.

Hamann, Byron Ellsworth. "The Social Life of Pre-Sunrise Things: Indigenous Mesoamerican Archaeology." *Current Anthropology* 43, no. 3 (2002): 351–82.

———. "'In the Eyes of the Mixtecs / To View Several Pages Simultaneously': Seeing and the Mixtec Screenfolds." *Visible Language* 38, no. 1 (2004): 68–123.

———. "Heirlooms and Ruins: High Culture, Mesoamerican Civilization, and the Postclassic Oaxacan Tradition." In *After Monte Alban: Transformation and Negotiation in Oaxaca, Mexico,* edited by Jeffrey P. Blomster, 119–67. Boulder: University Press of Colorado, 2008.

———. "How Maya Hieroglyphs Got Their Name: Egypt, Mexico, and China in Western Grammatology since the Fifteenth Century." *Proceedings of the American Philosophical Society* 152, no. 1 (2008): 1–68.

———. "Chronological Pollution: Potsherds, Mosques, and Broken Gods before and after the Conquest of Mexico." *Current Anthropology* 49, no. 5 (2008): 803–36.

———. "The Mirrors of *Las Meninas:* Cochineal, Silver, and Clay." *Art Bulletin* 92, no. 1–2 (2010): 6–35, 58–60.

———. "Inquisitions and Social Conflicts in Sixteenth-Century Yanhuitlan and Valencia: Catholic Colonizations in the Early Modern Transatlantic World." PhD dissertation, University of Chicago, 2011.

———. "Object, Image, Cleverness: The *Lienzo de Tlaxcala.*" *Art History* 36, no. 3 (2013): 518–45.

———. "Bad Chrisitians, New Spains: Muslims, Catholics, and Native Americans in a Mediterratlantic World." Unpublished manuscript.

Hanks, William F. *Converting Words: Maya in the Age of the Cross.* Berkeley: University of California, 2010.

Healy, Paul F., and Marc G. Blainey. "Ancient Maya Mosaic Mirrors: Function, Symbolism, and Meaning." *Ancient Mesoamerica* 22, no. 2 (2011): 229–44.

Hermann Lejarazu, Manuel A. *Códice Muro: Un documento mixteco colonial.* Oaxaca: Gobierno del Estado de Oaxaca, 2003.

———. "El sitio de Monte Negro como lugar de origen y la fundación prehispánica de Tilantongo en los códices mixtecos." *Estudios mesoamericanos* 10 (January–June 2011): 39–61.

Hernández, Esther. "El vocabulario náhuatl de Molina frente el vocabulario de Nebrija." *Iberoromania: Revista dedicada a las lenguas y literaturas ibero-rrománicas de Europa y América* 52 (2000): 1–9.

———. "En torno al diccionario americano más antiguo: El vocabulario de verbos nahuas de Fray Andres de Olmos (1547)." In *Filología y lingüística: Estudios ofrecidos a Antonio Quilis,* vol. 1, 1779–96. Madrid: Consejo Superior de Investigaciones Científicas, 2005.

———. "Influencias de método y concepción entre los vocabuarios novohispanos del siglo XVI." In *América y el diccionario,* edited by Mar Campos Souto, Félix Córdoba Rodríguez, and José Ignacio Pérez Pascual, 63–78. A Coruña: Servizo de Publicacións, Universidade da Coruña, 2006.

———. "La lexicografía hispano-amerindia del siglo XVI." *Philologia hispalensis* 22 (2008): 189–211.

———. "En torno al vocabulario hispano-maya conservado en la biblioteca

'John Carter Brown' (*Codex Indicus 8*)." *Revista de lexicografía* 14 (2008): 111–22.

———. "Vocabularios hispano-mayas del siglo XVI." In *Missionary Linguistics IV / Lingüística misionera IV: Lexicography: Selected Papers from the Fifth International Conference on Missionary Linguistics*, edited by Otto Zwartjes, Ramón Arzápalo Marín, and Thomas C. Smith-Stark, 129–45. Amsterdam and Philadelphia: John Benjamins, 2009.

Hernández, Miguel, S.I. *Vida, Martyrio, y translacion de la gloriosa virgen, y martyr Santa Leocadia. Que escrivio el padre Miguel Hernandez de la Compañia de Jesus, con la relacion, de lo que passo en la vltima translacion, que se hizo de las santas reliquias de Flandes a Toledo*. Toledo: Pedro Rodríguez, 1591.

Hernández de León-Portilla, Ascensión. "Nebrija y el inicio de la lingüística mesoamericana." *Anuario de letras* 31 (1993): 205–23.

———. "Hernando de Ribas, intérprete de dos mundos." *Revista latina de pensamiento y lenguaje (Número monográfico: Estudios de filología y lingüística náhuatl)* 2 (1995–1996): 477–93.

———, ed. *Obras clásicas sobre la lengua náhuatl*. Madrid: Fundación Histórica Tavera, 1998. CD-ROM.

Höpfner, Lötte. "De la vida de Eduard Seler: Recuerdos personales." *El México antiguo* 7 (1949): 58–74.

Hornkens, Heinrich. *Recveil de dictionaires françoys, espaignolz et latins*. Brussels: Rutger Velpius, 1599.

Houston, Stephen D. "Literacy among the Pre-Columbian Maya: A Comparative Perspective." In *Writing without Words: Alternative Literacies in Mesoamerica and the Andes*, edited by Elizabeth Hill Boone and Walter D. Mignolo, 27–49. Durham, NC: Duke University Press, 1994.

Houston, Stephen, and Takeshi Inomata. *The Classic Maya*. Cambridge: Cambridge University Press, 2009.

Houston, Stephen, and David Stuart. "Of Gods, Glyphs, and Kings: Divinity and Rulership among the Classic Maya." *Antiquity* 70, no. 268 (1996): 289–312.

———. "The Ancient Maya Self: Personhood and Portraiture in the Classic Period." In "Pre-Columbian States of Being," special issue, *Res: Anthropology and Aesthetics* 33 (Spring 1998): 73–101.

Houston, Stephen, David Stuart, and Karl Taube. *The Memory of Bones: Body, Being, and Experience among the Classic Maya*. Austin: University of Texas Press, 2006.

Houston, Stephen, and Karl Taube. "An Archaeology of the Senses: Perception and Cultural Expression in Ancient Mesoamerica." *Cambridge Archaeological Journal* 10, no. 2 (2000): 261–94.

Illich, Ivan. *In the Vineyard of the Text: A Commentary on Hugh's Didascalion.* Chicago: University of Chicago Press, 1993.

Jackson, Heather J. *Marginalia: Readers Writing in Books.* New Haven, CT: Yale University Press, 2001.

Jackson, Sarah E. "Continuity and Change in Early Colonial Maya Community Governance: A Lexical Perspective." *Ethnohistory* 58, no. 4 (2011): 683–726.

Jansen, Maarten E. R. G. N. *Huisi Tacu: Estudio interpretivo de un libro mixteco antiguo: Codice Vindobonensis Mexicanus 1.* Amsterdam: Centro de Estudios y Documentación Latinoamericanos, 1982.

Jansen, Maarten E. R. G. N., and Gabina Aurora Pérez Jiménez. *Codex Bodley: A Painted Chronicle from the Mixtec Highlands, Mexico.* Oxford: Bodleian Library, 2005.

———. *The Mixtec Pictorial Manuscripts: Time, Agency, and Memory in Ancient Mexico.* Leiden: Brill, 2011.

Jardine, Lisa, and Anthony Grafton. " 'Studied for Action': How Gabriel Harvey Read His Livy." *Past and Present* 129 (November 1990): 30–78.

Johns, Adrian. *The Nature of the Book: Print and Knowledge in the Making.* Chicago: University of Chicago Press, 1998.

———. *Piracy: The Intellectual Property Wars from Gutenberg to Gates.* Chicago: University of Chicago Press, 2009.

Johnson, Harvey Leroy. *An Edition of* Triunfo de los santos *with a Consideration of Jesuit School Plays in Mexico before 1650.* Series in Romance Languages and Literatures, no. 31. Philadelphia: Publications of the University of Pennsylvania, 1941.

Joyce, Rosemary. "Gender at the Crossroads of Mesoamerican Knowledge." *Latin American Antiquity* 10, no. 4 (1999): 433–35.

Karttunen, Frances. "The Roots of Sixteenth-Century Mesoamerican Lexicography." In *Cultures, Ideologies, and the Dictionary: Studies in Honor of Ladislav Zgusta,* edited by Braj B. Kachru and Henry Kahane, 75–88. Tübingen: Max Niemeyer Verlag, 1995.

Kingsborough, [Edward King], Viscount. *Antiquities of Mexico.* 9 vols. London: Robert Havell and Colnaghi, 1831–1848.

Klein, Cecelia F. "Not Like Us and All the Same: Pre-Columbian Art History and the Construction of the Nonwest." *Res: Anthropology and Aesthetics* 42 (Autumn 2002): 131–38.

Klor de Alva, Jorge. "Colonialism and Postcolonialism as (Latin) American Mirages." *Colonial Latin American Review* 1, no. 1–2 (1992): 3–23.

———. "The Postcolonization of the (Latin) American Experience: A Reconsideration of 'Colonialism,' 'Postcolonialism,' and 'Mestisaje.'" In *After Colonialism: Imperial Histories and Postcolonial Displacements,* edited by Gyan Prakash, 241–75. Princeton, NJ: Princeton University Press, 1994.

Laird, Andrew. "Aztec and Roman Gods in Sixteenth-Century Mexico: Classical Learning and Ethnography in Sixteenth-Century Mexico." Paper presented at the conference "Altera Roma: Art and Empire from the Aztecs to New Spain," Getty Villa, Malibu, CA, April 30–May 1, 2010.

Lastra, Yolanda. "El vocabulario trilingüe de Fray Alonso Urbano." In *Scripta philologica in honorem Juan M. Lope Blanch,* edited by Elizabeth Luna Traill, 39–46. Mexico City: Universidad Nacional Autónoma de México, 1992.

Lastra, Yolanda, Etna T. Pasacio, and Leopoldo Valiñas, eds. *Vocabulario castellano-matlatzinca de Fray Andrés de Castro (1557).* Mexico City: Instituto de Investigaciones Antropológicas, Universidad Nacional Autónoma de México, forthcoming.

Latour, Bruno. *The Pasteurization of France,* translated by Catherine Porter. Cambridge, MA: Harvard University Press, 1988.

———. "Drawing Things Together." In *Representation in Scientific Practice,* edited by Michael Lynch and Steve Woolgar, 19–68. Cambridge, MA: MIT Press, 1990.

———. *We Have Never Been Modern,* translated by Catherine Porter. Cambridge, MA: Harvard University Press, 1993.

Laughlin, Robert M., with John B. Haviland. *The Great Tzotzil Dictionary of Santo Domingo Zinacantán: With Grammatical Analysis and Historical Commentary. Volume 1: Tzotzil-English.* Washington, DC: Smithsonian Institution Press, 1988.

Leibsohn, Dana. "Seeing In-Situ: Mapa de Cuauhtinchan No. 2." In *Cave, City, and Eagle's Nest: An Interpretive Journey through the Mapa de Cuauhtinchan No. 2,* edited by Davíd Carrasco and Scott Sessions, 389–426. Albuquerque: University of New Mexico Press, 2007.

Leiva Soto, Francisco. "La imprenta de Antequera en el siglo XVI: Andrés Lobato, Antonio de Nebrija, Agustín Antonio de Nebrija y Claudio Bolán." *Boletín de la Asociación Andaluza de Bibliotecarios* 61 (December 2000): 29–45.

Levene, Ricardo. *Las Indias no eran colonias.* Madrid: Espasa-Calpe, 1951.

Levy, Evonne, and Kenneth Mills, eds. *Lexikon of the Hispanic Baroque: Transatlantic Exchange and Transformation.* Austin: University of Texas Press, 2013.

Lind, Michael. *Ancient Zapotec Religion: An Ethnohistorical and Archaeological Perspective.* Boulder: University Press of Colorado, 2015.

Lockhart, James. "Some Nahua Concepts in Postconquest Guise." *History of European Ideas* 6, no. 4 (1985): 465–82.

————. *The Nahuas after the Conquest.* Stanford, CA: Stanford University Press, 1992.

————. "Sightings: Initial Nahua Reactions to Spanish Culture." In *Implicit Understandings: Observing, Reporting, and Reflecting on the Encounters between Europeans and Other Peoples in the Early Modern Era,* edited by Stuart B. Schwartz, 218–48. Cambridge: Cambridge University Press, 1994.

————. *Nahuatl as Written: Lessons in Older Written Nahuatl with Copious Examples and Texts.* Stanford, CA: Stanford University Press, 2001.

Lope Blanch, Juan M. "Nebrija, primer lingüista moderno." In *Memoria del coloquio La Obra de Antonio de Nebrija y su Recepción en la Nueva España: Quince estudios nebrisenses (1492–1992),* edited by Ignacio Guzmán Betancourt and Eréndira Nansen Díaz, 39–46. Mexico: Instituto Nacional de Antropología e Historia, 1997.

————. "La lexicografia española y los vocabularios de lenguas amerindias." In *Lengua y discurso: Estudios dedicados al profesor Vidal Lamíquiz,* edited by Pilar Gómez Manzano, Pedro Carbonero Cano, and Manuel Casado Velarde, 555–66. Madrid: Arco Libros, 1999.

López Bernasocchi, August, and Manuel Galeote. *Tesoro castellano del primer diccionario de América: Lemas y concordancias del vocablario español-nahuatl (1555) de Alonso de Molina.* Madrid: Editorial Verbum, 2010.

Love, Michael. "Early States in the Southern Maya Region." In *The Origins of Maya States,* edited by Loa P. Traxler and Robert J. Sharer. Philadelphia: University of Pennsylvania Museum of Archaeology and Anthropology, forthcoming.

Lucas, Adam Robert. "Industrial Milling in the Ancient and Medieval Worlds: A Survey of the Evidence for an Industrial Revolution in Medieval Europe." *Technology and Culture* 46, no. 1 (January 2005): 1–30.

MacCormack, Sabine. "Ubi Ecclesia? Perceptions of Medieval Europe in Spanish America." *Speculum* 69, no. 1 (1994): 74–100.

————. *On the Wings of Time: Rome, the Incas, Spain, and Peru.* Princeton, NJ: Princeton University Press, 2007.

MacDonald, Gerald J., ed. *Vocabulario de romance en latín,* by Antonio de Nebrija. Philadelphia: Temple University Press, 1973.

Magaloni Kerpel, Diana. "Painters of the New World: The Process of Making the Florentine Codex." In *Colors between Two Worlds: The Florentine Codex of Bernardino de Sahagún,* edited by Gerhard Wolf and Joseph Connors, 47–76. Florence: Kunsthistorisches Institut and Villa I Tatti, 2011.

Mannheim, Bruce. "Lexicography of Colonial Quechua." In *Wörterbücher Dictionaries Dictionnaires,* edited by Franz Josef Hausmann, vol. 3, 2676–84. Berlin: Walter de Gruyter, 1991.

Mano González, Marta de la. *Mercaderes e impresores de libros en la Salamanca del siglo XVI*. Salamanca: Ediciones Universidad de Salamanca, 1998.

Manrique Castañeda, Leonardo. "La estructura del *Arte para aprender la lengua mexicana* de fray Andrés de Olmos." In *Memoria del coloquio La Obra de Antonio de Nebrija y su Recepción en la Nueva España: Quince estudios nebrisenses (1492–1992)*, edited by Ignacio Guzmán Betancourt and Eréndira Nansen Díaz, 96–106. Mexico: Instituto Nacional de Antropología e Historia, 1997.

Marcus, Joyce. "Archaeology and Religion: A Comparison of the Zapotec and Maya." *World Archaeology* 10, no. 2 (1978): 172–91.

———. *Women's Ritual in Formative Oaxaca: Figurine-Making, Divination, Death, and the Ancestors*. Memoirs of the Museum of Anthropology, no. 33. Ann Arbor: Museum of Anthropology, University of Michigan, 1998.

Mason, J. Alden. "Mirrors of Ancient America." *Museum Journal* 18, no. 2 (1927): 201–9.

Masten, Jeffrey. *Queer Philologies: Language, Sex, and Affect in Shakespeare's Time*. Philadelphia: University of Pennsylvania Press, forthcoming.

Matilla Tascón, Antonio. "Las impresiones de la 'Gramática' de Nebrija en los siglos XVII y XVIII." In *Varia bibliographica: Homenaje a José Simón Díaz*, edited by Concepción Casado Lobato et al., 467–82. Kassel: Edition Reichenberger, 1998.

McGann, Jerome. *A Critique of Modern Textual Criticism*. Chicago: University of Chicago Press, 1983.

McKenzie, D. F. "The Sociology of a Text: Orality, Literacy, and Print in Early New Zealand." *The Library*, 6th ser., 4, no. 4 (1984): 333–65.

———. *Bibliography and the Sociology of Texts: The Panizzi Lectures 1985*. London: British Library, 1986.

Mengin, Ernst, ed. *Bocabulario de Mayathan: Das Wörterbuch der yukatekischen Mayasprache; vollständige Faksimile-Ausgabe des Codex Vindobonensis S.N. 3833 der Österreichischen Nationalbibliothek*. Graz: Akademische Druck- und Verlagsanstalt, 1972.

Michelon, Oscar, ed. *Diccionario de San Francisco*. Graz: Akademische Druck- und Verlagsanstalt, 1976.

Mignolo, Walter. *The Darker Side of the Renaissance: Literacy, Territoriality, and Colonization*. Ann Arbor: University of Michigan Press, 1995.

Minsheu, John. *A Dictionarie in Spanish and English, first published into the English tongue by Ric. Perciuale Gent. Now enlarged and amplified with many thousand words. . . .* London: E. Bollifant, 1599.

Mintz, Sidney. *Sweetness and Power: The Place of Sugar in Modern History*. New York: Penguin, 1985.

Molina, Alonso de. *Aqui comiença vn vocabulario en la lengua castellana y mexicana.* Mexico: Juan Pablos, 1555.

———. *Vocabvlario en lengva castellana y mexicana.* Mexico: Alonso de Spinosa, 1571.

———. *Aquí comiença vn vocabulario en la lengua castellana y mexicana.* 1555. Edited by Manuel Galeote. Málaga: Universidad de Málaga, 2001.

Monaghan, John D. "Performance and the Structure of the Mixtec Codices." *Ancient Mesoamerica* 1, no. 1 (1990): 133–40.

———. "The Text in the Body, the Body in the Text: The Embodied Sign in Mixtec Writing." In *Writing without Words: Alternative Literacies in Mesoamerica and the Andes,* edited by Elizabeth Hill Boone and Walter D. Mignolo, 87–101. Durham, NC: Duke University Press, 1994.

Monaghan, John D., and Byron Hamann. "Reading as Social Practice and Cultural Construction." *Indiana Journal of Hispanic Literatures* 13 (Fall 1998): 131–40.

Montellano Arteaga, Marcela. "Culhuacán: El primer molino de papel en América." *Boletín de Monumentos Históricos,* 3rd ser., 16 (May–August 2009): 74–90.

Montero Cartelle, Emilio, and Avelina Carrera de la Red. "El *Dictionarium medicum* de E. A. de Nebrija." In *Antonio de Nebrija: Edad Media y Renacimiento,* edited by Carmen Codoñer and Juan Antonio González Iglesias, 399–411. Salamanca: Universidad de Salamanca, 1994.

Montes de Oca Vega, Mercedes. "Semantic Couplets as an Expression of Cultural Identity." *Collegium Antropologicum* 28, Supplement 1 (2004): 191–99.

Monzon, Cristina. "The Tarascan Lexicographic Tradition in the Sixteenth Century." In *Missionary Linguistics IV / Lingüística misionera IV: Lexicography: Selected Papers from the Fifth International Conference on Missionary Linguistics,* edited by Otto Zwartjes, Ramón Arzápalo Marín, and Thomas C. Smith-Stark, 165–96. Amsterdam and Philadelphia: John Benjamins, 2009.

Morales, Ambrosio de. *La vida, el martyrio, la inuencion, las grandezas y las translaciones de los gloriosos niños martyres San Iusto y Pastor. Y el solenne triumpho con que fueron recebidas sus santas reliquias en Alcala de Henares y su postrera translacion.* Alcalá: Andres de Angulo, 1568.

Morales, Pedro de. *Carta del Padre Pedro de Morales,* edited by Beatriz Mariscal Hay. Mexico City: Colegio de Mexico, 2000.

Morán, J. Miguel. *La memoria de las piedras: Anticuarios, arqueólogos y coleccionistas de antigüedades en la España de los Austrias.* Madrid: Centro de Estudios Europa Hispánica, 2010.

Moreno Fernández, Francisco. "Antonio de Nebrija y la lexicografía americana del siglo XVI." *Voz y letra: Revista de literatura* 5, no. 1 (1994): 79–104.

Morris, Earl H. "Description of the Temple of the Warriors and Edifices Related Thereto." In *The Temple of the Warriors at Chichen Itza, Yucatan,* by Earl H. Morris, Jean Charlot, and Ann Axtell Morris, vol. 1, 1–227. Washington, DC: Carnegie Institution of Washington, Publication 406, 1931.

"Motul II Dictionary." Codex Indicus 8. John Carter Brown Library, Brown University, Providence, RI.

Murray, Laura J. "Vocabularies of Native American Languages: A Literary and Historical Approach to an Elusive Genre." *American Quarterly* 53, no. 4 (2001): 590–623.

Nansen Díaz, Eréndira. "Nebrija en la descripción y prescripción de las lenguas de México durante la Colonia." In *Memoria del coloquio La Obra de Antonio de Nebrija y su Recepción en la Nueva España: Quince estudios nebrisenses (1492–1992),* edited by Ignacio Guzmán Betancourt and Eréndira Nansen Díaz, 81–96. Mexico: Instituto Nacional de Antropología e Historia, 1997.

Nebrija, Antonio de. *Introductiones latinae explicitae.* Salamanca, 1481.

———. *Introduciones latinas del maestro antonio de nebrissa contrapuesto el romance al latin.* Publisher unknown, 1488?

———. *Lexicon hoc est dictionarium ex sermone latino in hispaniense[m].* [a.i recto: *Esta tassado este vocabulario por los muy altos & muy poderosos principes. . . .*] Salamanca, 1492. [Copy consulted: BNE *I1778.]

———. *Dictionarium ex hispaniensi in latinum sermone[m].* [a.i recto: *Esta tassado este vocabulario por los muy altos & muy poderosos principes. . . .*] 1495. [Copy consulted: BNE *I1778.]

———. *Muestra dela istoria que Maestro de lebrixa dio ala Reina nuestra señora.* Burgos? 1490s.

———. *Vocabularius. Interpretatio dictionum ex sermone Latino in Hispaniensem, et dictionum Hispaniensium in Latinum sermonem.* Seville: Estanislao Polono and Jacobo Kromberger, 1503. [Copy consulted: BC 42-6-17.]

———. *Vocabularius Anthonii Nebrissensis.* Seville: Jacobo Kromberger, 1506. [Copy consulted: BNF Rés g.X.15.]

———. *Dictionarium aelij Antonij Nebrissensis.* Burgos: Fadrique de Basilea and Arnao Guillén de Brocar, 1512. [Copy consulted: BC 15-5-20.]

———. *Dictionarium ex hispanie[n]si in latinum sermonem.* Salamanca: Lorenzo Hon de Deis, 1513. [Copy consulted: BNE *R31797.]

———. *Dictionarium Aelij Antonij Nebrissensis.* Zaragoza: Jorge Coci, 1514. [Copy consulted: Chicago, Newberry Library, Case Collection Folio X 672.49.]

———. *Vocabulario de Roma[n]ce.* Seville: Juan Varela, 1516. [Copies consulted: BUC Res.270(1); BNE *R2700; BL C.63.c.14.]

———. *Vocabulario de Roma[n]ce en latin.* Seville: Juan Varela[?], 1516 [ca. 1520]. [Copies consulted: BUC FOA158; BNE *R2219; BL C.63.c.15.]

———. *Dictionarium Aelij Antonij nebrissensis.* Alcalá de Henares: Arnao Guillén de Brocar, 1520. [Copy consulted: BL *C.63.i.7.]

———. *Dictionarium Aelij Antonij nebrissensis.* Alcalá de Henares: Arnao Guillén de Brocar, 1520. [Copy consulted: BNE *R7701.]

———. *Dictionarium Aelii Antonii Nebrissen[sis].* Alcalá de Henares: Miguel de Eguía, 1528. [Copy consulted: BNE *R28553.]

———. *Dictionarium Aelii Antonii Nebrissen[sis].* Alcalá de Henares: Miguel de Eguía, 1532. [Copies consulted: BNE *R2505; BNE *R20560.]

———. *Dictionariu[m] Aelij Antonij Nebrissen[sis].* Valencia: Francisco Díaz Romano, 1533. [Copy consulted: BNE *R7691.]

———. *Homiliae per diversos avtores in Evangelia.* Granada: Sancho de Nebrija, 1534.

———. *Hymnorvm recognitio.* Granada: Sancho de Nebrija, 1534.

———. *Libri minores.* Granada: [Sancho de Nebrija], 1534.

———. *Vafre dicta philosophorum.* Granada: Sancho de Nebrija, 1534.

———. *Dictionarium Ael. Antonii Nebrissensis.* Granada: Sancho de Nebrija, 1536. [Copies consulted: BNE *R27141; Granada, Biblioteca de la Universidad de Granada BHR/A-005-027; Oxford, Taylor Institute Library DICT.C.1536.]

———. *Dictionarium Ael. Antonii Nebrissensis.* Granada: Sancho de Nebrija, 1540. [Copies consulted: RAE *2-B-6; BL Cup.410.aa.31.]

———. *Dictionarivm Ael. Antonii Nebrissensis.* Granada: Sancho de Nebrija, 1543. [Copy consulted: BNP RES. 2964 A, 2965 A.]

———. *Dictionarivm Ael. Antonii Nebrissensis.* Granada: Sancho de Nebrija, 1545. [Copy consulted: BNE *R28933.]

———. *Segmenta ex epistolis.* Granada: [Sancho de Nebrija], 1545.

———. *Dictionarivm Aelij Antonij Nebrissensis.* Antwerp: Jan Steels, 1545. [Copies consulted: BNP L.4251//1 V; Freiburg, Bibliothek der Universität D4735.]

———. *Aelii Antonii Nebrissensis gramatici triplicis dictionarii.* Estella: Adrián de Amberes, 1548. [Copy consulted: RAE 2-B-5.]

———. *Dictionarium Æ. A. Nebrissensis.* Granada: Sancho de Nebrija, 1550. [Copies consulted: Cambridge University Library, Peterborough.G.2.17; BNP L.4254 V.]

———. *Dictionarivm Ael. Antonij Nebrissensis.* Granada: Sancho de Nebrija, 1552. [Copy consulted: BNE *R28932.]

———. *Dictionarivm latinohispanicvm, et vice versa hispanicolatinvm.* Antwerp: Jan Steels, 1553. [Copy consulted: HSA.]

———. *Dictionarivm Ael. Antonii Nebrissensis.* Granada: Sancho de Nebrija, 1554. [Copy consulted: Silos, Biblioteca del Monasterio de Silos Le6-a8.]

———. *Dictionarivm Ael. Antonii Nebrissensis.* Granada: Sancho de Nebrija, 1555. [Copies consulted: BNE *U7684; JL 393374 III.]

———. *Dictionarivm latinohispanicvm, et vice versa hispanicolatinvm.* Antwerp: Jan Steels, 1560. [Copies consulted: BNE *R28876(1); BUC Noviciado *Res.22.III.]

———. *Dictionarivm quadruplex Ael. Antonii Nebrissensis.* Granada: Antonio de Nebrija 1567. [Copies consulted: JL 393373 III; Valencia, Biblioteca del Real Colegio Seminario de Corpus Christi-Patriarca SJR / 1138.]

———. *Dictionarivm latinohispanicvm,* et vice versa hispanicolatinvm. Antwerp: Viuda y Herederos de Jan Steels, 1570. [Copies consulted: BNE 4:109820; BL 1560 / 1776.]

———. *Dictionarivm quadruplex Ael. Antonii Nebrissensis.* Granada: [Antonio de Nebrija], 1572. [Copy consulted: BUC Noviciado Res.22243.]

———. *Aelii Antonii Nebrissensis dictionarium.* Antequera: Antonio de Nebrija, 1574. [Copy consulted: BNF Rés-X-874.]

———. *Aelii Antonii Nebrissensis grammatici, chronographi regii dictionarium.* Antequera: Antonio de Nebrija, 1578. [Copy consulted: BNE U8566(1).]

———. *Aelii Antonii Nebrissensis grammatici, chronographi regii dictionarium.* Antequera: Antonio de Nebrija, 1581. [Copies consulted: BNE *R28854; JL 393375 III; Stanford, Stanford University Library Rare Books PA2365.S5 N43 1581.]

———. *Dictionarium Aelii Antonii Nebrissensis.* Granada: Antonio de Nebrija, 1585. [Copies consulted: BPR VIII / 1284; BNF X-859; Nashville, Vanderbilt University Special Collections Library, PA2365.S5 N4 1585a.]

———. *Dictionarivm Aelii Antonii Nebrissensis.* Granada: Antonio de Nebrija, 1589. [Copies consulted: BNE 28925; Bristol, Bristol Reference Library, EPB 396 / D1 C Bookstack F.]

———. *Dictionarivm Aelii Antonii Nebrissensis.* Antequera: Agustín Antonio de Nebrija, 1595. [Copies consulted: BNE 28949; RAE *37-I-4.]

———. *Diccionario de romance en latin.* Antequera: Agustín Antonio de Nebrija, 1600. [Copy consulted: Granada, Biblioteca de la Universidad de Granada, FLA / A2 2.]

———. *Diccionario de romance en latin.* Seville: Alfonso Rodríguez Gamarra, 1610. [Copy consulted: RAE *29-I-6 (3).]

———. *Dictionarium medicum: (el "Diccionario médico" de Elio Antonio de Nebrija).* Edited by Avelina Carrera de la Red. Salamanca: Universidad de Salamanca, 2001.

Nelson, Zachary, Barry Scheetz, Guillermo Mata Amado, and Antonio Prado. "Composite Mirrors of the Ancient Maya: Ostentatious Production and Precolumbian Fraud." *The PARI Journal: A Quarterly Publication of the Pre-Columbian Art Research Institute* 9, no. 4 (2009): 1–7.

Niederehe, Hans-Josef. "La *Gramática de la lengua castellana* (1492) de Antonio de Nebrija." *Boletín de la Sociedad Española de Historiografía Lingüística* 4 (2004): 41–52.

Nieto Jiménez, Lidio. "Coincidencias y divergencias entre los diccionarios de Nebrija, Las Casas y Percyvall." In *Nebrija V Centenario: Actas del Tercer Congreso Internacional de Historiografía Lingüística,* edited by Ricardo Escavy Zamora, José Miguel Hernández Terrés, and Antonio Roldán Pérez, vol. 3, 351–66. Murcia: Universidad de Murcia, 1994.

Norton, F. J. *Printing in Spain, 1501–1520.* London: Cambridge University Press, 1966.

Nuyts, Corneille Joseph. *Jean Steelsius, libraire d'Anvers (1533–1575): Relevé bibliographique de ses productions.* Brussels: F. Heussner, 1859.

Odriozola, Antonio. "La caracola del bibliófilo Nebrisense." *Revista de bibliografía nacional* 7 (1946): 3–114.

Ogborn, Miles. "Writing Travels: Power, Knowledge and Ritual on the English East India Company's Early Voyages." *Transactions of the Institute of British Geographers,* n.s., 27, no. 2 (2002): 155–71.

Ogilvie, Sarah. *Words of the World: A Global History of the Oxford English Dictionary.* Cambridge: Cambridge University Press, 2013.

Olivier Durand, Guilhem. "The Mexica Pantheon in Light of Greco-Roman Polytheism: Uses, Abuses, and Proposals." Paper presented at the conference "Altera Roma: Art and Empire from the Aztecs to New Spain," Getty Villa, Malibu, CA, April 30–May 1, 2010.

Olmos, Andrés de. "Arte de la lengua mexicana." William Gates Collection, Rare 497.2017 051. Latin American Library, Tulane University.

———. *Arte de la lengua mexicana.* 1547. Edited by René Acuña. Mexico City: Universidad Nacional Autónoma de México, 1985.

Osowski, Edward W. *Indigenous Miracles: Nahua Authority in Colonial Mexico.* Tucson: University of Arizona Press, 2010.

Oudin, César. *Tesoro de las dos lengvas francesa y española.* Paris: Marc Orry, 1607.

Pagden, Anthony. *The Fall of Natural Man: The American Indian and the Origins of Comparative Ethnology.* 2nd ed. Cambridge: Cambridge University Press, 1986.

Pallet, Jean. *Diccionario mvy copioso de la lengua española y françesa.* Paris: Matthieu Guillemet, 1604.

———. *Diccionario mvy copioso de la lengua española y françesa.* Brussels: Rutger Velpius, 1606.

Panofsky, Erwin. *Studies in Iconology: Humanist Themes in the Art of the Renaissance.* New York: Harper and Row, 1939.

Peñalver Castillo, M., and Y. González Aranda. "Pedro de Alcalá, seguidor de Nebrija." *Revista de la Facultad de Humanidades de Jaén,* 4–5, no. 1 (1995–96): 55–78.

Pendergast, David M. "Ancient Maya Mercury." *Science,* n.s., 217, no. 4559 (1982): 533–35.

Percyvall, Richard. *Bibliotheca Hispanica: Containing a Grammar, with a Dictionarie in Spanish, English, and Latine.* London: John Jackson, for Richard Watkins, 1591.

Peterson, Jeanette Favrot. "The *Florentine Codex* Imagery and the Colonial *Tlacuilo.*" In *The Work of Bernardino de Sahagún: Pioneer Ethnographer of Sixteenth-Century Aztec Mexico,* edited by J. Jorge Klor de Alva, H. B. Nicholson, and Eloise Quiñones Keber, 273–93. Albany: Institute for Mesoamerican Studies, University at Albany, State University of New York, 1988.

Pezzi Martínez, Elena, ed. *El vocabulario de Pedro de Alcalá.* Almería: Editorial Cajal, 1989.

Phelan, John L. "Philippine Linguistics and Spanish Missionaires, 1565–1700." *Mid-America: An Historical Review* 37, no. 3 (1955): 153–70.

Piedra, José. "The Value of Paper." *Res: Anthropology and Aesthetics* 16 (Autumn 1988): 85–104.

Pillsbury, Joanne. "Reading Art without Writing: Interpreting Chimú Architectural Sculpture." In *Dialogues in Art History, from Mesopotamian to Modern: Readings for a New Century,* edited by Elizabeth Cropper, 73–89. Washington, DC: National Gallery of Art, 2009.

Pines, J. "Les médecins marranes, espagnols et portugais à Anvers, aux XVIe et XVIIe siècles." *Le scalpel: Journal belge des sciences medicales* 116, no. 26 (29 June 1963): 545–52.

Porras Barrenechea, Raúl. Prologue to *Léxicon, o vocabulario de la lengua general del Perú,* by Domingo de Santo Tomás, v–xxxii. Lima: Universidad Nacional Mayor de San Marcos, 1951.

Postma, Antoon. "Tagalog *Vocabularios*" (2001). https://sites.google.com/site/pinagpala/Vocabularios.pdf.

Rafael, Vicente L. *Contracting Colonialism: Translation and Christian Conversion in Tagalog Society under Early Spanish Rule.* Durham, NC: Duke University Press, 1993.

Revilla Rico, Mariano. *La Políglota de Alcalá: Estudio histórico-crítico.* Madrid: Imprenta Helénica, 1917.

Reyes, Fermín de los, and Marta M. Nadales. "The Book in Segovia in the Fifteenth and Sixteenth Centuries: Accident, Chance, Necessity?" In *Print Culture and Peripheries in Early Modern Europe: A Contribution to the History of Printing and the Book Trade in Small European and Spanish Cities,* edited by Benito Rial Costas, 345–62. Leiden: Brill, 2012.

Ricciardelli, M. "Review of *Antonio de Nebrija: Vocabulario de romance en latín.*" *Renaissance Quarterly* 28, no. 3 (1975): 408–11.

Richards, Jennifer. "Gabriel Harvey, James VI, and the Politics of Reading Early Modern Poetry." *Huntington Library Quarterly* 71, no. 2 (2008): 303–21.

Rider, John. *Bibliotheca Scholastica: A Double Dictionarie.* Oxford: Joseph Barnes, 1589.

Rojas Torres, Rosa María. "La categoría 'adjetivo' en el *Arte del idioma zapoteco* (1578) y el *Vocabulario en lengua çapoteca* (1578) de Juan de Córdova." *Historiographia linguistica* 26, no. 2–3 (2009): 259–79.

Romero Rangel, Laura. "La originalidad del *Vocabulario castellano-mexicano* (1571) de Alonso de Molina." In *América y el diccionario,* edited by Mar Campos Souto, Félix Córdoba Rodríguez, and José Ignacio Pérez Pascual, 137–51. A Coruña: Universidade da Coruña, Servizo de Publicacións, 2006.

Rouzet, Anne. *Dictionnaire des imprimeurs, libraires et éditeurs des XVe et XVIe siècles dans les limites géographiques de la Belgique actuelle.* Nieuwkoop: B. de Graaf, 1975.

Sáez Guillén, José Francisco, and Federico García de la Concha Delgado. "Obras de Nebrija impresas por Arnao Guillén de Brocar en la Biblioteca Colombina de Sevilla." In *El libro antiguo español: Actas del segundo Coloquio Internacional (Madrid),* edited by María Luisa López-Vidriero and Pedro M. Cátedra, 431–47. Salamanca: Ediciones de la Universidad de Salamanca, 1992.

Sahagún, Bernardino de. *Florentine Codex: General History of the Things of New Spain* [1547–1580], edited and translated by Arthur J. O. Anderson and Charles E. Dibble. 12 vols. Salt Lake City and Santa Fe, NM: University of Utah Press and School of American Research, 1950–1982.

Sahlins, Marshall. "Colors and Cultures." *Semiotica* 16, no. 1 (1975): 1–22.

———. "Cosmologies of Capitalism: The Trans-Pacific Sector of 'The World System.'" *Proceedings of the British Academy* 74 (1988): 1–51.

San Buenaventura, Pedro de. *Vocabvlario de lengva tagala. El romance castellano pvesto primero.* Pila: Thomas Pinpin and Domingo Loay, 1613.

———. *Vocabulario de lengua tagala.* 1613. Edited by Cayetano Sánchez-Fuertes. Valencia: Librerías "París-Valencia," 1994.

Sánchez-Fuertes, Cayetano. "El *Vocabulario de lengua tagala* de Fray Pedro de San Buenaventura, OFM." In *Vocabulario de lengua tagala,* by Pedro de San Buenaventura, i–x. Valencia: Librerías "París-Valencia," 1994.

Santo Tomás, Domingo de. *Lexicon, o vocabulario de la lengua general del Perv.* Valladolid: Francisco Fernandez de Cordoua, 1560.

Sarmiento, Ramón. "Antonio de Nebrija y la lingüística en la época del descubrimiento." In *La lingüística española en la época de los descubrimientos: Actas del coloquio en honor del Profesor Hans-Josef Niederhe,* edited by Beatrice Bagola, 157–74. Hamburg: Buske, 2000.

Schuller, Rudolf. "An Unknown Matlatsinka Manuscript Vocabulary of 1555–1557." *Indian Notes* 7, no. 2 (1930): 175–94.

Scott, William Henry. "Sixteenth-Century Tagalog Technology from the *Vocabulario de la lengua tagala* of Pedro de San Buenaventura, O.F.M." In *Gava': Studies in Austronesian Languages and Cultures Dedicated to Hans Kähler,* edited by Rainer Carle et al., 325–35. Berlin: Reimer, 1982.

Scott-Warren, Jason. "Reading Graffiti in the Early Modern Book." *Huntington Library Quarterly* 73, no. 3 (2010): 363–81.

Sellen, Adam T. "Storm-God Impersonators from Ancient Oaxaca." *Ancient Mesoamerica* 13, no. 1 (2002): 3–19.

———. *El cielo compartido: Deidades y ancestros en las vasijas efigie zapotecas.* Mérida: Centro Peninsular en Humanidades y Ciencias Sociales, Universidad Nacional Autónoma de México, 2007.

Sherman, William. *Used Books: Marking Readers in Renaissance England.* Philadelphia: University of Pennsylvania Press, 2008.

Silverstein, Michael. "Translation, Transduction, Transformation: Skating 'Glossando' on Thin Semiotic Ice." In *Translating Cultures: Perspectives on Translation and Anthropology,* edited by Paula G. Rubel and Abraham Rosman, 75–105. Oxford: Berg, 2003.

Slights, William W. E. "The Edifying Margins of Renaissance English Books." *Renaissance Quarterly* 42, no. 4 (1989): 682–716.

———. "Review of *Marginalia: Readers Writing in Books.*" *Journal of English and Germanic Philology* 102, no. 1 (2003): 126–28.

Smith, Jeffrey Chipps. "Repatriating Sanctity, or How the Dukes of Bavaria Rescued Saints during the Reformation." In *Crossing Cultures: Conflict, Migration, Convergence,* edited by Jaynie Anderson, 1084–89. Melbourne: Melbourne University Press, 2009.

———. "Salvaging Saints: The Rescue and Display of Relics in Munich during the Early Catholic Reformation." In *Art, Piety, and Devotion in the Christian West, 1500–1700,* edited by Virginia Chieffo Raguin, 25–33. Burlington, VT: Ashgate, 2010.

Smith, Mary Elizabeth. *Picture Writing from Ancient Southern Mexico: Mixtec Place Signs and Maps.* Civilizations of the American Indian Series 124. Norman: University of Oklahoma Press, 1973.

———. "The Relationship between Mixtec Manuscript Painting and the Mixtec Language: A Study of Some Personal Names in Codices Muro and Sánchez Solís." In *Mesoamerican Writing Systems,* edited by Elizabeth P. Benson, 47–98. Washington, DC: Dumbarton Oaks Research Library and Collection, 1973.

Smith-Stark, Thomas C. "Mujeres, música y mostagán: La vida alegre de los zapotecos decimoséxticos." In *Memorias: Jornadas Filológicas 1994*, 357–81. Mexico City: Universidad Nacional Autónoma de México, 1995.

———. "El 'primer Nebrija indiano': Apuntes sobre una nueva edición del *Vocabulario* de Alonso de Molina." *Nueva revista de filología hispánica* 50, no. 2 (2002): 531–41.

———. "Dioses, sacerdotes y sacrificio: Una mirada a la religión zapoteca a través del *Vocabvlario en lengva çapoteca* (1578) de Juan de Córdova." In *La religión de los Binnigula'sa'*, edited by Víctor de la Cruz and Marcus Winter, 89–195. Oaxaca: Instituto Estatal de Educación Pública de Oaxaca and Instituto Oaxaqueño de las Culturas, 2002.

———. "Lexicography in New Spain (1492–1611)." In *Missionary Linguistics IV / Lingüística misionera IV: Lexicography: Selected Papers from the Fifth International Conference on Missionary Linguistics*, edited by Otto Zwartjes, Ramón Arzápalo Marín, and Thomas C. Smith-Stark, 3–82. Amsterdam and Philadelphia: John Benjamins, 2009.

"Solana Dictionary." HSA, manuscript B2005.

Stallybrass, Peter, Roger Chartier, J. Franklin Mowery, and Heather Wolfe. "Hamlet's Tables and the Technologies of Writing in Renaissance England." *Shakespeare Quarterly* 55, no. 4 (2004): 379–419.

Steiner, Roger J. *Two Centuries of Spanish and English Bilingual Lexicography (1590–1800)*. The Hague: Mouton, 1970.

Subrahmanyam, Sanjay. "Connected Histories: Notes towards a Reconfiguration of Early Modern Eurasia." *Modern Asian Studies* 31, no. 3 (1997): 735–62.

———. "Holding the World in Balance: The Connected Histories of the Iberian Overseas Empires, 1500–1640." *American Historical Review* 112, no. 5 (2007): 1359–85.

Taube, Karl A. "The Iconography of Mirrors at Teotihuacan." In *Art, Polity, and the City of Teotihuacan*, edited by Janet C. Berlo, 169–204. Washington, DC: Dumbarton Oaks, 1992.

Tawada, Yoko. "The Translator's Gate, or Celan Reads Japanese." *Mantis: A Journal of Poetry, Criticism & Translation* 8 (2009): 223–32.

Tedlock, Dennis. *The Spoken Word and the Work of Interpretation*. Philadelphia: University of Pennsylvania Press, 1983.

———. *Popol Vuh: The Mayan Book of the Dawn of Life*, 2nd ed. New York: Simon and Schuster, 1996.

———. *Rabinal Achi: A Mayan Drama of War and Sacrifice*. Oxford: Oxford University Press, 2003.

Tellez Nieto, Heréndira. *Vocabulario trilingüe en español-latín-náhuatl atribuido a fray Bernardino de Sahagún*. Mexico: Instituto Nacional de Antropología e Historia, 2010.

Thiemer-Sachse, Ursula. "El 'Vocabulario' castellano–zapoteco y el 'Arte en lengua zapoteca' de Juan de Córdova: Intenciones y resultados (perspectiva antropológica)." In *La descripción de las lenguas amerindias en la época colonial,* edited by Klaus Zimmermann, 147–74. Frankfurt and Madrid: Vervuert and Iberoamericana, 1997.

Thomas, Keith. *Religion and the Decline of Magic.* New York: Charles Scribner's Sons, 1971.

Torero, Alfredo. "Entre Roma y Lima: El *Lexicon* quichua de fray Domingo de Santo Tomás [1560]." In *La descripción de las lenguas amerindias en la época colonial,* edited by Klaus Zimmermann, 271–90. Frankfurt and Madrid: Vervuert and Iberoamericana, 1997.

Torre, Antonio de la. "La casa de Nebrija en Alcalá de Henares y la casa de la imprenta de la 'Biblia Políglota Complutense.'" *Revista de filología española* 29 (1945): 175–212.

Tribble, Evelyn B. *Margins and Marginality: The Printed Page in Early Modern England.* Charlottesville: University Press of Virginia, 1993.

Urbano, Alonso. "Arte breve de la lengua otomí compuesto por el padre fray Alonso Urbano de la Orden de nuestro padre San Francisco." BNF, Département des manuscrits, Manuscrit Américain 8.

———. *Arte breve de la lengua otomí y vocabulario trilingüe.* 1605. Edited by René Acuña. Mexico City: Universidad Nacional Autónoma de México, 1990.

Valdivia, Luys de. *Vocabvlario breve en lengva millcayac.* Lima: Francisco del Canto, 1607.

"Vocabulario trilingüe." Vault MS 1478, Ayer Collection. Newberry Library, Chicago.

Vocabvlario en la lengva general del Perv llamada Quichua, y en la lengua Española. Nvevamente emendado y añadido de algunas cosas que faltaban por el Padre Maestro Fray Juan Martinez Catedratico de la Lengua. Lima: Antonio Ricardo, 1604.

Vittori, Girolamo. *Tesoro de las tres lengvas francesa, italiana, y española.* Geneva: Philippe Albert and Alexandre Pernet, 1609.

Warner, Michael. "What's Colonial about Colonial America?" In *Possible Pasts: Becoming Colonial in Early America,* edited by Robert Blair St. George, 49–70. Ithaca, NY: Cornell University Press, 2000.

Warren, Benedict, ed. *Diccionario grande de la lengua de Michoacan.* 2 vols. Morelia: Fimax Publicistas, 1991.

Webster, Susan Verdi. *Art and Ritual in Golden Age Spain: Sevillan Confraternities and the Processional Sculpture of Holy Week.* Princeton, NJ: Princeton University Press, 1998.

Wilkinson, Alexander S. *Iberian Books: Books Published in Spanish or Portuguese or on the Iberian Peninsula before 1601.* Leiden: Brill, 2010.

Wolf, Eric Robert. *Europe and the People without History*. Berkeley: University of California Press, 1982.

Wood, Francis A. "The Origin of Color-Names." *Modern Language Notes* 20, no. 8 (1905): 225–29.

Zeitlin, Judith Francis. *Cultural Politics in Colonial Tehuantepec: Community and State among the Isthmus Zapotec, 1500–1750*. Stanford, CA: Stanford University Press, 2005.

Zuili, Marc. *César et Antoine Oudin, deux polygraphes français des XVIe et XVIIe siècles: Vie, œuvre et ébauche d'une édition critique du* Tesoro de las dos lenguas española y francesa *(1607–1675)*. Nanterre: Université de Paris X–Nanterre, 2004.

———. "César Oudin y la difusión del español en Francia en el siglo XVII." In *La cultura del otro: Español en Francia, francés en España*, edited by Manuel Bruñas Cuevas et al., 278–89. Seville: Universidad de Sevilla, 2006.

Index

Page numbers in italics refer to illustrations.

217

BYRON ELLSWORTH HAMANN was born in Lafayette, Indiana. He was living in the Twin Cities for the Bicentennial, and spent the following decade in Green Bay, Wisconsin. He received a BA in history of art from Brown Unversity in 1994, an MA in anthropology from Vanderbilt University in 1998, an MA in anthropology from the University of Chicago in 2000, and a dual PhD in anthropology and history from the University of Chicago in 2011.